Reflections on Industry
and
Economy

Other Titles

Reflections on Industry and Economy

Issa Aremu

Malthouse Press Limited

Lagos, Benin, Ibadan, Jos, Port-Harcourt, Zaria

© Issa Aremu 2015
First published 2015
ISBN 978-978-53321-0-0

Malthouse Press Limited
43 Onitana Street, Off Stadium Hotel Road,
Off Western Avenue, Lagos Mainland
E-mail: malthouse_press@yahoo.com
malthouselagos@gmail.com
Tel: +234 (01) 0802 600 3203

Foreword

The collection of articles in this book, *Reflections on Industry and Economy*, x-rays decades of turbulent socio-economic developments in a rapidly globalizing world, most which however deal with the Nigerian condition, with passing remarks on some developing countries and constraints imposed by international division of labour. Issa Aremu here examines, dissects and probes policymakers and attendant policies and processes of local and international economic and financial institutions, and development agencies and consequences for economies and teeming millions of Nigerians.

On financial and monetary policies, the Federal Ministry of Finance and the Central Bank of Nigeria come into sharp focus in a wide-ranging critique of monetary policies, especially exchange rate regimes, debt equity and management of external reserves, the regulation of banks and other financial institutions and of capital market operations. While recapitalization of banks under Soludo as governor of the CBN receives a lukewarm approval, Issa thinks the former has difficulty seeing interest rate management as instrument for recovery, and mass employment. In fact, Issa Aremu insists that "the latest big-bang is the unnecessary increase in Monetary Policy Rate to 10 per cent ostensibly to tame inflation which reportedly jumped to 8 per cent in February under its nose. Increase in MPR will further reverse the gains recorded in interest-rate management that has witnessed some token increase in private sector leading. It is another arrogant class-bias policy to privilege the already over-privileged banks at the expense of the real value-adding sector of the economy." And "the neo-liberal least resistance policy of managing inflation through hike in interest rate is also at variance with current thinking in emerging economies that downward push in interest rate is indispensable to economic recovery, economic competitiveness and employment generation."

Discomfort over regulation of the financial and banking system escalates into alarm and bewilderment over the quality of bank management itself, how SMEs do not get funded and few individuals and corporate bodies could run up debts in billions of naira, sums the EFCC, NDIC and other investigative bodies can hardly fully ascertain. That this largely unproductive amalgam of a few rich bank-owners and handful of favoured borrowers/debtors and a generally badly performing banking system remains a severe drawback to meaningful economic development and a balanced economy is not a difficult conclusion to reach. A situation, one may agree with Issa, the emotive and poorly understood and badly argued case for and against Islamic banking can shed little light.

The naira re-denomination and the dollarization of state government accounts "which ran into the brick wall of seven-point agenda of President Musa Yar'Adua that include war on graft" are two policies Issa deprecates, and takes a swipe at the "dollarised" ministerial salaries of Dr Ngozi Okonjo-Iweala and Mallam El Rufai which stood in obscene contrast to prevailing public sector wages and much against long-established procedures and regulations on compensation of public servants.

The contending publicly aired arguments over myriad economic challenges facing Nigeria since the 1980s receive more than adequate attention: neo-liberal philosophy underpinning the IMF-driven deregulation and privatization policies, specific programmes subsumed under never-ending reform agendas and out-of-reach goals (NEPAD, MDGs, Visions 2010 and 2020, Seven-Point Agenda, Davos Declaration, etc.), erratic supply and conflict-inducing pricing of refined petroleum products and incomprehensible computations and politics of fuel subsidy removal, neglect of non-oil sector, deliberations and recommendations of the Nigerian Economic Summit, states-federal government's tussles over excess crude proceeds and level of crude oil theft, and those considerations covered by the Fiscal Responsibility Act.

While cheering on Obasanjo administration's measures for resuscitating a dying textile industry, including creation of a Textile

Revival Fund, and celebrating the reactivation of textile factory in Kaduna and proactive and sensible policies of the Bank of Industry, Issa Aremu contends in several articles that monetary and other economic policies have substantially led in the direction of de-industrialisation, pauperization and mass unemployment, claims which seem borne out by cost of living indices, rapidly declining quality of life and depressing statistics on unemployment. Even at that, Issa was able to see, through more than seven thousand jobs created across the country by the Dangote group and utilizing local raw materials, an investment genre that portends a better performing indigenous private sector in place of import-dependent organized private sector and skewed international trade, especially with China, against the national economy.

The tremendous growth of the telecommunications industry latterly, Issa cautions, is a mixed blessing. While ushering in more effective communication between individuals and between corporate bodies, "in fact GSM has further accentuated our technological dependency as a nation." And, "Teleconomy, just like oil economy, is a capital-intensive activity, labour-saving rather than labour-intensive." Not many of the jobs generated therein could be regarded as "decent jobs" by the International Labour Organization's standard, more of barely disguised underemployment for those selling recharge cards, and not-so well remunerated subcontracted and precarious jobs within the companies themselves.

Even a cursory read of this collection of articles leaves an impression of not only a badly performing Nigerian economy in spite of crude oil sales, but also of successive political actors and bureaucrats embracing not too well understood policy options advocated by the World Bank and the IMF and of the main industrialized countries sustaining them ideologically, recurrent talks of reforms and sloganeering for over three decades leaving substantially untouched the numbing degree of corruption, the dependency structure of the economy, and the lives of a majority of Nigerians. If you wish to have in one place and at a glance the debates that have raged in the last three decades in Nigeria over issues of any economic importance, then have a copy of this book.

Aliko Dangote

"There is no political democracy without economic democracy."
-Popular banner

Table of Contents

About the Author

Comrade Issa Obalowu Aremu, NPOM, mni was born in 1961 to the extended family of Mallam Mahmood Aremu and Hadjia Afusat Amoke of Alapata and Kasandubu compounds of Ilorin respectively. He attended Ansar Ud Deen primary school, Ijagbo. He had his secondary education at Ilorin Grammar School before moving to School of Basic Studies, Ahmadu Bello University, ABU, Zaria in 1977.

Issa's passion for organizing and activism started in the late 1970s and early 80s, decades of progressive and radical ideas in ABU. He was an active member of ABU students' unionism and rose to become the Secretary General of the reputable radical Marxist-Leninist Movement for Progressive Nigeria (MPN). He was among the score of students' leaders repressed with expulsion by Ango Abdullahi Vice Chancellorship in 1981 at his final year. He eventually obtained his BSc (Hons) degree in Economics from University of Port Harcourt in 1985 with Second Class Upper. He has his Master degree in Labour and Development studies from the prestigious Institute for Social Studies (ISS), The Hague, The Netherlands, in 1991. He is an alumnus of George Meany Labour Centre, Maryland, Washington, USA (1987 and 2003). He joined the labour movement as the Head, Economic/Research department of Nigeria Labour Congress (NLC) between 1987 and 1989. He later moved to the National Union of Textile Garment and Tailoring Workers of Nigeria (NUTGTWN), a private sector affiliate union of NLC in 1989. After 20 years of active union carrier, he rose from an organizing Secretary to become the General Secretary of the union in March 2000. He took over as the General Secretary of the union from Comrade Adams Oshiomhole mni, the Comrade governor of Edo State and two times former President of Nigeria Labour Congress (NLC).

Comrade Issa Aremu is currently one of the Vice-Presidents of the Nigeria Labour Congress (NLC). In 2013 In Johannesburg, South Africa, he was elected the Chairman, new IndustriALL Global Union, Africa Region with more than 50 million members in 165 countries with headquarters in Geneva, Switzerland making an Executive African Member of IndustriALL Global Union. Having attended Senior Executive Course 27 of the National Institute (mni) for Policy and Strategic Studies, Kuru, Jos in 2005, Comrade Issa Aremu is a Member of the National Institute.

In 2013 he was elected the Secretary-General of the Alumni Association of the National Institute for Policy & Strategy Studies, AANI.

He is currently the Chairman of the Interim Management Committee of First Guarantee Pension Limited and a member of the tripartite National Labour Advisory Committee (NLAC) made up of government, employers and trade unions. He also serves in the Board of Labour City Transport Service (LCTS). He is the Chairman, International Committee of Nigeria Labour Congress (NLC).

Comrade Issa Aremu, mni has served on the Board of Michael Imoudu National Institute of Labour Studies (MINILS) and Nigeria Social Insurance Trust Fund (NSITF). His contributions helped to reposition these institutions as leading labour market institutions in Nigeria. He had served on the tripartite Federal National Minimum Wage, in 2000 and 2010 and Petroleum Products Pricing Regulatory Committee in 2003 as well as tripartite committee on Revival of textile and Garment industry. He has led negotiations and signed hundreds of national collective agreements on salaries, allowances, gratuity and pensions of textile, garment and tailoring workers over the years.

A visible leading member of mass national actions on socio-political issues during the struggle for democracy and against military dictatorship in the 1980s and 1990s, Comrade Issa is a weekly columnist with Abuja-based, *Daily Trust* newspapers. His published works include; *The Social Relevance of Trade Unionism, The Crises of Pricing Petroleum Products in Nigeria, Collapse of Textile Industry in Nigeria: Implications for Employment and Poverty Eradication and Tears Not Enough.*

Comrade Issa Aremu, mni, was one of the labour delegates to the 2014 National Conference. He was the Deputy Chairman of the National Conference Committee on Civil Society, Labour, Youth and Sports. He is a strong activist and advocate on, Redistribution of national wealth, improved Productivity and Re-Industrialisation of Nigerian economy. Recipient of many distinguished awards and recognitions, the President of Nigeria, Dr. Goodluck Ebele Jonathan, GCFR, on August 21, 2014 in recognition of his contribution to national productivity improvement and consciousness conferred on him the National Productivity Order of Merit (NPOM) Award. He is married with children.

Money without Responsibility[1]

The 254-paged historic 'Report of the Political Bureau" has only a passing remark on 'Finance', under which the Central Bank is singled out for attack. The Bureau acknowledged the allegations of ineptitude and corruption against the bankers' banker and said its performance 'leaves much to be desired'. Such has been the obscurity of the other segments of the financial sector, namely the commercial, merchant banks and insurance companies that they escaped the commendable nation-wide efforts of the drafters of the Bureau Report.

The hurriedly prepared report on the "State of the Nigerian Economy" by Planning Ministry in 1983 certainly examined the effects in the performance of commercial and merchant banks. But the report did not bring to the fore, the outrageous activities of these banks in also ensuring the collapse of the Second Republic's economy; hence, cosmetic resolutions: appeal for long-term lending, weekend banking, two shifts during the week, overcoming the problem of "under banking", etc.

Thanks to SAP, ironically the handiwork of bankers (among others), which have brought bankers before the media searchlight. For one, the implementation of the measures of SAP, importantly exchange allocation is the banks' pet project and it has handsomely paid too.

Before SAP, an observer would have doubted the conclusion of the celebrated American economist, J. K. Galbraith, who said: "The process by which banks create money is so simple that the mind is repelled."

Dr. Ibrahim Ayagi, himself a controversial banker, now the chairman, Kano Endowment Fund, would go down as the

---

[1] *The Nigerian Economist*, 18 – 31 July 1982, pp. 19)

"inventor" of the term: "Lagos-Ibadan Bank". Surprisingly, the 'Lagos-Ibadan Press' (if you share my prejudice) some of which are reputable for financial sagacity as well as, spreading banking terms (remember 'liquidity squeeze'), refused to accord legitimacy to Ayagi's 'discovery'. In fairness though, he enjoyed publicity for his insidious occasional assault on SAP. It is surprising that such an apt objective term as "Lagos-Ibadan bank" would not gain currency. I beg to disagree that the media is not immune from our collective bias. It is, however, remarkable that a much more marketable term "Eaglet bank" was chosen to describe the glass-house banks (you could mistake some for cash-and-carry stores) which have been in "operation" in Lagos and Lagos alone since the inception of SAP.

The last time, the banks came under presidential attack for perverting CBN's credit policy guidelines and flouting SFEM Decree 23 of 1986, a mischievous observer said the money changers (or are they money-lenders) have all-purpose medicine to government's idle talk and scapegoatism. Remember that only the bankers enjoy the irresistible power of lobby even under the military. It means money is mightier than sword. It is convenient for government to occupy trade union's office than arraigning respectable banks' executive before anti-sabotage tribunal for blatantly keeping bad books or no books at all on purchase forex.

Ever heard that the security men swooped on the activities of respectable bankers committee? The unusual request that the dossier on depositors be forwarded to government in 1986, made bankers declare themselves "prisoners of conscience" who needed the solidarity of Amnesty International. Personal liberty was being threatened, we were told.

Closely related to the power of lobby is the ingenuity of advertisement. Thus corporate affairs departments of the banks favourably compete with Foreign Exchange Department in terms of budget and space.

Let both the commercial and merchant banks ensure rural banking not by mobilising scarce rural savings to finance dubious exports in urban centres but ploughing such savings back into community projects.

The argument that rural areas lack facilities doesn't hold water. Didn't the oil companies open up bushes and rivers for on and off shore exploration respectively?

Thus the banks should not see the new challenge as an excuse to retrench workers but create more money, open up frontiers and employ more hands.

Professor Dotun Philips recently put the banks' value added at meagre 2.4% above internally generated revenue. That was news.

Hitherto the public knew the banks for open-ended profits contained in complex statements of accounts, in which auditors' fees are inflated and income policy guidelines issued by productivity, price and income board are blatantly violated. When will there be banks with social responsibility in Nigeria?

Who Profits From Debt Equity?[2]

Perhaps, it may not be incorrect to say one unintended effects of the Structural Adjustment Programme (SAP) is that the programme has become a fetter on open-door policy proclaimed by the administration. A fetter it is, unintended it is, but a logical effect of the implementations of the policy instruments that constitute the SAP nonetheless. What with the secrecy and shrewd discretion major policy options, namely SFEM, privatisation, subsidy removal and various debt management options are being pursued in recent times.

When SFEM perverted open-door policy by escaping weekly media-searchlight, we were told it was because the scheme was no more a novelty. Yet that was when there was a dramatic shift to Dutch auction system and curiously enough, it was shortly after this shift, a leading statesman in the person of Dr. Nnamdi Azikiwe (who definitely should know) told journalists: 'SFEM sounds Greek'. It may well be the great Zik wanted to escape the mischief of media men after all, but not without saying: so much for the 'huge success" of the SFEM public enlightenment committee.

The argument against public scrutiny of financial issues is summed up thus: information required for analysis 'is beyond the knowledge of the common man'. Witness how 'experts' intimidated the 'ignoramuses' in our midst during the IMF debate – or was it the other way round? If that argument is taken on its face value, a question then arises: Why not provide information that would assist a meaningful discussion in a country blessed with a greater number of common men and common women?

---

[2] *Herald*, 10th June 1986

4

Debt equity is the latest term in the book of Nigeria's debt management. Again the new option was a veritable scoop to media men, true to character, quoting copiously the foreign press and "sources close to the finance ministry." We were told debt-to-equity swaps involve creditor banks offering debt owed them (in form of promissory notes) by Nigeria to an "investor" seeking to invest here. The CBN is expected to buy this debt at a discount and exchange this for local currency at the prevailing SFEM rates. Swaps, the explanation continues, rests on the profitable hope that holders of promissory notes on insured trade credit (put at US1.6 billion dollars) can retire their debts in naira with huge benefits. An example is cited.

Promissory notes purchased at pre-SFEM rate of $1.30 to N1 means N5.20k to one dollar today. Even the stakes are higher than it is realised that a dollar promissory note worth only 32 cents in the international money market. So 32 cents for a dollar promissory note worth N4.00 at the present conversion rate and by implication a dollar purchase of promissory note worth N12.50k. Now in case swaps could involve as small as only 5 per cent of the uninsured credit (about US$81.062m) holders would realise a billion naira rip-off from the swaps almost an equivalent of the total debit, (pre-SFEM). Any further evidence why the rate of applications being lodged with ministry of finance for this easy fortune by creditors is on the increase?

Hitherto, wages and salaries of poor workers had been falsely singled out as a source of inflation and in a gross contempt for reason and logic 'arguments' are in legion as to why wages should be cut or restrained. We can however, only contemplated the stag-inflation swaps will usher in at a go. Perhaps the SFEM proceeds already at the disposal of government can initially wet the speculative appetite of creditors. But it cannot be doubted that as buy-back deals increases (and it will), the pressure on CBN to permit more naira to buy these huge loans will increase. But the real issue is that debt-equity option can only serve a speculative purpose and not productive end. This is why the view according to which swaps enhance foreign investment is untenable. It is either policy makers on this score are self-serving and therefore hypocritical or ignorant of the dynamics of the present day world economy.

Why in spite of favourable conditions SAP has created, foreign investments remains at the level of encomiums for SAP by this or that visiting and departing envoys? Creditor-nations, notably USA and Britain are no less in deep recession and will certainly prefer to 'hog the cake'. Thus more than ever before, developing countries need inward looking patriotic development strategy that should necessarily suspect 'dumping' policies of creditors and their agencies. Definitely the speed at which holders of promissory notes respond to the buy-back deals indicates that it is another heed to cheap advantages characteristic of speculation and arbitrage as distinct from risk adventure.

Nor will SAP ease debt-burden either. On the contrary it complicates and postpones debt crisis at a high cost. It is significant to note that 'buy-back' comes at a time privatisation is being feverishly pursued and the already moribund effort at indigenization is being jettisoned once and for all. Will it really be desirable and constitutional for trans-nationals to bargain our national assets at cheap price? Are we to swap the economy for loans?

Debt-equity option underscores once again, Nigeria's least resistance (from the standpoint of sovereignty) in debt management. It may trample underfoot a national call for ascertaining dubious claims before commitment to repayment, swaps or repudiation. Coming shortly after an official acknowledgement that external debts might after all not be more than US7-10 billion (and not necessarily US20b), smacks of arbitrariness. At international level, it endorses the discredited baker's plan and subverts a genuine collective approach to debt crisis. If it has international precedence at all, it is not worthy of emulating; such is Chile under the heel of monstrous dictatorship, but which we are also told has the most comprehensive package on debt-equity swaps.

In the Abyss of Debts[3]

It is increasingly becoming difficult separating lies and hypocrisy on the one hand, and basic facts on the other, whenever "new" economic issue is billed for discussion in recent times. Government information mill has turned out a piece of news that there was no need for any World Bank loan for the operation of the celebrated Second-Tier Foreign Exchange Market (SFEM). That was in the wake of authoritative report that the bank's policy memo is the same as the government's Structural Adjustment Programme (SAP) and that 'made-in-Nigeria' tag on the "new economic policy" was a fraud.[*]

But going through the speech of the Finance Minister on the eve of independence celebration, and curiously too, at the time the veritable symbol of nationhood: naira, was billed for auction, one ponders who was fooling whom and why.

According to Dr. P. C. Okongwu, Nigeria has agreed to borrow additional $1.5 billion from World Bank, ostensibly to "finance various projects". Financial reporters chose to dub this "new package of assistance for SFEM".

A doubting Thomas might however legitimately not believe financial reporters who are only desperate to be known for a kind of economic sagacity. Yet the highest country's ruling body has put all such doubts to rest. AFRC has approved as much as N452 million World Bank loan at not a low rate of 8 per cent, for the initial take off of the SFEM.

---

[3] *National Concord*, Saturday 18th October, 1986, pp. 3
[*] See *African Business*, August 1986

Much has been written about SFEM by observers. But so far, one consequence of this "economic recovery programme" that is discernible to all and official acknowledged is *indebtedness.*

Of course, the economy is already in the blind alley of indebtedness, and perhaps this is why a so-called solution of debt-burden could further push the economy into more debts and yet does not make news.

But it was doubtful if the preoccupation of post-colonial leaders in 1960 was that of commitment to debt obligations. In 1960, total external debt was put at N82.4 million. When divided with the total population figure of Nigeria now, it would be about N1.00 per head, and a cent in American dollar value.

Chief S. B. Falegan put the country's total debt at N488.8m in 1970. Though the debt growth rate was 17 per cent within the decade, the total external debt was still modest enough. Contracted mainly in forms of long term loans from World Bank and host of Western countries, repayment period were generous; ten to forty years, with low interest rate of 2 per cent. Debt service ratio was also as low as 3.5 per cent.

And perhaps the most singular record of the first decade after the proclamation of Independence was that Civil War harrowing experience was financed through taxes imposed on workers and not loans from abroad.

It should however be pointed out that the relative small debt of the 60s had little to do with prudence of the then economic managers. Rather, it was due to the fact that the key determinant in Nigerian "development process" i.e. foreign investment, was then insignificant. In the developing countries, the process of indebtedness has its own politics and no less in Nigeria too. Creditors lend out money, if only borrowers can repay. Huge oil revenues of the 1970s made supplier-creditors to realise that Nigeria was credit-worthy.

Big trading houses sell where their products can be bought. Local patronisers are in great number in Nigeria; from importers of raw materials to office pins. Governments initiated projects which involved millions of foreign exchange to execute. Multi-million naira worth high ways were constructed simultaneously as assembly plants were being established. Experts drew industrial "plans" with emphasis on imported inputs. The $1 billion loan contracted by government in 1978 was not to resolve any balance of payment crisis (there was none) but rather to finance dozen of turn-key projects.

But if the military nurtured the idea of jumbo-loan, the civilian administrators deemed it fit to implement the idea. Between 1979 and 1983, politicians gave fillips for debts and mostly via massive imports and dubious loan contracts by both states, Federal Government and Central Bank put official debt commitment at N21.38 billion in 1984. It has been reported that in 1986, the total external debt per head is $125. That is what an innocent Nigerian owes.

But the question is where have all these billions gone to and who pays for them?

The 1978 $1 billion Euro-dollar was ostensibly meant for projects which included pipelines, cement factories, refineries, sugar projects and iron and steel. Studies have shown that disbursement and actual repayment of this loan has little to do with these listed projects.

On the contrary, as much as N178 million of the loan went into Lagos-Ibadan expressway. And by 1985, only 57.3% of the construction cost of the highways had been recovered through toll-fees. Also the Aladja Steel Complex which produces at low 18 per cent capacity has gulped N1.26 billion while Ajaokuta project is put at N3.5 billion.

Meanwhile, government has renegotiated a second round of Euro-market loan of $1.145 billion. One loan begets another loan, it seems, and a vicious cycle is set in motion.

The results of most jumbo-loans incurred by the politicians had been documented partially by various studies and government commissions. Where the loans were not used to rig elections, they were committed to such "bottom-less pits" called projects.

It is instructive also to note that the managing director of International Bank of West Africa, Mr. Oladele Olashore, revealed last year that "Nigeria does not get more than 25 per cent value for her huge expenditure on import." He knew better that the imports were financed through trade credits.

Yet, debts and its management by successive government constitute real burden for the ordinary Nigerians and the collective existence of a sovereign economy. Nigeria is currently 20 per cent above the critical 10 per cent debt service ratio set by the World Bank.

"Development Plans" have been abandoned for desperate solutions to meet the requirements, including whims and caprices of creditors. In the list of these solutions are devaluation, petroleum subsidy removal, retrenchment, levies and now auctioning of naira through SFEM, such that today it will not be incorrect to say, foreign creditors rule the economy, local debtors only preside.

Revisiting Economic Summit II[4]

In keeping with their promise, the organizers of the Economic Summit II did some press briefing during the months of May and June to elaborate on their deliberations and recommendations. One of such press briefings could not have escaped the attention of observers of the trends in the economy.

On Tuesday May 23, NTA popular programme, *Dialogue,* featured Messrs Paschal Dozie and Muhammed Hayatu-Deen. Whatever could have been the set objectives for featuring the distinguished private sector personalities, viewers were certainly intrigued to watch a popular network platform reputable for lively debate transformed to a 30-minute long monologue. For once, it was uninteresting to watch two principal designers and organizers of Economic Summit II, mutually complimenting and reinforcing each other's monolithic positions on controversial issues that affect corporate well-being of all.

The point cannot be overemphasised; Economic Summit II suffers not only from the limitations of a privatized discourse but also the inadequacies of privatization of public policies. Contrary to the advertised stance of heavy public sector involvement with the alleged inclusion of "academia and Nigerian labour", policy recommendations from the Summit address more of private concern than public welfare. This summit is permanently haunted by the self-centred orientation and biases of its organizers.

Its recommendation on the country's economic philosophy is true to designers' delight; "economy" we are told "will be market oriented." How this obvious reference to what is certainly not in

[4] *ThisDay*, Friday 6th September 1995, pp. 6

dispute passes for a recommendation confounds the reading public. What is 'market-oriented economy' in Nigeria's context? What has been the full impact of 'market-orientation' since the beginning of SAP in 1986? Is there a new rethinking about the market? How "internationally competitive" can the economy be? Policies on these issues may be desirable than some bogus declaration about market orientation.

It may, however, be useful to contrast the doctrinaire recommendation on "economic philosophy" to the measured position on "political philosophy". The summit envisages a political arrangement which "...all stake holders will be marching (pray, not on some military orders) and acting together towards the attainment of their common objectives." Good enough. But since politics and economics are two sides of the same national coin, it is again desirable that recommendations on the two should logically complement each other, otherwise, we are only being presented with a counterfeit coin. In what way does a favoured foot-loose market economy reconcile with a "marching" political order (or is it "suitable democracy")? Is "sustainable market economy" not as desirable as "suitable democracy" "governed by consensus"?

In fairness, the summit makes some concession to justice and even agrees that the economy shall be sensitive "to the less fortunate members of society". Yet, the fact that this concession is not more than a lip-service lies in the poverty of the summit's recommendations on poverty-alleviation. When compared with its recommendations on banking and insurance, the summit's considered options for improving living standards are not as robust and explicit. Indeed, for those who care, we are rather served with a stale menu. Witness these recommendations: "provide compulsory and free primary education", "substantially improve teachers' welfare" or "complete existing housing schemes". Are these actually new policy recommendations or policy day-dreams Nigerians are already fed up with?

Summit II lacks concrete measures on labour motivation and productivity improvement, two indispensable issues in any economic recovery. We were told that "remuneration of public servants should be increased substantially". How "substantial" will the remuneration be to motivate in the era of deregulation, "appropriate pricing" as well as "frequent and gradual adjustment of prices" of petroleum products?

Will remuneration be as "substantial" and sustainable as to change the miserable refugee image of the work force desperately waiting for occasional relief packages which are either grudgingly implemented or implemented in piece meal, together with sack-letters as sadly dramatised in Kwara State recently? Will the official contempt for the principle of minimum wage (still scandalously legally pegged at ₦250 per month) be abandoned for innovative measures such as wage indexation?

Lastly, it is regrettable that this summit sees the availability of major public funds as NSITF as veritable pools for improving "liquidity" in the stock market rather than meeting the pressing survival needs of tax payers and contributors of such funds. Is this not a case of putting public fund in service of private end? It is unfortunate that the perspective of shy-lock money-mongers would exert much dominance at a national summit. The National Economic Intelligence Committee certainly has a task at hand. The committee has the responsibility to unveil the private assumptions, which must have informed most policy recommendations at the Summit II. Future summits must also necessarily be seen to be more representative in conception, proceeding and outcomes.

Reflections on Camdessus' Exit[5]

What is in a job, that a resignation from it would elicit such reactions across the global village? Mr. Michel Camdessus, the CEO of the International Monetary Fund (IMF), we are told, resigned half way through his third five-year term in office due to 'personal reasons'. This, for once, is refreshingly newsworthy. It must go down as one riddle of the millennium that a long standing disinterested international banker that spends time and time elevating the virtues of 'impersonal market forces' into some precepts of Fund's catechism would fall for some 'personal forces'.

Few in financial cycles, however, attached importance to Camdessus overt reasons. Indeed, many insist we should locate the reasons for this sudden exit, in some hidden factors independent of his choice. The US has never concealed its criticism of Camdessus' less-than-thrift posturing for 'throwing money' at the distressed countries of Asia, (namely, South Korea and Thailand) and for sponging the former East European communists with generous credits in place of stiffer 'conditionalities'. Under his directorship (or is it dictatorship?) given that he is also accused of disregarding 'consensus', as much as $100 billion was mobilised for Asia to 'contain' the crisis. This sum dwarfs the peanut of $7 billion set for Africa's debt relief under the much publicised but selectively applied highly Indebted Poorest Countries Initiative (HIPC). Being the largest shareholder and the most influential member of the Fund, US opposed this bailout generosity.

---

[5] *The Guardian*, Sunday 19th December 1999, pp. 43; and the *Vanguard*, Wednesday 15th December 1999, pp. 11

America had reasoned, very well in line with the IMF's founding doctrine that Asia crisis, which has so far recorded unprecedented toll of human causalities, ought to get 'a little bit worse before it could get better.' In the languages of the salesmen, the Asians needed more 'discipline' and 'belt-tightening' rather than collecting IMF's money made up in a large part of some America's hard placed $40 billion quota. IMF therefore fell short of US expectation for not reminding the Asians that there is no free lunch even for the most desperately hungry in Washington (it is not by accident that the headquarters of the Fund is located there). In 1988, US majority Senate Leader Trent Lott not only reportedly called for the resignation of Camdessus, over his 'free-lunch' attitude to Asia, but also courted sympathy for such demand in the right cycles by invoking the phrase of McCarthy years. Camdessus, he hysterically declared, is a 'socialist from France'.

The resignation of Camdessus for whatever reasons nonetheless, exposes the myth of the invincibility of management of global 'development' agencies in general and importantly underscores the limit of the powers of their staff. The Fund's staffs have arrogantly carried on as some independent actors, when in reality they are minions and courtiers of those who appointed them. They often pose as policy originators when in truth they operate under strict 'conditionalities' that are no less vicious as those they are asked to impose on their victims, making them the victimised that deserve our sympathy than the bullies we love to hate. The Fund's staff do talk down on governments, especially of the debt-ridden Africa, as if they were the real lenders, when in reality they are merely recruited international debt collectors operating in conformity with their employers' brief.

Of special importance in Camdessus' exit also is the searchlight it beams on the condition of service of international civil servants. The question is when will the Fund leave up to its gospel of reform and set the pace by reforming self? IMF and the World Bank have, for instance, promoted considerable intellectual attack on the notion of permanent and protected jobs, in the process, scape-goating the trade unions as being responsible for 'rigidities' in the labour market. The two institutions actually invented the notion of 'labour market flexibility', under which millions of workers worldwide can be hired and fired in the true spirit of 'impersonal market forces'. It is certainly a great discovery that same Fund's staff enjoys stable and rewarding jobs as exemplified by the long service of its out-going director, even as millions of workers are losing their jobs worldwide based on its policy advice about the efficacy of labour market flexibility. Somebody must definitely unravel this one more millennium riddle that says: 'do what we say but do not practice what we do.'

Reflections on the out-going Fund's CEO remain incomplete without examining his Nigerian dimension. Camdessus will be remembered as the first chief executive to visit the country in recent time. Since Nigeria became a member of IMF at independence, it has been exposed to IMF intensive policy advice. But more than anybody else, Camdessus brought fresh life to the relationship between the country and the Fund with his May visit. Hitherto, Africa and indeed Nigeria, only featured in international financial discourse, once some desperate balance of payment crises necessitated some feverish mission-visits conducted often by some under-age, hard-nosed middle-level Fund's missionaries. It is gratifying that Camdessus broke the African jinx and proves that the continent matters beyond bailout handouts.

His Abuja lectures will be remembered, not only for the seminal issues raised therein, (good governance, democracy and the rule of law, equity and justice, economic restructuring, liberalisation and the debt crisis) but also the executive candour with which they were presented. The strong point of Camdessus' May visit lies in his pro-active orientation as distinct from the traditional reactive 'take it or leave it' recipes, the Fund's country missionaries are notorious for. But even with this acknowledged contribution, many observers still wonder if his Abuja ideas can actually lead to real movement in the direction of real development for Nigeria or will only further oil the existing grinding mill of no-growth, de-industrialisation, stagnation and poverty.

One of the controversial issues in Camdessus' lectures is trade liberalisation. Camdessus called for liberalised trade system to 'ensure that the private sector's decisions are not based on distorted prices.'

IMF staff papers have derided infant industry arguments, making a case for liberalisation ostensibly to usher in an era of competition, outward looking manufacturing and export diversification. Alluring, but this is one argument that is patently doctrinaire and in Nigerian context cancerous.

Camdessus described as 'historic scandal', the present Nigerian reality in which, the real per capita income is lower than three decades ago. Nobody can fault this 'point blank'. Yet, there have always been 'historic scandals', such that Camdessus need not act another Christopher Columbus rediscovering only one out of many historic scandals. One historic scandal lies in the fact that century-long colonial rule with its regime of trade-liberalisation not only killed emergent industry but did not establish a single industry. Infant industries and their protection are historic responses to the historic scandal of wholesale trade liberalisation under colonial economy in which Nigeria was assigned the ignoble role of a producer of raw materials for European industries and consumer of manufactured goods from the same Europe. To return us to the era of discredited mercantilism is not to learn from the lesson of one historic scandal. Sadly, the same historic scenario is being enacted. No thanks to Minister Anthony Ani under Abacha dictatorship who surreptitiously 'buy-us-back' to colonialism by signing WTO agreement in 1997 without any consultation with industry's operators. De-industrialisation now stares us on the face as dumped textile goods, food and beverages, furniture from Europe and Asia, litter Nigerian markets undermining local production and accentuating unemployment crisis. Nigeria's private sector's decisions are now based on worse 'distorted prices' and is caused by trade liberalisation contrary to Camdessus' assumption that it is caused by protectionism. It does not matter if the infant industries have now become old capable of facing up to competition as the IMF argues. The issue is that every country protects its own infant and old industries. All Western economies rightly disregard IMF's policy advice and protect their industries especially in agriculture, textile and construction. This explains why the cotton and textile industries in US fiercely opposed Clinton's Africa Bill, which tokenly tries to allow African imports. It explains subsidised agriculture in Europe and high level of protective and non-tariff measures for industries in Japan and South Korea. Nigeria needs not prove an exception.

IMF: Who Is Fooling Whom? [6]

A set of white teeth does not indicate a pure heart, goes a Nigerian proverb. Asked of the impact of Nigeria's withdrawal from IMF staff monitoring programme,[*] Dr Magnus Kpakol, the Chief Economic Adviser to the president reportedly snapped back; *Actually, Nigeria did not withdraw from anything.* Kpakol's disinterested response contrasts with Minister Ciroma's celebrated affirmative withdrawal notice elegantly premised on the preferred values of benefits of political stability, democratic consolidation, credibility and accountability, as distinct from IMF's 'narrowly defined macroeconomic targets'.

To what extent has the Federal Government's displayed 'white teeth' represented its 'pure heart' on the much talked about withdrawal from IMF's programme judging by advertised discordant views between bureaucrat Kpakol and adept politician Ciroma, two economic financial actors in the administration? Some observers maintain that the latest acrimony is vintage PDP, noting that what we are witnessing is a ruling party that has extended its habitual betrayal of consensus building in political arena to the sphere of economy.

Party Chairman, Audu Ogbe, ever short on categorical words on the war of attrition between PDP dominated legislature and executive, for once, engaged in straight talk by reportedly hailing the Federal Government for dumping the Fund's programme which he solely (and solely) held responsible for his party's inability to deliver on its promise to alleviate poverty. By this, Chief Ogbe created an impression, according to which, if there was no IMF and its monitoring programme, PDP could have picked one in its bagful of crisis-diversions, with the view of preventing searchlight from the

---

[6] *Nigerian Tribune*, 21st May 2002, pp. 12
[*] *Sunday Guardian*, 10/3/2002

fact that ruling PDP, awash with so much resources, has a token to showcase for them in terms of job creation and stable prices for the electorate.

International finance is an acknowledged game between politicians and bureaucrats in government on the one hand and presidents and spokesmen of multilateral financial institutions on the other. Nowhere is this game being feverishly played than Nigeria today.

It is the reaction to the latest development, IMF resident mission reportedly pledged support for Nigeria's decision with a promise to give 'technical' support for it s 'home grown' substitute programme. Some 'white teeth' indeed. But that was before the Fund's (pure) heart poured forth. Resident mission's seemingly supportive remark was quickly followed by more authoritative and rather combative press conference addressed by the Fund's Senior Adviser for Africa, Mr. Hiroyuki Hino (sounds as distant as Kpakol) disclosed that the Fund would have disengaged Nigeria anyway, due to, failure to meet some important macro economic benchmarks'.

Arising from this game of wits and war of nerves of Nigeria's withdrawal from IMF programme is the question; who is actually fooling who? Citizens must come to terms with the implications of the on-going Tom-and-Jerry-kind of money game in an economy urgently begging for recovery through original innovative policies and ideas and weigh the implications of the current drag for public well being.

IMF controversy, once again, points to how we are permanently hunted by incoherent economic policy formulation, the worst manifestation of which is multiple mutually exclusive official pronouncements such that one wonders who is actually responsible for Nigerian economy. The economy is under the strains engendered by multiple drivers, namely: unelectable bureaucrats, politicians and unaccountable officials of international financial institutions. Last year, the drama in incoherence on the economy was obscenely played out, when there was no official consensus on the external debt figure. The president, who has rightly not hidden his disdain for prohibitive debt, talked of 22 billion dollars, Vice-President Atiku Abubakar 25 billion, Finance Minister, Ciroma 28 billion, all in the presence of IMF, which predictably opted for the high figure of 32 billion dollars.

When do we put our house in order on critical economic issues? We may afford to be clumsy with the electoral law; Supreme Court is there to help us out. But who bails us out of the drain that ever constitutes servicing fees (as high as five billion dollars since the inception of civil rule) on debt that we do not agree on its sum total? Economic clumsiness pushes us deeper into poverty amidst abundant resource endowments and the earlier we come to terms with this, the better. We dare not push the economy into the current political Hobbesian state of nature in which everybody seems to be for himself and only God has been for us, the victims, so far.

There is still a discernible lack of openness on the part of the Fund officials even as they demand the same from their customers; governments. Thanks to the current controversy, critical information hitherto hidden is now an open knowledge. For once, we now know that Nigeria had 'formal' and 'informal' IMF programmes with 'conditionalities' that included higher fuel prices, privatisation, deregulation of downstream oil activities (read; fuel price increases) in particular. They had created a false impression of 'home grown' ideas even with some lip-service at patriotism, when in truth, it has all been about the legendry roadside birds dancing to some blues being played by Washington-based Bretton Woods Institution.

When Minister Ciroma accused IMF of bias for 'narrow macroeconomic targets', he inadvertently confirmed a well known fact that IMF is *not* a development agency and that the responsibility to develop Nigeria lies with those we elected to office and not with a debt collecting agency that IMF is. Time will tell if this administration will face up to the challenges arising from its reservation about the IMF programme. One immediate challenge is to creatively come out with alternative policies for recovery.

Vision 2010 without Abacha but within the context of the new democratic dispensation offers this administration as a serious point of departure at a real domestic economic initiative.

Meanwhile, it will be instructive to know IMF's reaction to the deep-seated resentment against its institution and programme in Nigeria. A seemingly divisive society and polity suddenly found common language in hailing the Federal Government for daring to snub IMF monitors. Only football unites Nigerians as official (lip-service?) rejection of IMF did recently. Perhaps this administration is only being populist with IMF card. And why not? Any government will act populist on the eve of an election. There is even some assumption the PDP might be acting ZANU-PF's notorious land question with IMF's monitoring programme. Either way, the spontaneous excitement that greeted the administration's current stance on IMF must certainly be a food-for-thought for the Fund.

The publicity blitz aimed at cultivating 'New Partnership for Development' in Nigeria launched by the Fund in 1999, has once again been undermined by its own very policy dogma. From an expectation of new partnership with Nigeria, IMF has taken some steps backward in the direction of old dictatorship with the attendant despair to the country and the Fund as well.

Mr. Hino, the Fund's adviser for Africa pointedly decried Nigeria's withdrawal and gave tutorial on how Nigeria should put its house in order by curbing excessive spending, merging the official and parallel market rates of the naira among other standard notorious policy prescriptions. While Nigeria may very well make do with some of this policy advice, the Fund may very well make do with some in-house reflections on its own policy prescriptions that are often observed in breach because they undermine real development. Vice President Atiku Abubakar disclosed that Nigeria met 11 out of 14 "points benchmark" dictated by the Fund, but that record level compliance still fell short of IMF's expectation. In IMF's school of recovery, in which 99 per cent is unacceptable, it is clear that no student can be successful. The painful reality however is that Nigeria is not a school with capacity for endless experiment.

This is a country of 120 million people groaning under the weight of a programme aimed at servicing dubious debts dutifully supervised by the Fund. IMF insistence that Nigeria devotes 3.1 billion dollars to servicing the debt that has been more than paid for means that we annually live below our means contrary to IMF's boring sermon that we live above means.

What Nigeria needs is not belt-tightening via freeze on recurrent and capital expenditure but loosening of the debt chain that will release scarce resources for growth. The $3.1 billion debt servicing, scandalous out-flow for a country that is paradoxically going around bowl in hand for foreign investment will be $28.4 billion by 2011. When Dr. Magnus Kpakol says IMF system is an 'open system in which everybody talks to everybody,' he is less magnanimous with his country. Nothing could be more closed-ended than when the creditors pressurise Nigeria to devote 65 per cent of country's capital expenditure, four times the total provision for health, to debt servicing.

NEPAD for Beginners[7]

NEPAD is one of Africa's development paradigms, which is true to type, increasingly caught between great optimism and deep-rooted pessimism. Indeed since its inception in July 2001 as a fruition of Millennium Partnership for Africa's Recovery Programme (MAP) and Omega Plan, NEPAD is already afflicted with the notorious malaise of African policy shouting match of 'yes' or 'no'.

First is the 'yes' group. The optimists and promoters of NEPAD are far more familiar as their arguments. Enthusiastically promoted by President Obasanjo, South Africa's Mbeki, Senegal's Abdoulaye Wade and Algeria's Bouteflika, NEPAD is seen as a new African initiative that raises the prospects of an African Renaissance. The goals are alluring; promote growth and sustainable development, eradicate widespread and severe poverty as well as halt marginalisation of the continent in the globalisation process. NEPAD's advocates insist that it is not a Fund raising project but in their words 'a holistic, comprehensive integrated strategic framework for the socio-economic development of Africa'.

It rests on three pillars for Africa's development to laying the conditions for development (with emphasis on conflict resolution, peace and democracy), sectoral priorities (bridging infrastructural gap, with emphasis on energy, transport, agriculture, environmental initiative, public investment and human resource) and resource mobilisation (through direct foreign and domestic investment, debt relief, overseas direct resource flows and market access initiative for agricultural and manufactured products from Africa). The advocates of NEPAD are proud to say that this new initiative departs from

---

[7] *Daily Trust*, Monday 29th July 2002, pp. 6

post-colonial import substitution strategy and the notorious adjustments programme of the late 1970s and 1980s. While the later was pushed and favoured by the IMF and World Bank, NEPAD proudly claims African ownership and insists it is one plan conceived and developed by African leaders.

The 'no' group is paradoxically being ably led from the reverse, by Gambia's Yahaya Jammeh. Jammeh, whose later-day civilian outlook seems more comic than real, is himself hardly reputed for hard-nosed humour. When he therefore, on the occasion of his recent anniversary on the throne, dropped what passed for a humour of the moment, it naturally turned a media delight. He told the BBC that the salesmen (no visible saleswoman yet) of NEPAD, which he perceives as 'bowl-in-hand project' needed sufficient 'KNEE-PADS' to go begging for their pet idea; NEPAD. The uncomplimentary joke marked the second pessimistic definition of NEPAD according to Jammeh. He had once underscored the dependency orientation of NEPAD by questioning a taunted notion of partnership, in which (as captured by a news agency picture) an obviously weather-beaten Obasanjo and Mbeki were seen standing in front of a rather relaxed Tony Blair during one of their NEPAD's salesmanship trips to UK. As a President of a tourism Republic, that survives on aids and handouts, new students of NEPAD dare not ignore Jamey's notion of the new programme. Jammeh knows as someone who lives on it, the frustration attendant of getting a token aid from still-necked affluent countries. With the ambitious expectation of as much as 60 billion dollars NEPAD annually as investment flows to the continent, the frustration might even more than double. The significance of Jammeh's attack of NEPAD lies in the fact that the scores of endless diplomacy of its chief advocates have only delivered token 6 billion dollars commitment of G-8.

The 'no' group has been reinforced by a number of African scholars and civil society organisations that have subjected NEPAD to remarkable scrutiny of late. They argued that NEPAD couldn't fashion out new partnership since it remains uncritical and even apologetic of the existing world economic and trade arrangement with all its inequities. It is seen as another attempt to once again resell the continent to the same neo-liberal economic agenda that for long brought it to ruination and underdevelopment. NEPAD is therefore seen as a continuation of the same structural adjustment programme it hopes to depart from. Critics fault the assumptions of African ownership of the programme given the conspicuous absence of Africans in the conception, design and formulation of the NEPAD, insisting that claim of African origin is a lip service; the main target of NEPAD is foreign donors, particularly in the G8. Significantly, the pessimists hold that by being uncritical of the existing world multilateral agencies and even seeking engagement with them, NEPAD further locks African economies to the disadvantaged globalisation process it atheistically strives to correct.

The challenge for new beginners to NEPAD is whence lies the truth about the programme? Is it another curse or a blessing as both the advocates and opponents of the programme want us to believe?

First point for new beginners to note is the return of development discourse in Africa after almost two decades of 'Do-nothing' but 'pay your debt' under the notorious SAP. There has been almost a conspiracy of silence about development since mid 80s as countries of Africa were made to grapple with survivalist strategy to cope with balance of payment crises, through currency devaluation, removal of subsidy, retrenchment and stripping of states assets via privatisation. The point here is that it is refreshingly new to see Africa talking about a vision for development and a programme of realising this vision with clear targets for growth rates human resource development, education and health among others.

It is also remarkable that via NEPAD, we are seeing a reinvention of developmentalist state in Africa, again after two decades of promotion of market orthodoxy, in which the state was vilified for being obstacle to development that must be rolled back to pave the way for private enterprise and market forces. Worthy of note is that if Africa will pass through the Rostow's 'stages of development', the state remains the engine for this push as the state has been a push for development in Europe, America and Asia, contrary to false hope about development through blind market process and promoted by creditors and their counterparts in Africa.

Even with its dependency orientation, we should note that the optimism of NEPAD's advocates lies with heads of government of G-8 and *not* the respective corporate institutions in G-8 countries, underscoring the fact that development has to be consciously directed through direct governmental action rather than market fundamentalism that we have been inundated with for the past decades.

Also significance is that through NEPAD, we are avertedly witnessing an ascendancy of political economy, albeit, a vulgar type, which has been long rubbished with the deafening collapse of soviet communism in late 1980s. NEPAD underscores that economic development is impossible without addressing the political question. This should rather be of great excitement to African radical scholars rather than wholesome criticism we have seen of late. Indeed one can talk of new Marxism without due acknowledgement to Karl Marx through NEPAD.

From 1960s up to date, holistic programme of transformation that insists that politics needs not be differentiated from economics and culture had been the preoccupation of few radicals that are often derided as utopian and unrealistic and in many respects seen as subversive by pointed dictatorship suffocating the continent then. Indeed this was precisely what the great late Bade Onimodes and Ola Onis and Bala Usmans demanded for in the 1970s and for which they were harassed and intimidated by the then Obasanjo as military head of state. At a point, authorities tried to ban political science and history from universities, as they were deemed subversive of development narrowly perceived as technocratic or technical. Indeed, in ABU and Uniport, authorities desperately tried to dismantle integrated schools of social science and arts which encouraged holistic view of development as favoured in NEPAD document. It is significant that with deepening poverty and lack of progress arising from past narrowly conceived economistic plans of the past we are now witnessing a convergence of perspective between adversaries that hitherto denied a worthy continent of robust perspective for development. The challenge for students of development is to see how to deepen the faith of newly converted advocates NEPAD to political economy rather than engaging in a

UN help analysis by paralysis that does not in any way address the practical problem of development in Africa.

Take the political component of NEPAD for instance. For African governments to concede that democracy is not just fashionable but indispensable for development is profoundly revolutionary. New beginners to NEPAD must hold the advocates of the programme to their new discovery through advocacy and insistence to deepen democracy. The issue is not to remain academic and dogmatic, begging the issue that NEPAD's conception of democracy is limited and 'Western', but to act for the realisation of a new timely and clear commitment to democratic process. NEPAD's document for instance, underscores accountability, freedom of association, and assembly, free and fair elections, and existence of several parties among others. In Nigeria, it will be very interesting how we translate this provision into reality. How does the NEPAD's provision relate to the existing silly, obscene and clearly undemocratic bureaucratic guidelines for party registration by INEC and the piecemeal registration of parties that ought to be inalienable right? The last three years of democratic process would have certainly brought out greater enterprise, if there had been unfettered party processes that would allow for real political parties as opposed to the existing 'electoral machines' (or are they rallies with apology to Audu Ogbe, Chairman of a ruling party that should know better). Thus the challenge is how we really domesticate NEPAD's programme and transform it from rhetoric's to reality, by supporting this democratic component and work towards its realisation.

NEPAD's economics however will task, the new beginners the more. Its economics is rather vague. On the positive side, it sets ambitious targets for growth, employment generation and poverty alleviation but its policy instruments to achieve these goals are rather assumed than explicitly stated. The challenge is to make NEPAD come out with practical proposals for real development. The advocates of the programme put their hope too much of scores of Ifs'; namely if the continent can mobilise, 60 billion dollars investment annually, if debt relief is granted, if overseas development assistance comes in, ad infinitum.

Yet there are considerably factors under the control of governments of the continent for development. They must come out with appropriate industrial policies that will protect existing small investment and attract more. For instance, lower interest rates. At Nigeria's 30 to 40 per cent rate of lending, only quick drug peddlers can borrow not long-term investors. Government must just do it to lower interest rate. In addition there must be protection for those labour intensive industries in which we have comparative advantages. Again it is within governments to impose restrictions and even ban to avoid the existing dumping of all sort of goods that are pushing the continent back to de industrialisation. Thus it is clear from the above that NEPAD provides a good platform for contestation as well as cooperation between governments and the citizens for development. The issue is that the citizens must claim ownership of the programme that in any case is being done in their name.

Naira: back to Dutch Disease[8]

What the Dutch and their auction system got to do with naira beats the imagination of every lay observer of the economy. And why not? Ordinary Nigerians rightly observe that Nigeria expends a whopping sum of 10 billion naira, 1.25% of 2002 budget on a National Identity card project, which remains more in the realm of potential than real. This project, they observe, is meant to differentiate Nigerians from *Nigeriens* no less than the Dutch. But it seems the only discernable return on this prohibitive investment so far is the growing crisis of confidence about the motive or intention of the project. To therefore put a Dutch stamp on the country's chosen mechanism for allocation of scarce foreign exchange further underscores profound national identity crisis of unimaginable proportion. Coming on the heel of the promise of a 'home-grown' economic policy by President's chief economic adviser, Dr Magnus Kpakol, cynics insist that applying Dutch method to allocate foreign exchange conveys an official hypocrisy of the worst bent. The question is; should national economic policy option not bear a national stamp, assuming that makes any difference to the substance of the policy?

Nigeria certainly has enough of Dutch disease. We had one in the 1970s, in which the problem was how to spend the oil money, thanks to oil windfalls. In 1987, another Dutch malaise afflicted the country, as the country was forced to adopt a notorious system of auctioning foreign exchange under an equally notorious programme of structural adjustment (SAP). To return to this Dutch ailment, almost 15 years after, underscores an outbreak of one Dutch disease too frequent in Nigeria. It makes nonsense of the Rostow's theory of

---

[8] *Daily Trust*, Monday 12th August 2002, pp. 6

growth according to which a country moves from one lower stage of economic performance to higher level.

Asked about his view, the late Nnamdi Azikiwe at the infamous height of the Dutch auction system in 1987 said the then Second-tier Foreign Exchange market (SFEM) (now IFEM) sounded 'Greek'. According to him, it was ' a clear devaluation of our currency'. Nothing has confirmed the validity of late sage's observation than the recent development in the country's money market. Two bidding sessions of Dutch auction recorded a significant devaluation of the naira. Indeed in January this year, naira exchanged for N112 to a dollar. Today, it exchanges for N131.01, a prohibitive 17% devaluation in six months. The only dramatic free-fall naira in comparison to latest development, was in September 1986, when a day after introduction of SFEM, naira took a plunge from N1.5535 to N4.6174, 197.23%. The country is yet to recover from that singular adventure into insanity.

The latest outbreaks of another Dutch disease as, it were, have certainly reopened the debate about the country's exchange rate management (or is it mismanagement?). It also brought to focus the role of the CBN in the on-going economic recovery efforts. With Dutch auction system, Nigeria's monetary economics must come under critical examination with public hearings that must elicit public concerns.

The often-repeated declared objectives of monetary policies are stable external value of the Naira, domestic price stability and a viable external balance of payment for the country. How our variously adopted mechanisms for allocating scarce foreign exchange (from fixed exchange regime to floating rates within SFEM, IFEM and Dutch auction) meet the requirements of declared objectives is one question begging for an answer.

In the 1970s up to mid-eighties, CBN maintained a regulatory function, which effectively shored up the value of the Naira against the vagaries of depreciation. CBN at a time severed link with the dollar in recognition of the unsettling happenings in foreign exchange markets. Due to inflation and disequilibrium in capital movements, major currencies continue to fluctuate erratically, which in turn undermined the value of the naira. The naira was actually floated but

CBN moderated the floatation by providing for adjustment and appropriate action. CBN introduced a managed floatation of naira in which exchange value of the naira was administratively determined on the basis of changes in the value of a selected group of currencies of different countries weighted on the volume of each country's trade with Nigeria. Freely fluctuating exchange rates was deemed incompatible with domestic price stability. This prevented imported inflation and sustained monetary stability that in turn allowed for economic planning and development of that period. Time has actually changed and so also the exchange rate mechanism.

We are told now that a regime of regulated exchange market is out of fashion and that what is desirable is deregulation in which through the interplay of market forces, 'true' value of the Naira will be determined. It is one irony of history that CBN today seems helpless to protect the value of naira against the increasing depreciation of the dollar even at a time the dollar is falling against other major currencies as it is now and as it was during September 11 terror attacks on World Trade Centre and the Pentagon. We are faced today with the spectre of imported devaluation of the naira.

The question begging for answer is; what is the objective of Dutch auction? Are the monetary objectives of price stability and stable exchange rate still valid? Certainly you cannot talk about price stability when, within six months, you record 17 per cent devaluation that further puts pressure on inflation rate officially put at 18 per cent by the government. Certainly the objective cannot be improved capacity utilization given that manufacturers now need more money to oil their ever-rising production cost for imported inputs, no thanks to devaluation. The muted reason that the Dutch auction rate will discourage round tripping and sharp practices can certainly not withstand the fact of history that shows that parallel exchange market will always coexist with the official market, giving incentive for sharp practices, for as long as the former is not sanctioned and is treated as if it is not a criminal activity.

The challenge lies in how the CBN must urgently resume its regulatory role especially with respect to the foreign exchange market. It is gratifying and commendable that we recently witnessed a new activist CBN that was willing to and indeed did sanction 20 erring banks and even sealed up a recalcitrant bank. That was a refreshing departure from a laissez-faire passive and almost irresponsible CBN of the old. The bank's deputy Governor Dr. Usman Shamsudeen in particular always raises the prospects of a new central banking with his active commentary that informs the citizens and puts financial operators on their toes about the danger of distress and upsurge in cases of fraud and financial crimes in general, including foreign exchange malpractices (round-tripping) inadequate quality and quantity of human resources, and dearth of experienced hands. His testimony in particular on the NITEL sale fiasco about how First Bank disregarded basic financial rules shows that we can have a CBN that knows its obligation to the economy and society as a whole.

CBN must return to basics. It must return to its core objectives of maintaining sound financial structure, promotion of monetary stability, safeguarding the value of naira and stable exchange rate and prove a financial adviser to the federal government, in the areas of price and exchange rate management.

The Asian currency crisis of two years ago, the terrorist attacks of September 11 in New York and the Argentina tragedy underscore the weakness of wholesale deregulation and liberalization of the financial sector.

Our current domestic 'round-tripping' and short-term frivolous financing of imports of consumables such as fruit juice, biscuits by banks that in turn put pressure on exchange rate of the naira must be treated as domestic equivalents of 'terror financing' which is wrecking havocs in terms of domestic factory closures, mass job losses swelling the ranks of armed robbers and communal and religious rioters. The policy goal should be the deployment of assets for development and not to move assets offshore.

Regulations must be introduced to stem the current capital flight. Relevant provisions of Bank and Other Financial Institutions Decree (BOFID) must be enforced. That law contains as many as 23 penalties for various contraventions which CBN is yet to apply to check recalcitrant banks.

Let the CBN chieftains know that Central Bank worldwide reads election results and *not* balance sheets. And election results are about inflation, employment, capacity utilization, social security and social welfare among others. Some of us have not hidden our disdain for a CBN headed by an accountant whose mindset is to balance books rather than balance objectives of development. It is only in Nigeria that on the eve of a presidential election, national currency will get devalued on the altar of an auctioning arrangement yet "opposition parties" remain indifferent. Indeed only NLC has warned about the danger of continuous slide in naira value.

Of what benefit is a consistent devaluation to a mono-cultural economy that exports nothing beyond crude oil, the price of which is fixed by OPEC? How does devaluation fit into the taunted NEPAD economics? What are the implications for inflation, capacity utilization and employment generation? Perhaps only the government benefits from the new Dutch auction through monetized oil receipts that will in turn fuel frivolous spending. Let CBN put an end to this Dutch disease, stabilise naira and kick start the process of economic recovery.

Re-Inventing the Industry[9]

President Olusegun Obasanjo, during the weekend presided over a Forum specifically dedicated to 'textiles'. Saturday Forum with the President is a programme introduced by His Excellency to critically examine a topical issue with a cross section of stakeholders with a view of finding some solutions. Whatever must have been the outcomes of previous forums, this last Forum was refreshing optimistic and revolutionary in its proceedings, its revelations and its possible resolutions of the identified problems of textile industry. It was a dream come true for investors and stakeholders who have been groaning under the negative effects of past government inaction.

Blazing the trail were two remarkable presentations by Honourable Minister of Industry Chief Kola Jamodu perhaps, the main facilitator of this forum and Mr. Victor Eburajolo, Chairman, Nigeria Textile Manufacturers Association. Never before have two presentations been unanimous on some grim statistics. The first generation industry, which had as many as 175 firms in mid-1980s, can barely enlist 44 today. Within the last five years the country uncritically jumped on World Trade Organisation (WTO) bandwagon, the industry lost as many as 60,000 jobs. Capacity utilisation is currently as miserable as 35 per cent. The bane of the industry is unfair competition from India and China reinforced by smuggling made possible by 152 land smuggling routes (Customs says it is actually 149 routes). In addition the problem of poor and inefficient infrastructure that in turn denied the industry much needed competitive advantage came to the fore. Then the sundry problems of prohibitive credit rates and multiple levies by state governments.

---

[9] *Daily Trust*, Monday 2nd September 2002, pp. 6

President Obasanjo at the opening of the Forum had underscored the significance of textile industry, thought provokingly tasking participants to prevent the nation from going 'naked' by averting the collapse of industry that should cloth all. But it was clear that confronted with 'naked' statistics by stakeholders, the President just like everybody at this Forum agreed as much that we are already being stripped 'naked' as the industry was on the verge of total collapse. President Obasanjo conveyed the concern of genuine stakeholders when he described unwholesome statistics as a 'disaster' and 'criminal'. He particularly impressed all that the neglect of the industry in recent past was 'unpardonable'. The President, who demonstrated an inclusive insight of the danger of foot-loose globalisation, accepted that the country had enough evidence of sufficient chronic injuries inflicted by dumping of goods in order to protect its industry within the WTO rules.

What came out of Saturday forum is that while it might be true that private sector is the engine of growth, the real lubricant of this engine remains the government. The President deserves commendation for restoring the activist developmental role of the state hitherto abandoned on the altar of SAP and do-nothing laissez-faire of the recent past. The truth is that contrary to falsehood promoted by IMF and its local megaphones, everybody protects its own industry. Whether the industry is in 'infancy' or 'adult-hood'. Why would America expend as much as a billion dollars a day to subsidise own farmers? Why would George W. Bush 'heartlessly' scorn Earth summit if it were not self-evident that the outcomes of the UN conference have adverse implications (in terms of industrial restructuring and job-creation) for the most polluting nation that USA is? Government after God, is the protector of citizens, cooperate citizens inclusive.

The Forum revealed how India subsidises its long dated industry through reduced energy tariffs and generous export incentives that made Indian products undersell Nigerian products at landing costs. Indeed India has a programme tagged as 'Focus on Africa' with a view of dumping its relatively cheaper goods. Conversely we saw how Nigeria remains unfocused until now, given that some state governments rather than giving incentives to industry, impose prohibitive levies of various wild imagination on industry, NEPA increases tariffs without corresponding energy output and raw-water desperately being sourced by industry is being taxed by some state governments.

UNIDO representative rightly pointed out that while protection is desirable in the short-run, the long-term challenge is that the industry must be competitive. He however rightly noted that a situation in which within two hours, there were four NEPA shut downs in an industry would not make the industry competitive. The challenge therefore lies in how the government will create the right policy environment for industry to thrive. It is the government that must fashion out appropriate industrial policy that must urgently underscore the imperative of domestic production rather than the existing unofficial imports and dumping, with huge revenue loss to the country. A situation in which according to the latest UNDP report, imports accounts for as much as 34 per cent of GDP, only return Nigeria to the colonial era in which we are exporter of raw materials and importers of finished goods. Even in the most celebrated of 'open' societies, USA, imports accounts for only 12.2 per cent of GDP making US economy, according to UNDP 'still insular'.

It is the government that must further push for greater power generation. NEPA certainly has shown the capacity for some improvement but as the MD of this public monopoly must have seen from Saturday forum, NEPA's improvement is still far cry from industrial requirements. Indeed, NEPA's slow and still erratic delivery is undermining production, encouraging idle capacity, creating unemployment and deepening poverty. It is also the government that must enforce quality standard and put appropriate legislation that must make violation of import requirements punishable. It is also the government that must manage the exchange rate and not auction the exchange rate as it is being done by the CBN with attendant implication for exchange rate and the effects on industrial planning. So much for market forces, we have seen how do-nothing approach by government in the past has virtually killed the first ever generation industry.

On the whole, what comes out of this timely forum is that the country must urgently halt the existing de-industrialisation process. If it is done for textile it must be done for all sectors of the economy. Indeed this is the acid-test for industrial revival. Textiles cannot be overemphasised given its linkage and employment fall-outs. It is self-evident that when it comes to discourse on production and development, unity of purpose is required. Which explains why the survival of cotton producers in Zamfara is intrinsically linked to the performance, or lack of it, of textile mill owner at Isolo Lagos. It is also clear that in the long run the only resource we must control is certainly not just oil and gas that are evidently non-renewable but industrial inputs and outputs that are clearly inexhaustible. Given the multi-dimensional approaches required to uplift textile alone, we can make do with more co-operation and many hands are required to do this.

The only missing link in the weekend forum is the loud and conspicuous absence of members of the relevant committees of the two houses especially dealing with commerce, industry and labour. Let there be disagreements since the strength of democracy lies in its capacity to make tolerable disagreements. However, as we disagree, we should also know that cooperation is needed even to resolve conflicts and above all to cope with the challenges of development confronting the country. The point here is that, we must move away from the ever-acrimonious politics of distribution of oil money (budget appropriation) to cooperative politics of production in the real sector of industry and agriculture. Put in another way, for all we care, let's 'impeach' the mounting problems of development rather than dissipating scarce energy hounding the dramatis persona that are in short-supply to address the problems before us all. The hope is that four-terms of reference given to the all-inclusive committee at the end of Saturday forum will come out with concrete ideas that must reinvent the industry.

Reducing poverty through paper work? [10]

"The world has enough for everyone's need, but not everyone's
greed."
– *Mahatma Ghandi*

Good programme must have good image. Poverty Reduction
Strategy Paper (PRSP) profoundly suffers from poverty of image.
Estimated whopping two-thirds of Nigerian population (some 80
million) adjudged poor wonder how their deprivations will be
reduced via some paper work. *Na paper work we go chop?* They rightly
ask. Perhaps the poor are ignoramuses after all but it is debatable
whether he or she that is not poor will know poverty than the poor
themselves. We can only ignore the perception of the poor at the
peril of any programme we design for them. *Na paper we go chop?* Is
certainly a legitimate question by the poor. After all, promoters of
poverty reduction do not measure poverty by paper but in dollar
terms.

We are told that "of world's 6 billion people, 2.8 billion (almost
half) live on less than $2 a day, and 1.2 billion (a fifth) live on less
than $1 a day. Of the 1.2 billion living on $1 a day, 23.3% live in sub-
Sahara Africa, the second worst off region to South Asia (World
Bank: 2001)." To build house, to combat illiteracy, the poor need
money not paper work. How the promoters of PRSP resolve this
image crisis determines the future of this 'new' programme. In
another breath, we are told it is a National Poverty Reduction
Strategy (PRS) Process. Paper to process - six and half a dozen. The
difference is not as clear. But this playing around with words only
deepens the image crisis of this programme among the growing poor
of our richly God-given world.

---

[10] *Daily Trust*, Monday 4th November 2002, pp. 6

If poverty reduction strategy is a process, then it becomes endless, another rolling stone that gathers no moss. Is reduction of deprivations not time-bound? Is it an endless process? The practical questions are; when will 80 million Nigerian poor reduce by half? When will 50% of our children less than five years of age adjudge malnourished reduce to 5%? This in turn raises the fundamental question about the sincerity of purpose of PRSP. Why must we beg poverty through proposal for its reduction when we can and should eradicate it through practical direct actions? The rich do not have their wealth piecemeal, so why should the poors' poverty be divisible into some percentages to be reduced over time? The poor do not desire an iota of poverty no less than the rich is willing to part with an iota of riches.

This then points to the real drivers of PRSP. PRSP is a programme conceived by government and "external development partners" (read IMF and World Bank). Nigeria's variant started early this year although government had unilaterally initiated a similar programme with fanfare (NAPEP) earlier. It has been terminated but we are just being told that it will be resuscitated soonest.

Critics have argued that the problem is not with PRSP but with its promoters, namely government, World Bank and IMF. They argue that government and Bretton Woods Institutions, via omission and commission, are the very institutions that promoted poverty in the land. Nigeria's welfare indicators were quite impressive in the 1960s, 1970s and up to mid-1980s, until the country got exposed to policy advice of IMF and World Bank. How Nigeria's GNP per capita of US$1,160 crashed to miserable US$260 in 1995 has been attributed to grand twin conspiracy of both the government and these institutions through currency devaluation, subsidy removal, reduction of public expenditure, wage-freeze, trade liberalisation, dismantling of developmentalist welfare state and its replacement with law(less) and (dis)order state, wrapped up in the notorious policy of Structural Adjustment Programme (SAP). Critics then maintain that these institutions, whose actions and inactions wiped off middle-class, fuelled inflation, promoted riots (remember SAP riot?) deepened poverty within the context of military dictatorship and lack of freedom, cannot today claim to be poverty-conscious or poverty concerned. Recent IMF/World Bank/Government *Volte-face* on poverty is said to be another public relations exercise that raises expectations of the poor again to dash them. Perhaps critics are right or wrong but what is clear is that PRSP faces profound crisis of legitimacy. For one, this programme is for the poor and *not* by the poor. It is top-down by conception and formulation. Hunted by its board-room origin, efforts are being made to reform PRSP by taking it to the streets where the poor are, through series of "stake-holders" fora at hotels and conference centres, again not at village squares and town halls where the malnourished children and their poor parents are. It is this conceptual problem that is the bane of PRSP.

Why should a country like Nigeria be preoccupied with poverty reduction when it should be busy with wealth generation and wealth distribution? Every poor knows that the key to eradicating poverty is wealth creation. What Nigeria needs is Wealth Creation Direct Actions (WCDA) and not Poverty Reduction Strategy Paper (PRSP). This calls for a halt to existing de-industrialisation of erstwhile promising industrial power-houses of Africa. We need sustainable growth with jobs not the existing jobless growth. Industry must be revived to generate enough goods and services. When supply exceeds demand, price must fall. When people work, they earn wages enhancing their purchasing power for produced goods and services. The poor don't need charity. What they need is value addiction based incomes.

The key then lies in real production and not another round of paper work on poverty reduction. President Obasanjo's administration has taken some bold and commendable steps in the direction of rebuilding the energy sector, telecom minus roads of course (ask Mr. Fix it?). Let it intensify efforts in the direction that progress has been made and overcome other short-comings. Infrastructural revival will boost capacity utilisation and attract new domestic investment. President's intervention has commendably forced bankers (or are they shylocks?) to reflect on their ruinous prohibitive interest rate but 25% official ceiling interest rate *cannot* still ensure recovery. If America following September 11 and the attendant recession the terrorist assault engendered could crash interest rate to 2.6% to ensure recovery, Nigeria that has been in vicious cycles of crisis will only fall into abyss of deeper crisis with "reduced" 25 per cent interest ceiling. Nobody can attract new funds at this so-called reduced but still prohibitive rate and break even.

Furthermore, without delay the Federal Government should implement the forthcoming report of the technical committee on key growth inducing labour intensive sectors like textile. There must be prohibition of some imports, at least in the short-run especially on goods we can and must produce at home. Customs reform must continue to empower custom-men and women *not* to turn the other way while smugglers ruin a nascent economy. America with all its preference at openness is still an insular economy with trade accounting for meagre 21 per cent of total GDP while in Nigeria it is as high as 75 per cent.

We must build common-wealth today such that individuals will have some wealth as distinct from today where few have huge private wealth but majority grapple with common misery. We must move from zero-sum/lootocracy (oil) economy to job provider/sum-sum economy. Let's today heed that Mahatma Ghandi's words that: "The World has enough for everyone's need, but not everyone's greed."

However, if we must insist on paper work given our penchant for conference, keynote addresses, opening and closing ceremonies, vote of thanks etc, kindly let's discuss Wealth Generation Strategy Paper (WGSP) and not PRSP. The poor are not inherently disabled, it is our policy/or lack of it that disabled them. Even disabled when enabled have gotten Olympic medals. Why not able critical but poor mass of our people?

Not yet interest rate management[11]

One key macro-economic target of the newly announced Federal Government's Economic Recovery Programme 2003-2007 is interest rate. The new programme envisages "Interest rates to be market responsive, with attempts to direct low interest funds to the real sector." And therein lies the problem; the ambivalence of the new programme about interest rate management. While the targets for inflation and real GDP in the new Economic Recovery Programme are more categorical; 'around' 10% and 7% respectively by year 2007, the new programme still acts the legendary ostrich with interest rate and of course, exchange rate, for which we are told to expect "exchange rate management that assures a stable currency and seeks to eliminate significant parallel market activity" (sounds Dutch).

Interest rate is a quantifiable item, so why are we shy of fixing a desirable interest rate target for urgent economic recovery? The ambivalence and ambiguity of the new policy on interest rate underscores the seeming official un-seriousness to combat the ever-destructive impact of soaring interest rates for the real productive sector of the economy. If there is no target what then do we work towards? The point cannot be over-emphasised that the real acid test of any economic recovery plan is interest rate management.

By the current lending rates of between 35 and 40 per cent, we have inadvertently locked up scarce financial capital in financial markets (banks) rather than in productive investments (industries - small and medium scale alike). According to the CBN, funds in banks have only fuelled speculative 'economics' in foreign exchange leading to "round tripping" totalling as much as $503 million in 2002 alone.

---

[11] *Daily Trust*, Monday 25th November 2002, pp. 6

'Round-tripping' is a glorified word for speculation and value-subtraction as distinct from production and value-addition.

At a time industries and labour-intensive small enterprises are begging for funds for recovery and expansion, monetization of banks' deposits without real value-addition that can enhance goods and services and job creation underscores the futility of our interest rate (miss) management.

In fairness, President Olusegun Obasanjo has been consistent in his strident criticism of regime of high interest. Rightly, the President insists that the existing prohibitive lending rates are unhelpful to real productive sector upon which rests production of goods and services and employment creation. Indeed the President has matched his words of concerns with direct actions of change. In April this year, in an unprecedented but welcomed "undiplomatic soldiering", President Obasanjo stormed the lions' (or are they lairs?) den. He attended Bankers' Committee to head-on challenge the banking operators on the desirability of high interest rates. The President literarily did the job of CBN's boss, Monsieur Joseph Sanusi, who ad-infinitum, rationalizes rather than frontally confront the regime of high rate.

For those who care, central banks world-wide do read election returns to be determined by how many jobs politicians create, how many industries they open or revive, etc. But in Nigeria, CBN is ever concerned with reading balance sheets in which domestic objectives of job creation and industrial production tend to assume less importance. Indeed, CBN has inadvertently substituted real interest rate management for empty rhetorical references to "market-determined" interest rates and do-nothing approach that profits the bankers at the expense of real producers.

The truth is that no where in the world is interest rate market determined. It is either interest is managed (hence interest management) or it is not managed (hence interest non-management). America is the most cited celebrated "market-economy". Yet we see how interest rate management serves as a worthy instrument of economic recovery since September 11-terror attack. The American Federal Reserve through orchestrated economic engineering (not empty verbal rationalization and rhetorical helplessness) has more than five-times in 1 year progressively reduced interest rate to all-time low-level of 1.4%. Literarily, American businessmen and women and foreign investors, now have access to free-funds for economic recovery from profound recession engendered by a singular terror-attack of September 2001.

Nigerian economy has been in recession for the past two decades. It is an irony that Nigeria's CBN still requires presidential prodding before seeing interest rate management as instrument for recovery.

It is however refreshing that the President's persistent stubbornness on the issue of interest rate understandably on the eve of election, is yielding some results. The hope is that like the President, CBN will also read election results not its ever-boring balance sheet. And what matters in election results include the extent the President turns the economy around.

With effect from 1ˢᵗ of this month, Bankers' Committee (note: not Bankers' market) announced a cut in rate to maximum lending rate of 22 per cent. By Nigeria's ever bizarre standard, this capping of rate at 22 per cent has been dubbed "lowering of rate". By world economy standard, 22 per cent is not an interest(ing) rate in any respect. With 1.4% interest rate in USA, average 6% in EU and 16 per cent in South Africa, Nigeria's "lowered" rate of 22 per cent only makes sense in a non-producing oil-rentier economy. Yet we must encourage the President in pushing for investment-friendly interest rate regime amidst low capacity utilization and de-industrialization of erstwhile promising economy even when his economic advisers remain cynical and even serve as stumbling blocks to the realisation of deserved goal.

One first challenge is to rescue the President from his advisers. The President's economic advisers and managers alike still have the unhelpful mindset of do-nothing about-interest rate that has produced ruinous interest rates. In July this year, CBN reluctantly cut the minimum rediscount rate (MRR) from 20.5% to 18.5%. In addition, it reduced the cash reserve ratio from 12.5% to 9.5% for commercial banks that reportedly increased lending to the real sector by at least 20%. One would have expected that the CBN in response to bankers' committee would further lower the MRR, the interest rate at which it lends to banks, in a way that interest rate will be further lowered. The point here is that the moves by President's men are still slower than the president's speed to reach the preferred bus-stop of a single digit interest rate in a depressed economy begging for economic recovery.

Government and its financial agencies should look for alternative ways to fight inflation and desist from using the blunt instrument of high interest rates to fight inflation. The broad objective should be substantial reduction of interest rate, to increase the purchasing power of consumers, facilitate the shift of capital from financial markets into productive investments and substantially reduce the burden of public debt. The bane of most states of the federation saddled today with low public investment and non-payment of workers' salaries is huge domestic debt occasioned by high interest rates charged by banks. Let us reduce the greed of the banks and meet the needs of the economy.

Nigeria is in dire need of industrial revival and employment creation. Yes there is the Bank of Industry (BOI), expected to support the real sector. But we should not forget that large pool of investable funds resides more in commercial banks. The cost of funds in commercial banks is therefore more decisive to the revival of the economy.

Fuel scarcity or Deregulation disaster? [12]

Whatever happened to deregulation of the down stream sector of the oil industry and the promised Eldorado that this magic wand policy will resolve "most of the issues involved in cost structure, pricing and subsidy of petroleum products in Nigeria?" Better still, whatever happened to "market forces" or "market fundamentals" according to the priests and drivers of the doctrine, Chief Rasheed Gbadamosi…and Kupolokuns among others? These are fundamental questions the media refused to ask in the wake of the return of fuel queues of "yesteryears", fire outbreak, absentee spouses (who readily found excuses in fuel's stations), 'black markets' and everything associated with "fuel scarcity."

When the NLC chieftains were ruthlessly defeated and even prosecuted after the second fuel crisis, the official explanation is that at N26 per litre – import-parity price, "level playing field" had been created for oil major marketers which will awash the land with abundant quantity and quality fuel.

Barely a year after, we are back to ground zero with respect to product supply while we are again being confronted with discordant voices, on "return of subsidy", search for new prices (371), product-diversion ad-infinitum. Watching the spectacle of NNPC boss, Gaius Obaseki, talking down on chieftains of seemingly deaf-and-dumb representatives of Mobil, Chevron, Texaco and other major marketers, one comes to the conclusion that deregulation has run a full cycle from the promises to near disaster.

---

[12] *Daily Trust*, Monday 17th March, 2003, pp. 6

Yet while we witnessed a lot of official activism to 'kick-start' deregulation policy, today we are witnessing loud official resignation and silence as the policy ushers in stagnation and discredit to an elected government on the eve of another elections. Instead of the Kupolokuns, Gbadamosis who enthusiastically sold a policy we are left with Obaseki and the President himself who must choose between a new mandate and a dummy policy satisfying the greed of oil dealers.

Honourable Minister of Information, Professor Jerry Gana, true to tradition, has identified another conspiracy behind the present fuel scarcity. Like the previous uncovered 'plot', yours sincerely has no ground to doubt the efficacy of this new conspiracy. But like other conspiracies, the latest is from within and not from without as the Honourable tended to do. While one finger must point to political opponents who understandably would be delighted to puncture a touted achievement of this administration in the area of fuel supply, the remaining four fingers point to President's policy advisers who conspire to sell an undesirable as well as unsustainable policy.

The bane of deregulation as presently conceived, is that it is one policy based on two factors outside the control of government, namely international price of crude oil (at all-time high level of $35 per barrel no thanks to impending aggression against Iraq) as well as exchange of the naira which has further nose-dived to N127 to a dollar. It is a great conspiracy that government will be made to adopt a policy by factors outside its control. Nothing could be more conspiratorial. It is to the eternal discredit of deregulation that we are back to the same very "trauma" and "economic disruption usually associated with adjustments to petroleum products' pricing."

Given the volatility of the products prices in international market and naira exchange rates, well-meaning Nigerians with NLC as spokesperson, had argued that deregulation of prices is impossible and clearly undesirable.

The other dark side of deregulation as presently packaged is that it relies solely on the profit motive of major oil marketers rather than the country's national requirements and needs. The present-day advertised obstinacy and difference of oil companies in the face of another national tragedy called fuels scarcity underscored the

48

vulnerability of a dependent policy as deregulation. As yours sincerely has pointed out in his book, *The Crises of Pricing Petroleum Products in Nigeria* (2001), that

> "Multinationals, by definition, cannot be loyal to any particular nation-state. They are driven by only on consideration – profit maximisation. As experience has shown in many countries, these oil multinationals have constituted themselves into cartels to undermine supply and fix monopolistic prices."

What we are witnessing today is that we have inadvertently replaced one notorious NNPC monopoly with another profit-driven foreign monopoly that almost today hold the country to ransom on the altar of a preferred dubious price.

The challenge today is that Obasanjo government must abandon existing doctrinaire oil companies' favoured policy of deregulation for a pragmatic policy that tasks our national creativity and public welfare. Within the first six months of this government, fuel supply commendably improved. This was made possible by a combined effort to restructure domestic refineries and stamp out corruption within the supply-chain. We have seen how even more affluent countries of Europe and America are stocking reserves in case of American war in Iraq. Oil is certainly too oily to be deregulated. It is always a regulated product and Nigeria cannot and should not be an exception.

PPPRA'S Dictatorship of 'Prices'[13]

One paradox of the recent fuel price increase is the 'academic' of (is it doctrinaire approach?) of its proponents to what is mainly a practical policy dilemma (or is it a policy scandal?).

Asked about the impact of what international media acknowledged as 'massive' increases in the prices of petroleum products, the chairman of the Petroleum Products Pricing Regulatory Agency (PPPRA - break your jaw) reportedly said inflation was a "monetary issue". Perhaps this standard textbook answer to an inflation riddle occasioned by fuel price increase had some relevance for the embattled American marines in Baghdad. But it was certainly an unhelpful literary escape by the chieftain of an agency charged with the practical responsibility to save the government and the citizenry alike the 'trauma' and 'economic disruption' associated with previous price adjustments. Remember that one cardinal objective of the agency was to prevent price volatility associated with past increases. PPPRA will certainly go on record as one agency that has caused more traumas to the government that set it up while fuelling more inflation than previous notorious discredited price control boards of the 1970s. In fact the greatest paradox is to have a self-declared regulatory agency pushing for deregulation. Witness the speculation that trails its 'consultation processes' agency from the 'stakeholders' to the Council of State. Never before has a proposed price adjustment proved so alarmist with all the attendant implication for hoarding of products and price speculations. Some industry watchers actually noted that the announced price increases by the agency were reflections of speculation fuelled by the lousy posturing

---

[13] *Daily Trust*, Monday 30th June, 2003, pp. 6

of the agency than the so-called stale menu of "market fundamentals" we have been fed with.

The problem is with the PPPRA no less than its method. We have actually witnessed some 'consultation'. But PPPRA's method of consultation is excessive on the side of monologue but filled with huge deficit on the side of dialogue. The agency talked at, talked against but not talking with the citizenry. Which explains why its representation at the House of Representatives left the Honourable members more in the dark than the way the agency met them. Pray, if Chief Gbadamosi could not convince the representatives with his omnibus template of prohibitive 40 naira per litre that generously made provision for demurrage (read: inefficiency) and highway maintenance, is it ordinary people, the Honourables represent that would be better informed in the PPPRA's school of monologue?

Even within the oil sector, PPPRA could simply not build the necessary consensus as NNPC's chieftains (who know better), insisted that only paltry sum of $150 million had been made available for refineries' repair, but the industry interlopers in PPPRA are slamming us with typical alarmist figure of N750 million if only to push 'a mind set' that refineries are 'citadels of waste'. The agency said the NNPC was a disaster in the past four years, while NNPC's Chief Executive, Gaius Obaseki, insisted he still deserved his job by saying that he had elevated the corporation from the miserably low level to its present enviable status of 14th position in the league of world's public corporations. Who then do we believe amongst these gladiators of deregulation?

The desperate manner the agency dragged the NLC from Abuja to Lagos to court over the matter of socio-economic policy underscores the gross incapability of the agency to engage in social engineering. The attempt at criminalization of social protest has never worked. Social disagreement calls for social dialogue not judicial blackmail. The present PPPRA is certainly a complete departure from the all-inclusive socially sensitive quantity, quality product regulatory agency labour had envisaged during the 2000 struggle. How President Obasanjo would be sold to an untidy agency that could not build internal consensus, not to talk of making its case in the public arena, is the first wonder of this renewed mandate.

If however, we are made to groan under the weight of the clumsy leadership and methodology of PPPRA, what will be intolerable is the dependency economics of the agency with all its attendant disaster for the Nigerian economy.

Chairman Gbadamosi was proud to flaunt his economic credentials, which in turn underscores the imperative of unhelpful academic/doctrinaire orientation and what the agency needs is problem solving constructive and innovative original ideas to seemingly intractable problems of products. Read him: '...refineries are not performing, we are looking outside our borders to fulfil a growing demand for petroleum products.'

In another breadth, he was blunt about the fallout of his repressive economics. 'It's going to be sorrows, tears and blood'.

According to Vision 2010, 'Nigeria's downstream oil activities should have become significant earner of foreign exchange and a supplier of a different range of raw materials to local industries.' Seven years to go, it is the same business as usual approach of periodic punitive increases in prices based on same outworn, boring you-know the reasons (removal of subsidy, stopping waste, etc). In 1999, President Obasanjo commendably declared his commitment of self-sufficiency in refining, ensuring regular and un-interrupted domestic product supply, creating value-added and providing gainful employment for Nigerians to acquire technical know-how in refining and distribution process. Remarkable is the fact that the president actually initiated activist measures, which brought domestic refining capacity to all time high capacity utilization of 53%. Regrettably, the same forces of import represented by PPPRS have further blackmailed the president. He seems to have abandoned the path of recovery and oil industry control. Which means it has been motions without movement? The new price regime is to attract import of product with all the attendant implication for domestic production and employment. 'We can now import fuel' was the enthusiastic remark of MD of Unipetrol, Adewale Tinubu, (note) *not* that 'we can now set up refinery'. Dr, Gaius Obaseki, GMD, NNPC recently lamented the abysmal low level of local content in the industry, given the huge level of public investment. 40 years after, there is very little progress in terms of technology transfer and domestic know-how.

Import and wholesale import of products take us far away from addressing his concern. Nigerian government is yet to move from 'income generating' to 'industry control', as government still remains a passive tax collector while the oil multinational companies still predominate. And even at that, government concern is miserably about pricing, not even quality of products and of course quantity is far from being guaranteed given that supply rests on twin-issues of international price of crude and exchange rate of the naira.

The Curse of Oil[14]

"Oil illustrates that if a strategic commodity is strategic, people will go to war over it." – *John Saul*

The country has witnessed the third avoidable shutdown via a national strike on account of third arbitrary pricing of petroleum products within four years by the Obasanjo administration.

Whatever happened then to market fundamentalists and their make belief that petroleum products are just products subject to the vagaries of the market? There is nowhere in the universe a product proves itself as strategic as in Nigeria. It was strategic to USA and its allies and that was why they went to war with Iraq. Saddam was no less a terrorist than Sharon. If Israel continuously enjoys the protection of USA against all reasons and logic, it was because of the assigned role of the Jewish state as a policeman for an unrestrained flow of crude from Middle East to West. Conversely if Iraq had to be bombed back to Stone Age, it was because of its recalcitrance to disrupt the flow of oil. Even at that, the dependence of Nigeria on oil is far more total than that of the big world powers. There is no country in which a product (oil) serves as a profound test of will as in Nigeria.

In Nigeria, oil remains the main source of revenue, despite the boring rhetoric of diversification. We are all road dependant (i.e. fuel dependant either by cars or *okada*) no thanks to the criminal neglect of railways and other alternative mass means of transport again despite rhetoric to the contrary and even scandalous appropriation of public funds in the name of same mass transits. When John Saul

---

[14] *Daily Trust*, Monday 7th July 2003, pp. 14

wrote 'oil is a commodity we consume on our way to buy more while driving on a petroleum-based surface he had in mind Nigeria perhaps more than Canada.

Ironically there is nowhere in the world that a government remains so casual and almost irresponsible in its attitude to a strategic product like oil than in Nigeria.

Recently Shell Petroleum Development Company of Nigeria (SPDC) (note; not NNPC or DPR or PPPRA) had a paid advert warning the nation about the danger of persistent thievery of Nigerian crude. According to the MD of Shell, Mr. Ron Berg, in the last two months alone Shell lost as many as 120,000 barrels of crude, a day to organised syndicates. To this end, Shell (again not NNPC) canvasses for international certification of Nigerian crude through finger printing in an attempt to smash the oil theft-gang. Shell's revelations underscore the curse of oil for the Nigerian nation. For one, it is an open knowledge that Shell together with all its other sisters, namely, Mobil, Texaco, AP among others, only extract crude to later inform NNPC.

In 2000, Engineer Hamman Tukur, the Chairman of National Revenue Mobilisation Commission revealed 20 hidden oil wells illegally operated by reputable oil companies, Shell inclusive. According to him, Nigeria lost as much as N280 billion due to this open illegal activities of the companies. Similarly the last House of Representatives indicted DPR of 'malfeasance' in not supervising joint venture companies, which engage in over-lifting of crude oil.

Now that acknowledged foul players in the upstream sector now cry out against other more deadly foul players, it is clear that over-take don overtake overtake (apology to Fela). It also means that as far as upstream sector is concerned, Nigeria has moved from crisis to profound tragedy. Think about it, if we could not do simple monitoring of crude as NNPC failed to do, what happens to the corporation's capacity to do independent exploration. Better too, if we are found wanting in policing oil wells, (as Shell seems to have given up, by demanding for finger printing of our crude) then what happens to our increasing incapacity for technology and industry control? The tragedy of Shell's revelation underscores the failure of Obasanjo's administration no less than the failure of the Nigerian state. If we now add the seeming collapse of the downstream (read: damned stream) operation, no thanks to fuel scarcity, prohibitive price increases and attendant mass protests and industrial actions, is there any further evidence that oil is a curse to Nigeria than a blessing to other OPEC countries?

Rethinking Reform[15]

Economic reform discourse is back to the centre stage as Nigeria Economic Summit Group (NESG) holds its tenth summit this week in Abuja. Both President Obasanjo and Vice-President Atiku Abubakar have of late been beating the drum of reform for those that care to listen. At the coronation of the new *Oba* of Lagos, Atiku once again underscored the resolve of the administration to initiate reform measures almost in the spirit of Mr. President's submission during the last media chat.

Quite reassuring that government is converted to reform. What however is not so clear is the nature of preferred reform, for whom by how and why? The challenge for the forthcoming Economic Summit lies therefore in rethinking reform with a view of defining the content of this reform, identifying its drivers and laying bare its benefits and costs to the nation.

The importance of reform cannot be overemphasized. With 70 per cent living below the poverty line, a sermon is not needed for us to critically re-look at policies that push the majority on the margin. There is so much work to be done. Yet there is so much unemployment and abysmal underemployment in the country. It is self evident that we must reform economy and society or we all get deformed with high incidents of robberies, communal gangsters and other related crimes arising from increasing deprivations in the land. Inspector General Tafa Balogun had every cause to celebrate the gallantry of his men in recently smashing the robbery gang. But when robbers operate in tens and scores and even hundreds, then we must be worried about the 'popular' character of robbery. Is robbery an exception practiced by the demented few rascals like Oyenusis or

---

15 *Daily Trust*, Monday 8th September 2003, pp. 8

57

Aninis of the old or is robbery 'employment' for the army of the unemployed and unemployable? Sixth world producer of oil, yet we are unable to meet domestic demand for products leading to imports and all its attendant problems such as pricing and products' diversion.

Nigeria's entrepreneurs and entrepreneurial skills dated back to late nineteenth century. But capacity utilisation averages today at miserable 30 per cent. No thanks to absence of industrial policy, collapse of infrastructure (energy, water, telecom, etc.) and of course dumping of smuggled goods of varying types and different countries. All this underscores why reform is absolutely desirable.

Paradoxically, people are sceptical about official reform rhetoric. Few actually think government is not sincere, noting that the imperative of reform is not officially shared as such. Reform, they say, is just another passing fad made possible by the insistence of creditors and donors. Indeed, cynics say regardless of official posturing, the official mindsets and actions are still as conservative as before and that reform is far from being internalised. We, for instance proclaim the desirability of 'lean' and smart government, yet we assemble motley of advisers and political jobbers with unwieldy portfolios making government the feet of clay. Why should anybody agree to downsize when we are not ready to up-size? We proclaim 'supply-side economics' according to which private producers 'can stimulate economic growth better than the governments'. The cliché is that private sector is the engine of growth. Yet the official policies and actions are weighted on the side of 'demand' side in which government spending is still the main 'stimulant' in the economy with all the attendant implications such as fuelling inflation, corruption and capital flight. We are eager to build a new stadium, host a sport fiesta (COJA) and even throw eight billion dollars at the Liberian campaign than visiting the collapsing factories, commissioning new mills and evolving creative ideas and policies that will truly make private sector the real engine of growth.

Mr. President and his Vice are evidently reform converts. Do other government officials share their reform vision? Recently UNIDO made public its findings on how to revive textile industry as a follow up to the initiative of Mr. President in August 2002. Yet most relevant ministries to implement the reform measures contained in UNIDO report were conspicuously absent while those that attended did so by proxies. The unhelpful attitude of some of these ministers was a radical departure from the passion and commitment to fix the industry as demonstrated by the President that personally sat down with all the stakeholders in 2002 to find solutions to the problems of the industry. Whence then the reform, when the reformists are in huge deficit? It is interesting to discover the level of indifference and even gross cynicism about new taunted monetization policy among top government officials even why the President pushes it with so much passion. If there is lack of cohesion upstairs about reform, how do we legitimise it below?

This then raises the question about who drives reform. Should the reform vision be consensual or individual driven? Vision 2010 represents the most far-reaching consensual reformist vision so far. Why then would government committed to reform ignore this great reform document and be reinventing the wheel through some abridged reform agenda the latest of which is NEEDS? Economic Summit group is known for inclusiveness in economic discourse by involving all stakeholders. Government however is still top-down unilateral in its approach to reform. And when government 'consults' as says it did with fuel pricing, it is more of formality than to benefit from the suggestions and ideas of the citizens. Take-it or leave-it approach of government to reform is fuelling the entrenched reform cynicism as citizens have come to realise that their opinions never matter after all.

Lastly and even more worrisome is the speed and rather spontaneous manner government pushes reform measures. Joseph Stiglitz, winner of the Nobel Prize in Economics in his latest bestseller on *Globalisation and Its Discontents* warned against '*Bolshevik approach to market reform*'. Stiglitz must have had Nigeria in mind, in which officialdom wants to correct the decay of 40 years in 4 weeks with immediate effects. The Leninists could afford 'shock therapy' approach to reform after all, the Bolsheviks envisaged revolution and not reform. But here reform with immediate effects is proving counter productive in Nigeria as we have seen with deregulation of the downstream petroleum sub-sector and NITEL sale fiasco. It is time we take a 'gradualist' approach to reform such that the process is all-inclusive and implemented within the complex reality of the country.

Rethinking Business[*]

The rich history of Nigeria's businesses and professions is also well recorded, Tom Forrest's 1995 *The Makers and Making of Nigerian Private Enterprise* dating it to the 1880s. Nigeria has thrown up great entrepreneurs from Jaja Opobo, Nana Olomu of Itsekiriland, Mobolaji Bank-Anthony, Doherty, Alhassan Dantata of Kano, Mohammed Shitta-Bey, Odutola, Oni, Banjoko to modern day Dangotes, Adenugas, Ekene Dili Chukwus, Ibrus, and so many others.

The tremendous growth and significant contribution of these businesses to GDP in post-colonial Nigeria can be attributed to high ethical standards in product and service delivery by businesses and professions alike.

But today, there is a huge deficit in ethical standards in businesses and professions such that the challenge is to reinvent ethics in standards *now* or we imperil businesses altogether.

J. K. Galbraith, the great American economist once wrote that the process by which banks create money is so simple that the mind is repelled. If Galbraith had observed modern-day banking profession in Nigeria, he would have written that: "process by which banks create money is so scandalous that robbery is preferred."

Remember 'round-tripping' according to which banks bid ostensibly on behalf of foreign-exchange users, only to divert this to parallel market for prohibitive profits. Whatever happened to project lending and risk-taking we used to know traditional banks for? Banks feverishly run after money in captive markets, namely; government and oil and gas sector and with the recent findings of the financial

[*] *Daily Trust*, 1ˢᵗ September, 2003

crime commission, even banks draw from the dirty fountain of 419 and even drug money. Not until the CBN spiritedly and commendably rose to insist on some ethics, banks almost without exception used unethical means that are not exclusive of turning young lady "customers' officers" into prostitutes to 'source' these funds.

The recent scandal rocking the Bank of the North (BON) underscores the dearth (or is it death) of ethics in banking businesses. The sacked MD of the bank allegedly loaned self ₦450 million and reportedly "used" ₦150 million "out of the bank's funds as a bribe to enable him secure a loan of ₦4 billion with which to recapitalise BON."

As it is in banking so also in petroleum the downstream sub-sector, billions of naira worth of imported oil (not locally refined products in 6th largest producer of oil) products are smuggled out by oil businessmen, big and independent marketers. The more new filling stations are built, the less fuel is available there and the more we see children selling fuel in jerry cans. Some business indeed, whereby products are sold outside the market place! Only in Nigeria's 'market-economy', sorry, 'black market' economy can this be possible.

Products are "diverted" just as they are adulterated killing and maiming innocent consumers, without compensation, thus making it lucrative for the perpetrators of this mass murder.

Mrs. Akinyuli's NAFDAC has commendably done a great and acknowledged job by exposing how patent medicine dealers and even drug 'manufacturers' are killing the country through fake drugs of different types. Big names were once named among multinationals importing expired inputs for production.

An American oil service company reportedly evaded taxes to the tune of millions of dollars in Nigeria. We are yet to hear the outcome of the probe feverishly set up by the presidency in the wake of the scandal.

COJA is already 'a feet of clay', but little did anybody contemplate that the clay is imported from South Africa. BMW reportedly gave 900 cars free to COJA in an attempt to outbid PAN. To what extent does BMW's method conform to ethics of competition and level playing field? How free are the free cars by a company in business for profit? What does this open corruption of the market mean for industrial capacity utilization, job creation in Nigeria? Meanwhile PAN is closed, Long Live COJA that lives on 'charity' of BMW South Africa.

Unethical behaviours in government business and public sector professions are even better imagined.

Some custom men and women reportedly turn the other way, as smugglers wreck the economy, with dumped inferior hazardous second-hand goods such as textiles leading to revenue loss, factory closures and attendant job-losses.

The increasing disregard for standard is making mail-practices addictive. Indeed the "businesses" and "professions" are themselves businesses of 419 or Advance Fee Fraud.

The most recent celebrated case of unethical business behaviours is that of the Vaswamis brothers. According to report, "The Vaswamis brothers are sleek lots."

It is time Nigerian businesses and professions get reformed or they get ultimately deformed.

Yet, are we not assuming so much, when we think professions and business must go with ethics and morality? Whose business? Whose ethics?

With LPO-crony capitalism like Nigeria's in which some use their connections to transfer public wealth to themselves pushing ethical standard is a tall order.

Even at that, the best apostles of the market agree that market economy does not mean chaos. On the contrary, there is a shared value that "courts must enforce contracts, police must punish insiders' dealers and manifest and public agencies must collect taxes"

Which explains why President Bush has not hesitated to put in jail corporate criminals in USA. Which explains why we must support the Ribadu's Financial Crime Commission for putting 419 king pins and banking robbers in detentions where they rightly belong.

Business must generate wealth and add value, create jobs and goods and services and not add to the ruination of our already accursed oil economy. President of General Motors (GM), Charles

Wilson (1890-1961) once remarked, "What is good for the country is good for General Motors, and vice versa." When will our businessmen and women make such commitment to Nigeria?

Tel (Economy)[16]

A visitor to Nigeria from outer space today confronted with GSM card-selling youths on the roads, 'ubiquitous umbrella-stand operators', mobile-set wielding citizens in the markets, churches and mosques, watching TV network with telecom ad (and telecom ad alone) would not hesitate to say this is undoubtedly a Tel(economy). Teleconomy is hereby defined as a phone-driven economy for phone users, by phone subscribers for telephone operators. We can truly talk of Telecom revolution of the 90s in which like manna from heaven, the country made a leap-jump from digital ineptitude to unprecedented digital activism. People have asked the question; how were we living before the emergence of GSM? This question underscores the new found liberation of subscribers compared to the tyranny under hitherto dictatorship of monopoly NITEL.

The statistics is also very liberating. From a miserable tele-density of 0.4 lines per 100 people before 1999, today it is 2.6 per 100 people. In absolute terms Nigeria boasts of 3 million lines, 2.3 million of which are reportedly to be mobile telephones, compared to less than 400,000 lines before 1999. Today we can speak freely with our mothers and fathers in villages and cities where private telephone providers and mobile service providers have facilities. Investment is also reported to be on the increase in telecom industry, second only to oil industry. There is no better evidence of the ascendancy of telecom industry than the way in which petrol-hawking youths compete feverishly for space with mobile recharge cards hawking-youths on our streets.

---

[16] *Daily Trust*, Monday 16th February 2004, pp. 6

The question is to what extent has this communication revolution advanced our development? Engr. Ernest Ndukwe, Vice Chairman NCC represents the optimists who insist for those who care that teleconomy has advanced national development. In fact to him, recent development in telecom sector underscores what Nigeria has been missing without the recent digital revolution. They refer to over 2000 jobs directly created by GSM operators and well over 400,000 indirect beneficiaries from GSM operations.

Reference is also made to increased competition and efficiency as well as enhanced direct investment in the sector. As encouraging as these referred positive results are, there are those who point to how unknowingly the digital telecom revolution may be under-developing the economy. First technology and expertise, just like oil sector, are still foreign. In fact GSM has further accentuated our technological dependency as a nation. Pessimists insist that through GSM, we have once again joined the globalisation train from the last coach, in which we have become a dumping ground for technologies that we don't produce and we are not eager to acquire either. It is a scandal that budget 2004(4th in 1999) just appreciates the imperatives of producing recharge cards in Nigeria. How about the handsets? When are we going to assemble handsets, not to talk of when we are going to produce them at home? Secondly, do the jobs generated so far reflect the quantum of investments?

Teleconomy just like oil economy is a capital-intensive activity, labour saving rather labour intensive. Mass goods sectors like textile and food and beverages would have certainly created more millions of jobs with this volume of investment. Also, what is the quality of jobs being created? The spectacular pictures of able bodied youths menacingly hawking GSM cards just like petrol hawking youths once again shows our preference for unsustainable non-skill acquisition casual jobs that can only under-develop the economy. Thirdly, we celebrate the new found communication channels occasioned by GSM operations, but what value has this added to the economy? Yes, business activities (at least for those businesses that are yet to close down) have been enhanced through relatively easy communication. But what is the cost of communication and the return on investment? As a matter of fact, there are those who will argue that GSM has brought more distortions to the economy. Today students that would rather buy books and enhance their knowledge will rather buy recharge cards that only enhance talking for talking sake. Housewives that will ordinarily buy mass goods such as beverages and textiles will rather allocate more resources to handsets and recharge cards. The bane of GSM is that it has advertently made us to switch scarce resources from the real wealth generating, labour intensive, value adding sector to capital intensive, capital flight promoting sectors such as telecom.

Recently, MTN raised as much as 350 million dollar facilities from a consortium of 16 banks to expand its facilities. Perhaps this is good for MTN just as it is good for banks. But this is certainly bad for the entire economy. Notable operators such as MTN have been accused of non re-investment and capital flight out of huge turnover they generate in Nigeria. It is a double jeopardy that the remaining scarce resources desperately built up by other surviving businesses are put at the disposal of a capital repatriation sectors like MTN while those that generate these resources are being denied such resources by our banks. It is the case of the poor financing the rich without conscience. When last did consortium of banks raise money for the real sector of the economy? The hope is that we will not be afflicted with the same curse of telecom just as we are already afflicted with curse of oil. Telecom sector is proving another enclave just as the oil sector.

Dollarisation of Discourse[17]

Most vested interest driven comments over the controversial dollar pay for Ministers Ngozi Okonjo-Iweala and Olu Adeniji, so far only elicit heat rather than light. We have once again brought to the fore the unhelpful Nigerian extremes of bad belle on one hand and official arrogance and ignorance on the other hand, with very little space for reasons. So far true to character, we have only talked at each other rather than talking with each other. Monsieur El Rufai's recent *'What kind of people have we become?* (*Daily Independent*04/03/04) scandalises some of his distant admirers. How a perceived incomprehension of critics would make a Minister of the Federal Republic questions altogether the stuff we are made as a people underscores a great slide into free fall in official commentary. Had the Honourable Minister not cultivated an image of a well meaning independent public officer, his latest *neo-Fani-(or is it fascist?) Kayode's trite* on ministers' dollar pay passes for another zero-tolerance level for alternative views in governance. This is neither useful to the two ministers El-Rufai pretends to defend nor public good he is paid to promote. The promise of reform and the reformers also is that civil society is encouraged to critically engage the reform agenda and the reformers with a view of deepening the reform and making it work for all it worth's. Some civil society engagements may certainly not be flattering no less than the same reform that we are officially reminded up teeth time not to be flattering (or in reform language) painful. The current compensation crisis tasks our capacity for reflections, communication, tolerance and not the same outworn

---

[17] *Daily Trust*, Wednesday 10th March, 2004, pp. 6

unrewarding 'capacity to fight back'. We should be fighting back fatigue by now. Critics of preferential pay are what they are; critics, they are *not* illegal structures' in the Honourable Minister's Abuja Master Plan that must be demolished at all costs. The ever-humorous Finance Minister Dr. Okonjo-Iweala with her social science background is not and cannot be averse to strident criticism on development issues. She had more than once (even before being a minister) challenged the citizens against complacency when good governance is in recess to demand for accountability and explanation. Let's address people's concern and not close the debate through threat as El-Rufai officially exhibited.

It is instructive that the first 'peer review' of the two Diaspora-ministers' performance by the citizens is over their dollarised pay. This should be thought for food or vice versa. NEPAD authors could not have imagined this perverse peer review, as it were. This is a singular paradox too naughty in particular for Dr. Ngozi Okonjo-Iweala. Since the tenure of Dr. O.O. Soleye, then Finance Minister under Buhari regime, we have never witnessed an activist Finance Minister like Dr. Ngozi Okonjo-Iweala. We may not necessarily agree with the thrust of her preferred options (and yours sincerely remains a passionate critic of her neo-liberal *wahala* (not *Nwuala* please). But we cannot doubt her activism and enthusiasm to make a difference. What with the initiation and popularisation of NEEDS. What with almost 'subversive' but courageous and transparent periodic popularisation of state and local government finances and allocations since 1999 and what with her modest force of example about originality and simplicity in a country in which up-town and Aso-rock women are epitome of fashionable vulgar indulgence. What with her sermons about the need to reform our values. She may very well deserve her dollar pay. But that active commentary trails this activist Minister of Finance only in the wake of disclosures of her dollar pay and not through her identified imprints on public policy above is the greatest paradox of our compensation crisis. Whatever the policy implications are, one thing is clear; we only ignore compensation crisis at our own peril. It is Pope John Paul II and *not* Karl Marx who said: 'A just wage for the worker is the ultimate test of whether any economic system is functioning justly.' The questions begging for answers are many and they need explanations not arrogant end of the debate official posturing. How just (in Papal sense) is preferential pay for some ministers? What does this mean for level playing field? Minister El-Rufai compares like with unlike when he reminded us of the wage gap between him and some staff of BPE? Ministers' pay is a function of some constitutionally defined remuneration mechanism and not some executive initiative via Diaspora Trust Fund under the dictatorship of UNDP. If Minister Ngozi had received $247000 per annum in pre-Adjustment/Reform Nigeria, when there was exchange rate parity, would there have been any outrage? Certainly no body would have cared. Put in another way, with stronger currency, Minister Ngozi does not need apartheid wage with all the embarrassment to a worthy worker like her? What are the policy implications for our exchange rate management? We have known the family budget of the two ministers to include payment for school fees for four kids at Harvard, have we pulsed for once to ask about family budgets of anonymous Nigerian workers and the extent the current minimum wage can hardly meet their needs and the level of sacrifices they bare? If there is the will, there will always be the way. We find the will to attract the best through Diaspora Trust Fund, when will there be the will to pay scores of thousands of abandoned pensioners in and around FCTD? Will our compassion (if any?) and sensitivity as well as motivation be all inclusive for once?

Economy in Discourse[18]

Last week could very well be declared *Nigeria's Economic Week* and that will not be disputed even with our ever-murky environment of partisanship. For once, in recent time, political headlines (read – murder – lines) gave way to grim economic statistics and rational economic discourse. The week started with the formal presentation of much muted National Economic Empowerment and Development Strategy (NEEDS) by President Olusegun Obasanjo. The 200-page document promises *seven* million jobs in the next three years, average of two million per year. This is a refreshing departure from 'government-does-not-create-jobs' dogma we have been hitherto assaulted with.

NEEDS says: "it is a development strategy anchored on the private sector as the engine of growth – for wealth creation, employment generation and poverty reduction." Even as NEEDS hopes to put all its eggs in private sector's basket, it also agrees that it is the government that must grow the private sector, before private sector will add-value and create jobs for us all. With this self-realisation, the hope is that the President's economic team will strip itself of the illusion that private sector is the means and ends of reform. Private sector may or may not create jobs, generate wealth or reduce poverty. The private sector's main goal is profit maximization. It is the government through macro-economic policies, dealing with interest rate, exchange rate, regulatory framework as well as leadership by examples that give the direction for private sector to follow. Yes, private sector is the engine of growth, but government provides for and oils this engine. Private sector can dump goods including fake drugs from abroad, exporting jobs and killing domestic

---

[18] *Daily Trust*, Monday 22nd March 2004, pp. 6

jobs and even kill precious lives in the process. Conversely private sector can re-invest, lower costs, backwardly integrate, mass employ and even contribute to charity. Either way, it is the government that will give the direction, which the private sector must follow. But government cannot lay-off workers uncritically without safety nets only to expect private sector to mass recruit the mass of unemployment. Government cannot deny good governance and expect miraculous cooperate governance. NEEDS' romanticism with the private sector is undoubtedly alluring but it must be balanced with the knowledge that Adam Smith wrote about *Wealth of Nations* and *not* Wealth of Cooperate Individual. The hope is that by the time NEEDS moves to the six geo-political zones, it will have a fuller picture of the real needs of the nation. The seven million jobs mark is commendable as it is courageous. It is the acid test for the success or otherwise of this new initiative.

The visiting World Bank President, Mr. James Wolfenson added colour to the unofficial economic week with is remarkable optimism about reform in particular and Nigeria's economic recovery in general. At a time, not a few see Nigeria a drag of the continent, Wolfenson's observation that we are the "Juice of Africa" was uplifting and departure from boring story of despair. Even significant was his remark that growth rests on partnership between private and public sectors, a thought for food for those who ideologically see private sector (and only private sector) as engine growth. According to him: 'The fundamental issues are to build capacity in the government and in the private sector, to allow people to be trained to do things effectively and to build a judicial system that protects rights …' This message from washing ton is for government and *not* private sector, making the point that even the Bank knows that the real engine of growth is government. Even more revolutionary was his declaration of the support of the Bank and all international financial institution for Nigeria-daring Nigeria to hold him 'accountable' and even challenged us to arrest him if he does not deliver on promise. Not even our government has dared with accountability and sanctions in case of failure (and they always fail) as World Bank President did.

Yet as dramatic as Wolfenson's submission was, it was all on forms than substance. His singling out of corruption as Nigeria's 'cancer' was predictable. It's the same old story that we are poor because we are corrupt. It's time we redefined corruption to include perverse-flow of resources from the poor to the rich through repayment of dubious debt that kept increasing by the hour; the supervision of the Debt crisis is the bane of our development efforts. Paradoxically, Yet Wolfenson parried the question on debt relief and even threw it back at us as our burden. The bank has undoubtedly changed its rhetoric's to include some concerns, but it methods and purpose remain intolerably conservative. This is not to say that corruption is not a cancer, but debt obligations and repayments that never end are even more cancerous.

CBN: Return of an Economist[19]

'Central Bankers Read Election Returns, Not Balance Sheets'- *Robert Z. Aliber*

The enthusiasm which seemed to have greeted the appointment of a professor of economics, who is also the economic adviser to the President, Mr. Charles Soludo, as the new governor of CBN underscores the groundswell of support for change in the administration of the bank. The apex bank had hitherto been under the heel of an accountant. For a considerable part of Chief Joseph Sanusi's tenure, (true to the callings of an accountant), he successfully tried hard to balance the books but not without ignoring the development objectives the bank was set up to achieve. The sanitisation of banks from the dirt of foreign exchange round tripping, his drastic albeit controversial measures such as closure of some non-performing banks and forced resignation and persecution of some bank's executives are part of the commendable legacy of the outgoing governor with respect to bank supervision. But Central Banking worldwide has been likened to a good (economic) driver, which must keep an eye on the road and maintain steady hands on the wheel for a good (economic) ride.

Countries preoccupied with issues in development use their central banks to keep the economy on course through activist macro economics with respect to pricing, (inflation), exchange rates, interest rates, capacity utilisation, employment, debt management etc. Sanusi's CBN failed woefully with respect to macro economics and it offered endless excuses and buck passing rather than answers to depressing economic situation. Through the instrumentality of Dutch

---

[19] *Daily Trust*, Monday 17th May, 2004, pp. 6

Auction (read: Nigeria variant of the Dutch Disease) naira had a free fall from 85 naira at Sanusi's ascendancy to 138 naira to a dollar. Do nothing approach to interest rate management brought rate to all time high level of between 25 to 30 per cent. In fact the battle to lower interest rate was left to President Obasanjo (and the President alone) who more than once had to exchange hot words with bankers for them to appreciate the imperatives of investment-friendly interest rate.

The return of an economist (hopefully the man with biggest picture) as distinct from the limited horizon of an accountant is expected to make some difference. Even at this, assuming all is about bigger picture of development and the economy, observers note that the bank has enough in-house economists to run the affairs of the bank. The hope is that Soludo's appointment is truly meant to make the bank return to the path of an all round development of the economy.

The point cannot be overemphasised; 'Central bankers read election results and not balance sheets.' Soludo should know that elections results are about macroeconomics, namely stable price, stable exchange rates, full employment, improved capacity utilisation, debt management and not necessarily about bank supervision which his predecessor occupied self with. Indeed, only in Nigeria can the existing riotous macro economic variables, the most notorious being unemployment rate of 55 per cent, deliver 'landslide election results'. South Africa's Federal Reserve and its remarkable performance with respect to macroeconomics are central to the recent globally acknowledged victory of ANC government during the recently concluded election results. Thus, the issue is not the return of the economist to CBN but the *economics* of the returned economist.

The challenge before Soludo is not to reinvent the wheel nor look for central banking model that has nothing to do with our miserable reality. He should rather look inward. He should find out how late Dr. Clement Isong, Harvard-trained economist, together with the then finance minister, late Chief Obafemi Awolowo managed the war economy without external borrowing and without inflation and naira devaluation. With existing level of unemployment, factory closures, low capacity utilisation and social deprivations occasioned by poverty, the present day economy can be likened to a war economy. We need a CBN that will be part of recovery and this call for activist bank regulator and *not* a passive CBN that bemoans economic decline through periodic reports of despair.

The new governor must be wary of received wisdom, British colonialists (Fisher's Report in 1952) actually objected to setting up a central bank with full functions of managing the economy. Indeed, the World Bank favoured "Central Bank with limited functions." Nigerian nationalists however insisted on full-fledged Central Bank for Nigeria as a tool for economic liberation from exploitative dependency on London money and capital market, which explains the establishment of an Act of Parliament in 1958.

CBN must return to basics and take up the great challenges it was engaging in the 1970s and 1980s. The CBN must return to its core objectives of maintaining sound financial structure, promotion of monetary stability, safeguarding the value of naira and stable exchange rate and prove a financial adviser to the federal government in the areas of price and exchange rate management and employment creation.

Economicide[20]

My dear friend, *Thursday Trust* columnist, Indang Alibi, the other day spiritedly celebrated the 'successes of deregulation of downstream oil sector. Citing the 'availability' of products nation-wide and 'disappearance' of black market, he wondered why labour had chosen to be an obstacle to a worthy reform. Many readers were as unexisting as the unexciting policy he chose to defend. In a point-scoring (as distinct from problem-solving) essay, Indang demanded for an apology from Adams Oshiomhole and NLC, for not giving deregulation policy a benefit of doubt and even daring to block it. Not even the combined propaganda mills of the Presidency, PPPRA and NNPC were as enthusiastic about their taunted policy as Idang.

Proverbial water has overflown deregulation bridge since Idang Alibi's trite. But even before his pen of clay dried up we are back to ground zero a la deregulation. Last week, Market fundamentalists were back to the centre stage with their same old terror story of 'market fundamentals'.

International price of crude, we are told, is in upward swing, ostensibly compounding products' landing costs and invariably making upward review of prices inevitable. You wonder why seemingly good news for oil producing countries should turn to despair for Nigeria. Once again Nigeria comes out as the weakest in the OPEC chain, no thanks to a downstream deregulation policy that is shamelessly import-informed, selfishly vested interest propelled and uneconomically import driven. Consumers are once again being

---

[20] *Daily Trust*, Monday 7ᵗʰ June 2004, pp. 6

called upon to bear the brunt of higher prices arising from a policy choice made in spite of their protestation.

Consistent free fall of the naira and prohibitive interest rates in the past five years (in spite of Mr. President's one-man protestation) had fuelled an economic crisis, manifesting in forms of rising production cost, factory closures and rising unemployment.

One year of deregulation of downstream sector has however pushed us from economic crisis to the brink of economicide, defined here as conscious match to economic suicide and economic ruination through suicidal policy option of import based deregulation.

Following the court truce over the notorious fuel tax, a joint assessment and verification committee of Federal Government and NLC was set up to find out the socio-economic impact of deregulation. This report is a compulsory reading for the remaining import-driven deregulation policy like Indang.

The findings include scandalous sub-optimal performance of all refineries one year after deregulation. Old Port Harcourt is down while the 'new' one operates at 50 per cent capacity. In a feverish response to recent NLC query, we now know through Rasheed Gbadamosi, that PH 1 & 2 had gulped $170,847,972 since 1999.* Kaduna TAM had gulped $205 million since 2002 with 1.2 million litres compared to its 5 million litre capacity while Warri is also down after as much as $108 million had been sucked in. Whatever happened to the promise of repaired functioning refineries and establishment of private refineries once deregulated prices were in place? Marketers renege to join the import chain contrary to their promise once 'market' pricing was allowed. NNPC still supplies well over 80 per cent of the imported products. Only in the dictionary of petroleum industry's market fundamentals, we come to realise that marketers can sell what they don't source but even collect on credit. The fraud was so intolerable such that Engr. Kupolokun, NNPC GMD at a time had to cut off their supply to compel the major marketers to join the import chain. But Kupolokun's strike against marketers was short-lived. He actually lost the battle with marketers and passed the burden to consumers through increase in prices for

---

* *Daily Trust* June 4

consumers. Some regulation for marketers, full deregulation of prices for consumers. If marketers are so import-shy a year after deregulation, when will they set up refineries? The most revealing however are the sharp practices of marketers. They include pump under delivery of products to consumers that average about 1.5 litres losses for every ten litres of petroleum products. Your guess is as good as mine how many sharp fortunes these rampant sharp practices had conferred on marketers. NNPC has not sanctioned any of these sharp practitioners. On the contrary, NNPC has rewarded them with new price increases. The only investment so far since deregulation is in import (and only import) reception.

The most revealing however is how in the one year of deregulation capacity utilisation had sharply declined due to increasing production cost arising from persistent products' price increases. NEEDS promises 'growing the private sector'. Deregulation grinds the private sector to a halt completing the cycle of economicide.

Capital Base or Capital Controls? [21]

So much heat (as distinct from light) has been generated around the new capital base. The return of an economist at the CBN has brought to the fore hitherto endangered development discourse and the role of banks therein. What makes Soludo's new radicalism (as it were) undue is not that his radicalism is not desirable. On the contrary, Soludo's bold initiative underscores a remarkable CBN's paradigm shift with respect to the role of finance in development. While the bank's ancient regime spent time reading balance sheets, (a good lot reportedly manipulated, sorry, re-engineered), Soludo with big bang serves different notice; central bankers must read election (or is it selection?) results; price stability, stable exchange rate, full employment, capacity utilisation and debt management among others.

Soludo raises the banner of bigger picture, challenges us with quality as distinct from abysmal quantity banking. He certainly deserves some benefit of doubt, if not unconditional encouragement. Pat Utomi's seemingly vested interest-driven cynicism about the prospects of prolonged stagnation[22] and Ayo Teriba's 'facts for facts' with respect to the new initiative[23] must give way to some broadmindedness and constructive engagement. The bane of development in Nigeria is the absence of vision and road map. We simply muddle through in greater quantity (the most populous nation. the most over-banked nation; the nation with highest filling stations) with dismal outcomes in quality of life.

We may disagree with Soludo's shock therapy/immediate effect approach and even his undue process. Some observers are even more

---

[21] *The Guardian*, 9th August 2004
[22] *The Guardian*, July 25
[23] *ThisDay*, July 19

benign; they urged us not to expect democratic practices from unelected governor of CBN. Key issues in financing however must be urgently revisited even with imperfect processes. Utomi gives the impression the CBN's capitalisation proposals are anti-thesis of proclaimed market economy approaches. Idolisation of the market should not make us forget that market forces are means and not the ends. We must overcome prisoner's dilemma (no thanks to our high walls). Cynically, restricted and domesticated Adams Smith's *Wealth of Nations* (happily Smith wrote not about Wealth of Banks) must give way to holistic Adams Smith, inclusive of his *Theory of Moral Sentiments*.

Market is a dynamic human social institution. Mature view has long replaced eighteenth century neoclassical unhelpful textbook notion of getting the price right at equilibrium. The greater advantage of the market lies in its function as the transmitter of knowledge. We must draw profound lessons from the current pitfalls of two decades of wholesome uninformed 'deregulation' of financial market. CBN can be accused of over dramatising banks' irresponsibility, but to assume problems are elsewhere and *not* with the banks as Pat Utomi did, is simply self-righteous. Asset-liability mismatch, capital inadequacy, weak internal controls, fraud and poor management, contributed to the lingering distress syndrome in the banking sector. At one breath, directors reportedly hold 89 per cent of non-performing credits in one bank.

Soludo's sermon to the bankers about the imperatives of capitalism with human and social 'face' is for me a tall order. Kenneth Galbraith, American economist once observed that the 'process by which bank create money is so simple that the mind is repelled'. Delinquent banking which rests on twin legs of government deposits and foreign exchange "round-tripping" with political solutions to bail them out in case of distress is certainly mind-boggling and could have bewildered Galbraith the more. Short term frivolous financing of imports of consumables such as fruit juice, biscuits by the banks are domestic equivalents of terror financing which is wrecking havoc in terms of domestic factory closures, mass job losses. Indecent jobs are the norms as some banks put their female staff in unprofessional use in the name of marketing contrary to their spirited denials to the contrary. Crony capitalism needs not have a social face. There is a lot that is asocial about it.

Interesting those accused of arm-chair, theoretical un-helpful banking are the very vocal against impractical proposals of CBN. Bankers under the auspices of Bankers Institute derided CBN's as ivory tower directive, taking exception to CBN's seemingly comparison of likes with unlike. If Soludo's initiative seems unsustainable it is not because it is not desirable (it is long over due) or that banks resist change (banks have always been reactionary anyway). The litmus test of CBN's recapitalisation proposal rests on its seemingly vulnerable assumptions. First was the assumption that capital inadequacy is the problem. This is diversionary. The real issue is capital application and capital control. Only public control of capital can make it socially responsible. Capital, (minimum or maximum) without control is capital on the loose; it can finance cocaine growing as well as finance terrorism as America came to realise in the wake of 9/11.

Malaysia survived the Asian financial turmoil of late 1990s while Indonesia is yet to recover because of the former's active capital control measures compared to the latter's passive de-control measures as advised by the IMF, (now with its belated apology after the misery in Indonesia). Rapid liberalisation of 1980s and 1990s was not complemented with enhanced regulatory capacity of the CBN. Indeed the growth of banks was inversely related to the sharp decline in CBN's regulatory framework. While the nation awaits other complementary measures of CBN, what is needed is capital control and not capital decontrol. The burden here is more with CBN than the banks. CBN must reform itself before it reforms others.

Today's relatively developed money market can be attributed to CBN's control measures of 1960s and 1970s. Not withstanding the enormous powers of the then international banks that dominated the system and the indiscipline and sheer inexperience of the then "indigenous" banks, CBN successfully in the 1970s and 1980s, employed measures to sustain expansion of credits to more productive sectors to stimulate productivity. Even though loans to preferred sectors fell bellow prescribed ratios, loans were nonetheless directed to real production sector, services, real estate and construction. The upward quality of life index of 1970s and 1980s was in large measure attributable to tamed and purposeful capital.

Soludo's celebration of mega-banks as ends in themselves is grossly misplaced. It is partly the frustration with mega-banks of old which led to clamour for uncritical dispersal in 1986. We cannot be moving from pillars to post in a periodic impulsive cycle. South Africa's mega banks must be presented within the context. Mega-banks are products of apartheid economy, which privileged the few white through wealth concentration. Liberated South Africa has a lot to learn from our disperse banking in principle and not the other way round. Un-wholesome mergers and acquisitions, a kind of 'compulsory love', lead to monopoly capitalism, which everywhere has anything but human face.

Lastly, shock therapy approach to reform is counter-productive. Even communists have realised that gradualist approach preserves reform/revolution compared to Bolshevik's rule of the thump that may even consume the revolutions themselves. Memory is the best guide. In the 50s, following banks' failures, colonial authorities raised the capital base from approximate ₦4, 000 to ₦50, 000. The colonial Banking Ordinance of 1952 however gave three years period for all banks to correct their inadequacy. Colonialists needed not be too kind to us than we are kind to ourselves in 2004. Reform must be properly phased with appropriate time for all to adjust.

Excess Crude[24]

We are in the season of excess crude defined as excess proceeds from oil in a typical fiscal year. No thanks to war of aggression against Iraq, the term; *'excess crude proceeds'* had entered into Nigeria's budget vocabulary hitherto notorious for *'ways and means'* and 'budget deficit'. Something akin to *excess proceeds* was *oil wind fall* of the Gulf War in the 90s, again no thanks to war on Iraq.

According to my friend, Paul Nwabuikwu, special assistant to the Finance Minister, as at the end of August, excess proceeds stood at ₦386 billion in 2004 year alone. Larger than many budgets of many states. Contrary to popular view, the bane of excess crude proceeds is not necessarily the controversy surrounding how to 'share' it, though this more than anything else dominates the headlines. Observers insist that the real bane of excess crude is its non- excessive (i.e. narrow) definition. Excess proceeds should be as clear as common sense but critics insist that common sense is far from being common in the oil sector and indeed in Nigerian economy, where excess proceeds are made. The issue is even complicated the more by the slavish usage of dictionary of IMF and World Bank whose crude meaning of excess means locked up surplus in the face of starvation, collapse of infrastructure, infant mortality rate and worsening poverty and its attendant desperation. In fact, cynics insist that in the final analysis, the real excess crude is our excessive crude intellectual dependency on definition of everything as simple as excess oil proceeds.

At what point does a nation talk of having excess revenue? Is it when revenue outstrips a projected budget that is ever premised on deficit financing (totalling ₦101billion this year alone and ₦110

---

[24] *Daily Trust*, Monday 27th September 2004, pp. 6

billion in 2003) or when surplus accrues after mass needs have been met? Can a nation groaning under the weight of blackouts occasioned by miserable power output in turn a fall out of poor funding talk of excess revenues? Are we truly living above our means or living below our earnings?

Whence excess crude proceeds when we are confronted with outstanding pension liabilities of all tiers of government which scandalously include almost one trillion naira arrears to millions of voiceless pensioners? Can a country whose external debts hit all time level of $34b (according to Debt Management Office (DMO) pride self with excess revenue? Budget watchers note that once we are liberated from the clutches of straight jacketed/book balancing approach to budget and move on to consider the socio-economic flow, it becomes self-evident that excess proceed is more academic and crude than real and elegant.

It is a great paradox that the era of excess crude (with all the problematic of its definitions) is also characterised by crude, sorry, (not so refined) methods in official handling of this ever naughty issue of excess crude proceeds. Whatever Federal NEEDS and the states' SEEDS strive to knit together, excess crude has crudely turned asunder. While predictably, states want proceeds 'shared', the Federal preferred them 'saved' to be in turned pilfered.

The reported apology to the national assembly by Mrs. Ngozi Okonjo-Iweala, the Finance Minister over the alleged back door pilfering of excess 2003 proceeds reportedly being saved is one apology too many from the members of the 'great' economic team, sorry, 'the 12 disciples'.

National assembly may have been immunised (or is it hypnotised?) against foolery, but it certainly still suffers one apology too many. A school of thought maintains that excessive apologies after crude erosion of the basic rights of legislators (in this case the right to appropriate budget spending) make an apologetic (not necessarily a serious) national assembly.

No one can doubt the seriousness and genuine commitment of Minister Ngozi to due process and reform of budget process. Yours truly was a living witness to her presentation of Budget 2004; simple and graphic with clear cut budget assumptions and performance targets, a refreshing departure from the crude products of the recent past.

But to the extent that the commendable Minister's efforts and indeed the budget process *wahala* (sounds Iweala) are still not error free underscores that the *12 disciples* are as vulnerable as we the lesser mortals. Yours sincerely was amused with the spirited explanation of the minister on the controversial ₦72.6 billion excess proceeds; 'I want us to look at the intent of what happened. It does not mean that there was malicious intent.' There are unconvinced reform cynics who would remind the Honourable that the road to hell, (no less than the road to undue process as in the case of this alleged spending of excess proceeds) is often inspired by 'good' and not necessarily 'malicious' intention. Unlike cynics, I certainly have no doubt not to believe her explanations. The question however is; will the Honourable queen of the disciples also grant other concerned citizens same benefits of doubt whenever they legitimately ask questions about the logic of downsizing, threat of mass sack, non payment of pensioners in the wake of mounting excess crude proceeds? We cannot plea for understanding and appreciation when at the same time we dismiss and even despise others demanding to know about reform that they know is deforming them. Honourable Finance Minister was not in a hurry to loose her job no less than FCT minister spiritedly defended his portfolio through an apology to an offended national assembly. Will the duo allow millions whose jobs have been threatened through their reform measures, which increase are not error free same opportunity to explain and even apologise so that they can also keep their jobs in this era of end of work? A little bit of this shared generosity is certainly preferred than any excess crude.

Economic Dialogue and Its Discontents[25]

Trust Dialogue predates the current national variant (or is it national appropriation?). Its second edition held last Thursday at Abuja. This singular exhibition of vision flies in the face of an absolutist assertion of Professor Mike Kwanashie according to which '*Nigerians are not working*'. *A seemingly failed (or is it catastrophic?) state* is certainly not synonymous with an ever resilient people. *Trust Dialogue* on the economy was timely. Against the background of the ongoing mutually assured destructive (PDP's) political load shedding, *Trust* proves that even if discoursing economy was seemingly 'stupid' to the political gladiators as Kabir Yusuf rightly observed last Monday, citizens maintain that it is still not yet a farewell to productivity in rentier oil state economy. The challenge lies in evolving a structure of incentives that would further unleash the creative value addition of Nigerians.

Kwanashie's paper was very tall in official reform dogma but miserably short on new policy proposals for economic renewal. It was a classical rendition of *apparatchik* top-down make-belief that nothing-works-unless-our-NEEDS even as he did not dispute the open knowledge that things were moving from bad to worse.

I am yet to come to terms with the professor's claim that we have 'little-choice' over globalisation but to 'get incorporated' into a process for which we have no control. What happens to the elementary teaching that economics is primarily about scarcity and 'choice'? The re-invention of the notorious long discredited TINA (there is no alternative) by Professor Kwanashie does violence to the theme of the dialogue; Reforming Nigeria; which model? In the sense that as far he is concerned only neo-liberal model is it. The Nobel

---

[25] *Daily Trust*, Monday 17th January 2005, pp. 6

Prize winner for economics, Professor Stiglitz, adviser to Clinton administration has shown that both Poland and China reform successfully without subjecting themselves to the tyranny of neo-liberal Washington consensus.

His romanticisation of due-process was certainly unhelpful in the light of the growing frustrations with a process that is increasingly proving undue. The issue is not whether due process is desirable or not. We are all due process converts even in our homes.

Due process is certainly indispensable for a hospital director no less for a governor or the President. But the point is that what are the due products of the due process? We are told we have saved billions of naira that would have been stolen on accounts of due contracts tender. This is good and commendable. But economists must see beyond this book-balancing approach to consider the balancing of objectives. Development and growth economists are certainly out of fashion.

But Paul Baran's warning in the 1950s to developing economies about avoiding getting bogged down by *actual surplus* while ignoring their *potential surplus* retains its validity on due process debate. We may certainly be saving money from a hospital denied funding on accounts of due process, but do we pause to ask the impact of hospital workers and patients alike. The recent strikes in the public hospitals and the attendant wastage of human lives (a disaster indeed) must make us to be as concerned with due products of the due process. The ends which we all agree must be the people must be as important as the means.

The emerging dogmatic approach to due process must give way to creative suggestions by the likes of Aluko and Awoniyi that we should rather mainstream due process in all government departments rather than creating a command desk in Abuja under the heel of some disciples counting some actual surpluses while down the ladder the nation is denied even greater potential surpluses.

By and large all the three speakers at Trust Dialogue failed to answer the question; which model of reform? On the contrary my dear friend, Sanusi Lamido who pointedly took an exception to neo-liberal prescriptions of SAP ended with the same neo-liberal old nostrums, especially with respect to his do-nothing *bazaar*-approach to interest rate management. All his commendable recommendations with respect to reinventing production (return of EEG, etc.) come to nothing if the existing interest rate regime subsists. Next time economy discourse is too important to be left to some select economists.

Economics has long been described as a '*dismal science*'. But what will save economists from being '*dismal*' like the dismal science itself is the economists' socio-political temperament. Between political opportunism of Kwanashie's economics and unapologetic dictatorship of Aluko's mantras (he is ever full of Hitler war economy) we need some political economists to put things in perspective.

Branding of NEPAD[26]

Ever heard of new development virus, Britain's Commission for Africa, under the directorship of Prime Minister Tony Blair and Finance Minister Gordon Brown? Invented in February last year, it courageously sets to 'manage globalization for Africa'. Quite alluringly, it sets to position the continent to meet the all-important Millennium Development Goals on poverty reduction due for mid-term review this year. Assuming it is all about public relations, Commission for Africa is one huge success before its document is even finalised. The global (read; Western) media is already talking of 2005 as Blair's Year of Africa. Not even the President of Africa Union is so attributed with the Month of Africa.

We are told that the British Prime Minister is motivated by the twin presidency of G-8 and European Union to mainstream Africa in global agenda. This means this is another passing fad rather than any sustainable commitment. The totalitarian orientation of the Commission for Africa is the most intriguing. A Commission for a whole continent. Not even during the Berlin Conference of 10th century was Britain so privileged with such totalitarian claim on the continent. How an island of 60 million in continental Europe would as a matter of fact and without reservation lump a continent of a billion populations into a 'development' straight jacket passes for a millennium riddle. Even more intriguing is that the key drivers of what is loudly dubbed Blair's new initiative are enthusiastic Africans which include the Tanzanian President.

When Lord Lugard invented indirect rule, it was doubtful whether he imagined the natives would subscribe to it willingly half a century after 'independence'. While the content of the Commission's

---

[26] *Daily Trust*, Monday 28th February 2005, pp. 6

document is being finalised, Tony Blair is already assuming some
original thinking and even a vision for a seemingly intractable dark-
continent. The poverty of Africa he said constitutes a 'scar on the
conscience of the world'. The indiscriminate characterization of all
countries of Africa as being poor is one thought for food. I am not
sure about the cultural dimension of Lugard's colonial campaigns
which undoubtedly involved looting of African arts, brutal violence
and banishment of those who ventured to resist. But Tony Blair has
showed that control paradigm can have some lighter side. One
notable commission member is Bob Geldof of the Band Aid and
Live Aid for the legendary Ethiopia's famine victims in the 1970s, a
rude reminder that, two decades after, Africans are still perceived as
some miserable victims. And why not? Note that this is a
Commission for Africa *not* Commission by Africa or Commission of
Africa.

Emerging facts indicate that the only thing original about Blair's
initiative is the original smartness to appropriate the latent Africans'
aspirations using willing Africans. This truism is acknowledged by
discernable Africans no less by the British economist. In its edition of
Jan 22nd 2005 the weekly journal was short of accusing Tony Blair of
plagiarism citing how his Commission's draft document wantonly
pillaged NEPAD document. 'It's (read; NEPAD's) content is mostly
copied by the Britain's Commission for Africa…' wrote the
Economist.

Two weeks ago, NEPAD business group held in Abuja.
President Olusegun Obasanjo rightly challenged participants on
'branding of NEPAD'. According to Mr. President, NEPAD
branding involves '…deliberate and strategic efforts to popularise
NEPAD and investing in products that are used in homes, offices
and for export that carry the NEPAD brand'. 'If I may so ask; what
is wrong with NEPAD motorcycle or bicycle?' the President added
rhetorically. As desirable as the President's challenge was it
simplistically assumed that NEPAD patent is in itself guaranteed
which is a misplaced assumption. I think the first task is to
deliberately patent NEPAD against plagiarism and crude
appropriation by the very people NEPAD's chieftains put enormous
hope to realise NEPAD's goals. Commission for Africa is at best a

copy of NEPAD without acknowledgement and at worse a subversion of the latter through resource dispersal and resource diversion without apology. Witness the fact that its proposals dealing with good governance for aid, democracy for debt relief are the same as NEPAD's. Branding NEPAD should start with this self realisation.

Above all, branding NEPAD calls for its domestication. NEPAD's chieftains must let it be owned by Africans themselves rather than G-8 which is eager to remove its cover and claim its ownership. Furthermore, patenting NEPAD calls for prohibition of willing African leaders and experts, from serving multiple masters at the same time. Africans serving on Blair's Commission should chose between Britain's usurpation of an idea and a continent's attempt at development. History shows that Lagos Plan of Action was subverted by Brandt Commission and ECA's popular participation was undermined by SAP.

Return of Vision 2010[27]

Anti-corruption campaign suddenly assumes a special importance in recent time. Thanks to the big-bang radical move by President Olusegun Obasanjo which had overnight landed former Senate President, Adolphos Wabara, former education Minister Professor Fabian Osuji and police Chief Tafa Balogun among other notables in the court of law. Commentaries still trail this official bold departure from official rhetoric to practical actions on graft-curtailment. We have read the sycophantic (in praise of Mr. President), to the most cynical (too late, too token) and conspiratorial (to impress creditors and international community). Whatever the truism, what is not disputable is that more than ever before, re-energised anti-corruption war has once again brought to the fore the spectre of Vision 2010.

Vision 2010 aptly characterises corruption as a scourge that must be dealt with if Nigeria would enlist in the comity of producing nations. Perhaps if this singular characterization had been internalised we would have been saved the deep-seated cynicism that trail the disclosures on corruption. Yours sincerely agrees with Col Ahmadu Ali of the infamous students' massacre that you don't need external prodding to appreciate that corruption is a scourge.

Vision 2010 has shown that corruption is a zero-sum game in which the community loses all while the corrupt is the only winner. What passes for bribes (*sorry lobbying*) in the Ministry of Education will certainly not be available for improved training facilities for students in our schools. What passes for '*loan*' to a Vice Chancellor for on-ward transfer to assembly men, to pass an education budget, will certainly not be available to improve library facilities.

---

[27] *Daily Trust*, Monday 25th April, 2005 pp. 6

Inadvertently we kill the education sector while we swell the pockets of the few via corruption. This is the issue that tasks our imagination.

Conversely if Vision 2010's impact assessment of corruption is appreciated then the praise-singers of the Mr. President's move will be out of jobs. In fact the President accepts as much. According to him the corrupt are not his enemies but enemies of Nigeria. The best way therefore for the praise singers to demonstrate that they are truly with the President is not to indulge in the usual eye-service (as distinct with heart-service) but to follow the president's foot steps to ensure further full disclosures about corruption.

This then raises the point about the real strength of Vision 2010 process. Vision 2010 is consensual to the extent that the vision was expected to be shared by all who help in formulating it. Those who formulated the vision were drawn from all stakeholders in Nigerian enterprise that include public and private sector operators. The beauty of the all-inclusive process of 2010 vision is that it was owned and expected to be promoted by all the stakeholders. Anti-Corruption crusade was therefore expected to be the preoccupation of all. Recently the ICPC chairman, Justice Mustapha Akanbi alluded to how anti-corruption campaign has become a one-man orchestra, all around the President while most of his lieutenants are on-lookers. The promise of Vision 2010 could have reversed the emerging trend so decried by Justice Akanbi.

Lastly the definition of corruption by Vision 2010 is inclusive of political corruption via rigging and election manipulation. Given that most present day leaders were not truly elected and are therefore under no obligation to be accountable to anybody other than themselves (Wabara was once quoted as saying politicians must recoup their investment in politics) any further evidence then that we are confronted with corruption scandals of unprecedented proportions? It is refreshing that Vision 2010 document is among the background documents sent to National Political Reform Conference (NPRC). Are we to expect the return of Vision 2010 five years after it has gathered dust? Better late than Never! Anti-Corruption is one out of other critical success factors considered by that historic document. Others include manufacturing, agriculture, labour-management relations, environment, private, public sector partnership.

UN Seat or Millennium Development Goals? [28]

The contest for UN seat under the proposed new reformed UN system and the realisation of UN Millennium Development Goals, MDGs, (due for mid-term assessment this year) are far from being mutually exclusive. On the contrary, they should compliment each other in a country in which things operate in compliment and not in contest. But this is Nigeria, a country where complimentarily is an exception and neo-liberal competition is the rule. In terms of conceptual framework, the concepts and principles with heuristic device in this inquiry are located within the social action frame of analysis. Both Dunlop and Marx have been criticised for their disposition towards reductionism. They emphasize primarily the structures and systems at the expense of the actors. Dunlopian 'industrial relations systems' sums up the 'system thinking' according to which 'a system of rules and institutions... operate to regulate the way work is done'. In the Dunlopian frame, human agency is only assumed away in the system of rule making. 'Supra-individual structure' is also central to Marxian theory. Primary importance is accorded to 'objective structure', which exist not only independently of human actions but also considerably influences the direction of the latter in a predetermined way. Thus this functionalist perspective in Marxian frame understandably and inadvertently assigns motives and intentions to people only by their class position, which is an 'objective structure' defined only in relation to the relation of production (Barbalet: 404 and Clegg *et al.,* 28). Since the primary objective of this inquiry is a preoccupation with "subjective meaning" in terms of how workers through collective actions have acted to

---

[28] *Daily Trust*, Monday 16th May 2005, pp. 6

change their environment, functionalist system thinking of either 'rules' or 'objective structure' cannot be useful concepts.

The social frame is formulated out of the recognition of the limitations of sociology of system. It stresses the fact that the orientations of actors should be the focus of analysis. When applied to workers, we have to know how they order their wants and expectations relative to their employment. The usefulness of this approach lies in the fact that it allows us to see the relevance of the union from the notions and orientations of the members as distinct from the requirements of the 'system'. This approach has got significant application in industrial relations and labour studies. Watson (1988) observed that social action frame is dated to Weber's sociology. There is however a recognition that even in the Marxian paradigm, the great "dramatis personae" are no more 'proletariat' and the 'bourgeoisie' but 'managers', 'supervisors', 'shop-steward', trade unions and other groups separated not on the basis of ownership of means of production but by access to authority' (Burris: 1987: 98 & Hyman: 1975). Crouch emphasizes that 'sociology of social action' takes as the point of departure, 'actors with goals which they seek to realize through certain available means and in relationships with other social actors whose own pursuit of goals either reinforces or conflicts with the attempts of the original actors.' It is added that 'once we start specifying goals and means we can begin to make theories about the ways actors are likely to act.' Colin also points out that the strength of social action frame lies in its deference to those approaches that choose to reduce actors' expectations and objectives to 'ideology, consciousness or imagery; or from one which makes inferences from the structure of relations between social actors without examining the implications of that structure for behaviour.' Indeed this framework of analysis also stresses the role of cognition, social perceptions and consciousness but it is not held that these offer 'automatic explanations' for the activities of active individuals. Important too is the understanding that this approach to appreciating union performance does not preclude the notion of social structure and the context in which the union operates. It is a method that acknowledges the ... structural imbalance in social relations, such as the fundamental inequality between capital and labour.' The notion of balance and power is not ignored no less than the fact that it is a notion of social structure that is 'more subtle, complex, and less dogmatic' than the system thinking has it. The issue is the extent the imbalances in power structure enter into the 'pattern of action chosen by different social actors' as I hope to show in the performance of the NUTGWN. This research perspective points to the fact that while the employment relations in the textile industry imposes a considerable number of limitations on the workers, through their unions, they have demonstrated that '...potential always exists for human beings to act in ways which serve to change and modify the existing social order' (Watson D: 1988:182).

The Federal government has just constituted an enlarged national committee on the reform of UN system headed by the former Head of States, retired General Abdulsalami Abubakar with Chief Emeka Anyioku as the secretary. Among other things, this historic committee is expected to aggregate national inputs on the proposed reform as well as strategise on how the country can get the well deserved seat on the Security Council.

Yours sincerely is never in doubt that Nigeria more than any country in the continent deserves a seat on the Security Council, given our tested commitment to multilateralism and global peace. However observers believe that we need to do more than panel-beating to be taken serious in the new UN reform system. Paradoxically the number one observer who shares this perspective is Mr. President himself. President Olusegun Obasanjo in Katsina last week was reported to have said that:

> 'If Nigeria has been what it should have been, nobody will be contesting that seat with Nigeria, it should never have been...But because we have under-performed in the past, now others are saying they are suited for UN seats. It should never have been. And we should largely blame ourselves for that."

The questions are; what should Nigeria have been which it has not been making others saying they are suited for UN seats? In what area have we under-performed in the past? Are we still not under-performing now? Or better still have we over performed? Who are the *others* and how have they performed?

According to UN Human Development Index for 2004, Nigeria is ranked 151 with war torn countries like Sierra-Leone on low human development. South Africa and Egypt ranked 119 and 120 respectively making them listed on the medium human development. GDP per capital for Nigeria was $860 while South Africa and Egypt were $10,070 and $3,180 respectively. Life-expectancy was 51.6 in Nigeria while it was 48.8 and 68.6 in South Africa (no thanks for prevalence Aids rate of 25%) and Egypt respectively. Combined gross enrolment ratio for primary, secondary and tertiary schools was 45 per cent for Nigeria and 76 and 77 per cent respectively for Egypt and South Africa. Against this background of grim statistics of the UN any further evidences how we have performed? When we add other well-known facts that over 70 per cent live below poverty line, that Nigeria ranks fourth among the world's 22 countries with high tuberculosis burden and ranks among countries with low spending on health and education, is there any doubt that we are still under-performing?

This is why some observers have argued that the national committee Nigeria needs urgently is an all inclusive committee on meeting the Millennium Development Goals. In fact, such committee may get us closer to UN seat than the one on UN reform that in the long run does not reform our life. MDGs, we all know, "constitute a set of 8 goals, 18 targets and 48 indicators – that establish concrete, time-bound targets for advancing development and reducing poverty by 2015 or earlier." The world must see that we are truly committed to making this great potential for prosperity called Nigeria into a reality of prosperity, willing to release the energy of this huge human resource for development through supportive (power supply, health, water, education) not repressive policies (mass lay-offs, increases in prices of petroleum products, budget cuts etc). By the way, whatever choice we make, the struggle for UN Security Council seat cannot be separated from the struggle for social and economic security for mass of Nigerians.

Between Hunger and Famine[29]

There is no famine in Niger. And that is official. According to Niger President, Monsieur Mamadou Tandja, '*The people of Niger look well-fed as you can see*' he reportedly told *BBC*. News in the final analysis is an expression of language. Conscious of the fact that the Republic of Niger is officially French-speaking one would be right to think that the head-line news was a deliberate English distortion of the French meaning of the word; famine as seen by President Tandja. My *French English dictionary* however indicates that the meaning of famine is not divisible in both languages. On the contrary, 'famine' seems a borrowed French word that means dearth and acute shortage of food resulting in hunger. There is no doubt that President Tandja is familiar with this value- free meaning of the word; famine, which is clearly acute hunger. But true to his political callings, he opts for the value-loaded/political meaning of an ordinary word in an extraordinary political dictionary exclusive to the Presidential Library in Niamey.

According to him, famine is no famine but something close to it, namely food shortages occasioned by usual endemic poor rains and locust invasions in Niger. He accused the media, aid agencies and opposition parties of exaggeration and smear campaign against his administration. Paradoxically Monsieur Le President's assigned meaning (as distinct from the real meaning) is not fundamentally different from the explanation of the aid agencies. In the true spirit of the new Presidential Orwellian double-speak in Niamey, aid agencies also avoided calling a spade a spade but some agricultural instrument. World Food Programme (WFP) spokesman Greg Barrow apparently on the word-defensive following Presidential word-offensive

---

[29] *Daily Trust*, Monday 15th August 2005, pp. 12

reportedly said that: "We have not spoken about famine but about pockets of severe malnutrition.'

Observers are at liberty to spot the differences between the President's "*food shortages caused by poor rain and locusts*" and WFP spokesman's "*pockets of severe malnutrition and famine*". The only caution however, is that the peripatetic pictures and images of desperate food starved mothers and children we saw recently on television are not about use of language or exercise in some study of semiotics but about real life story of human deprivation in the new millennium that promises abundance for humanity. It is also not clear what President Tandja's self-serving remark that '*people of Niger look well-fed*' means for the commendable upsurge of African humanitarian solidarity for the thousands of malnourished and the dying in Niger. What is however clear is that the humanitarian support in Nigeria for the deprived in Niger was not inspired by President Tandja's broadcast but by the desire to come to the aid of many in that country hunted by the spectre of hunger due to acute food shortages. To this extent the humanitarian support for the people of Niger must intensify rather than slow down unless we all want to indulge in the luxury of "politics of hunger" when what the sick, the weak and the dying of Niger need urgently is food, food and food.

The controversial remark of President Mamadou Tandja about zero-hunger in Niger has invariably brought to the fore the poverty of leadership and leadership challenge in Africa. According to the 2004 Human Development Report, Niger was 176th, i.e. second to the last (war-weary Sierra Leone) on the Human Development Index. The life expectancy at birth of President Tandja's "well-fed people" was 46 years, adult literacy was 17.1% and combined gross enrolment ratio for primary, secondary and tertiary schools was as miserable as 19 per cent, 85.3% are bellow income poverty line while as many as 41 per cent of children are under weight for age. These solemn statistics are NOT manufactured by the opposition nor aid agencies as President Mamadou was quick to make cheap political capital (or was it blackmail?) from the misery of his own people.

The question is that given the above poverty figures even without shortage of rain and droughts, does he need any further evidence that people of Niger are far from being "well-fed" given the country's miserable underdevelopment? This question further points to the hypocrisy of the entire global hype and instant humanitarian activism about the Niger famine. Why should we be rudely woken up to the burden of poverty and underdevelopment by corpses of our fellow beings and carcasses of their animals? Can we not see that when as many as 70 per cent of the population live less than a dollar per day (as they do in many African countries, Nigeria inclusive), the country is actually one huge cemetery as many are in daily famine and acute hunger due to income poverty? The official mind set and ego-peddling in Niamey is certainly the type that will not get Niger and indeed Africa out of misery. To say that Niger is experiencing "like all the countries in the Sahel, a food crisis due to the poor harvest and the locust attacks" underscores failed leadership. There are virtually no countries that are disaster-free. Cuba lives permanently under the spectre of hurricane and tornadoes, yet it is top on UN Development Index. Burkina Faso in the sub-region was also disaster-prone but we have not seen gory pictures of failed state as we saw in Niger. The challenge of governance is to deliver prosperity for the people in spite of disasters not for elected President to be telling us the difference between famine and hunger or comparing the scale of misery as if misery to one is not misery to all. The world cannot resolve on end to poverty while some miserable politicians in the continent play politics of poverty.

Debt: Costs of a Relief[30]

The seemingly (or was it for real?) peripatetic picture of debt-negotiation-fatigued Mr. President and his Honourable Finance Minister, Dr. Ngozi Okonjo-Iweala on a national television network once again confirms the old saying that she that goes a borrowing must ultimately go a sorrowing. The ordeal of the torturous road to debt relief contrasts sharply with the relative ease the first debt was incurred in the 1970s. The official debt stress may however be just be a tip of the iceberg. If the road to debt relief tasked the energy and imagination of the officialdom so much, we then imagine the actual burden imposed on the people by the two decades of deprivations, which characterized the previous callous regimes of debt repayment, debt servicing and debt rescheduling.

The rich cried for once, (the Honourable Minister reportedly shed tears amidst additive verbal conditionality of Paris Club), we should not forget that millions of poor Nigerians actually bled under the crushing weight of dictatorship of conditionality of currency devaluation, wage freeze and SAP riots, cut in public expenditure, "budgetary belt-tightening for patients much too poor to own belts" (according to UN envoy, Jeffrey Sachs), withdrawal of subsidies, down sizing and all that constitute what the recent LIVE Aid concert organisers called evil of Structural Adjustment Programme (SAP). It is certainly morally acceptable that we make Poverty History, but let nobody assume that it means memory loss about the unforgettable avoidable imposed poverty on the poor. In fact there is wisdom in the argument that the real commendation arising from the recent debt relief should go to Nigerians who in the first instance, had to contend with mass misery by living for three decades perpetually

[30] *Daily Trust*, Monday 18th July 2005, pp. 6

below their true means (even though they were falsely accused of living above their means by SAP regimes) due to resource constraints and resource denials the perverse flow of resources external debt endangered. And that is precisely the issue; it is time we counted the costs of debt, debt payments and debt relief to know if the problem is actually over. True to expectation the new debt relief has been trained with same typical but simplistic polarized uncritical (almost psychopathic) official commendation on the one hand and habitual cynicism about the government efforts on the other hand. But what is needed is neither of this binary exhaustion but deeper reflections about the debt road hitherto chosen.

The strength of the recent debt deal is that contrary to the neo-liberal dogma that there is no alternative (TINA) to debt debacle beyond rescheduling and repayment, there are certainly alternatives that include debt reduction and outright cancellation. Once there is the will there will always be countless ways out. We also see the limit of the market logic with respect to debt management. The neo-liberal tool kit prefers casino-like interest charges and repayments, defaults followed by penalties approach but both the creditors and debtors know that this road only makes debt unsustainable and un-payable. It takes the public intervention and debtor-states' activism to put common sense to a potentially chaotic mutually assured destruction.

Closely tied to this is the fact that in a globalize world, options are never foreclosed *if and only if* we dare to struggle and persevere. The debt deal is not a product of a night-long negotiation as such or the moral rectitude of the creditors but the outcome of decades-long global activist campaigns for total debt cancellation by mass organisations like Jubilee 2000, trade unions, Africa Union (AU), NEPAD's advocacy for debt reduction, the tenacity of President Obasanjo's singular campaign for debt forgiveness since 1998 and the strike "notice" by the national assembly. The question is: does the deal worth the battle? The weakness of the debt deal is that it came so late and so token. Nigeria deserves unconditional total debt cancellation both from point of view of economics and sociology and not just debt reduction. According to the Debt Management Office (DMO), in the past 38 years as much as $42 billion had been paid to

Paris Club as interests and penalties on $13.5 billion loans to Nigeria. Simple wisdom here is that the debt has been well over paid such that debt reductions, discounted partial pay back only legitimise further extractions from what has been over paid. If Ghana and Tanzania with lower population and size and therefore relatively less debt burden could get debt cancellation, Nigeria (which is also a lowest recipient of foreign aid according to Professor Sachs, the UN Secretary General on Millennium Development Goals (MDGs) certainly deserves a better deal. Finance Minister was "thrilled" to say that Nigeria saves a "potential $8 billion" following $18 billion debt relief with Paris Club. This sounds like alchemist's temptation.

The whole truth is that in real times, the net outflow of initial actual (not potential) $6 billion arrears and buy back of $8.2 billion outstanding even at discounted rates dwarf the "potential" marginal savings. The Honourable Minister is encouraged to temper the excitement of the deal with the impact assessment of its implementation on existing NEEDS targets, annual budgets and the existing financing gaps.

We dare not raise expectations which are difficult to fulfil. Business-as-usual such as debt rescheduling is certainly untenable but business-unusual that still promotes perverse resource transfer from poor Nigeria to the rich Paris Club a day longer is untenable and unexciting. President Obasanjo not concealing his frustration with slow response to his campaign for debt forgiveness once noted a country needed not be bombed to stone-age like Iraq before its debt is cancelled.

The systematic damage debt management did to Nigeria's industrial sector, state capacity for service delivery, public education and health sector in the past three decades are equivalent of declaration of war on Nigerians. The question is: does Nigeria have to incur such huge cost of being devalued from a middle income earner to the poorest of the poor before we have a debt deal that is less far reaching in putting an end to the debt burden?

Reforming the Reform[31]

"When an orange tree bears bitter oranges, cut down the tree not just the fruit"- Swaziland Proverb

Chief Ernest Shonekan, Chairman Interim National Government (ING) once remarked that the pricing (then; "appropriate pricing") of petroleum products was a 'test of will' between his government and the people of Nigeria. Watching the new Information Minister, Frank Nweke Jnr. making a case for why consumers must pay for more under the new regime of the appropriate pricing called "deregulation" shows that a decade after, we are still hunted by the spectre of adjustment/reform that pitches the people against their government. Shonekan Interim contraption laid no claim to popular legitimacy (it was unelectable anyway). It is however debatable if Obasanjo administration which owns its acceptance to the electorate (affirmed by Supreme Court recently) could afford the indulgency of permanent war of attrition with the citizenry, through the weapon of mass provocation like addictive fuel price increase.

Time and *dramatis personae* (Ministers after Ministers) have definitely changed. It is however remarkable that the official rhetoric with respect to why products' prices must reach the roof top remain completely frozen. The rhetoric bears features like; "necessary 'tough' decision to allow for private operators", "need to ensure cost recovery" and sustainable supply, "removal of subsidy" and freezing of resources for health, education and road, etc. There is definitely a need for a change of official rhetoric.

It is certainly time to rethink the reform process in which government remains at pain (or is it fun?) to impose sustained painful

---

[31] *Daily Trust*, Monday 29th August, 2005 pp. 6

products' price increases which apart from undermining necessary consensus for development but does great violence to the very government's acclaimed objective of wealth generation and poverty alleviation. The first point of departure is the language and the image of reform. We are told that deregulation is part of the 'tough' measures that for now remain painful but will prove amenable with time. Hour arable Minister...compares like with unlike, when he likened fuel price to telecom products' prices which once went up but eventually 'came-down'. Apart from the fact that one half-decade price-climbing in petroleum sector makes short and long run economics indivisible thus belying the Minister's simplistic claim, the real problem is in the official mind-set that proudly holds that things must get 'tough' for the already toughened populace before they will get better.

Amartya Sen, 1998 Nobel Prize Winner for Economics warns us against a development process as a war (and in his own words), as a "fierce process", the regular trade marks of which are "blood, sweat and tears... a world in which wisdom demands toughness." Our creditors in IMF and World Bank are certainly not accountable to us. They may thus irresponsibly task and insult us on "tough" policy measures of subsidy removal, devaluation and international pricing (which their home countries' citizens won't accept)

But our government officials must necessarily critically access the impact assessment of the received "tough" wisdom for public welfare on their own citizens that are already down and out and begging desperately for upliftment. NTA network news reminds us everyday of the obvious; children who are out of schools briskly mopping windscreens and simultaneously making away with car mirrors on our major high ways. How will additional fuel price hikes get these children back to schools and not get those in schools currently to the streets is the critical question begging for answer from government officials and not a rendition of mantra of "international market price". The qualitative aspect of the much taunted accountability and transparency is the extent of the "softness" of government policies on its people.

Recent serial "tough"' talks of Chief Rasheed Gbadamosi, Chairman PPPRA that prices must go up now and now... cast reform process in the mould of *new-terrorism* in which citizens' concerns don't matter. The real reform of the reform must therefore start with the language and refurbished image of reform that must stress "softness" in place of "toughness", diverse concerns of the nation in place of sectoral vested interest. Paradoxically it is "Mass communication" and "sociology" subjects so much reportedly diminished by Mr. President that can salvage public officials from this identified malaise. Mass communication teaches mass-language that is people's sensitive while sociology teaches all important social sensitivity of development for our seemingly frozen and insensitive public officials.

Secondly we must revisit the unhelpful official notion of market fundamentalism that pitches the state against the market as if the thin line that divides them in our context is as clear. What manner of the market is the market for petroleum products in which imports constitute 90 per cent of supply and is handled mainly by NNPC, itself a government monopoly? John Mcmillan rightly observes that in "the problem in the developing countries is not that the markets are absent but that they are working badly.' In fact, the challenge of governance is to first reinvent the market by getting domestic supply chain in place through refinery fixing rather than lazily peddling rhetoric about market forces that in the first instance are not at play. Adam Smith did not place his optimism of the *Wealth of Nations* on the dubious "market forces" currently bandied by non-market forces in Nigerian government.

Lastly reform is not an end but a means to an end. This then calls for holistic approach to every policy especially as critical as petroleum products. If we recover cost in down stream sector, which costs does it induce in others? If queues of the past truly disappear, at what costs to other sectors in which cost-pushed inflation has imperilled many industries and elongated the unemployment queue? These are the questions elementary to a sociology student which our government officials must find an answer for.

Nigeria-China: the Widening Gap[*]

President of China visits Nigeria this week. President ... visit is part of a global tour that took him to notable countries like United States, Saudi Arabia etc. The fact that this historic visit has not captured the imagination of the media dominated in recent times by transition politics once again shows how development discourse is fast taking a back stage. Notwithstanding the distance and geography, Nigeria and China share significant traits worthy of acknowledgement. In terms of population, the two are giants in their own rights. With a population of 1.5 billion (official 1.3 billion) China is the largest in the world. Conversely Nigeria, with estimated population of 150 million people, (before the last census) is the largest concentration of black people in the world. In fact, one of every two Asians is a Chinese, while the expected census figure may reveal that one in every three persons in Africa is a Nigerian. Nigeria's population is as diverse as China's in terms of languages, cultures and religions. The two countries also boast of remarkable resource endowment and whatever the parameters, the two are regional powers, with China as actual power no less than Nigeria still more of a potential power.

This is however where the similarities stop. Until recently the two shared common brand-name of "third world" countries but today, the world witnessed China's unprecedented race to the top while Nigeria had a free fall to the bottom of development index. China sustained unprecedented 10 per cent growth rate in the 90s while Nigeria recorded double digit negative growth rate during the period. Between 1990 and 2000, China uplifted as many as 200 million out of poverty while in Nigeria 70 per cent of that population

* *Daily Trust*, 24th April, 2006

were pushed from prosperity into poverty in Nigeria. Paradoxically Sino-Nigeria bilateral relations are long dated. Yet development observers have never imagined that the gap between two friendly nations would be widening with age. As a matter of fact, China has benefited more from the relations that started with formal diplomatic ties on 10 February, 1971 as much as Nigeria has recorded losses in quantitative and qualitative terms. Put in development language, Nigeria keeps paying the China price, while China remains a smart price-taker.

It is bad enough that the balance of trade has always been in favour of China but worse that the quality of this trade more than the quantity under develops Nigeria. Dumped substandard goods *from* China are the rule than exception judging by the discoveries of both National Agency for Food and Drug Administration and Control (NAFDAC) and Standards Organisation of Nigeria (SON). The railway refurbishing scam under Abacha dictatorship underscored the dark side of Sino-Nigeria relations with Nigerian side's preference for greed and corruption.

The issue here is not that China is a bad player and Nigeria a victim of unfair relations. The issue is that while China is development conscious, Nigeria is development-shy and at worse anti-development in orientation and policy formulation. In the seventies because the two countries were driven development, the relations were mutually benefiting. For instance, China and Chinese businesses were eager to set up factories especially in textile sub-sector while Nigeria was eager to provide enabling environment such as protection of domestic market, power and water supply, with a view of providing jobs in the labour-intensive industry. However from late eighties, while China kept to development dogma, Nigeria infested with Dutch disease occasioned by cheap oil money preferred import to domestic production with all the attendant policy summersault. The result is that today in place of *Chinese factories* producing and employment millions of Nigeria, we now have *China towns* trading in dumped goods amidst factory closures and mass unemployment. Thus the critical issue in the widening gap between Nigeria and China lies in the parallel roads to development in the two different countries.

In his celebrated book, *Globalization and Its Discontents,* winner of Nobel Prize in Economics, Joseph Stiglitz, shows that the miracle of China lies in good governance, public-private sector partnership and a genuine home-driven policy agenda as opposed to branded neo-liberal IMF/World Bank policies contained in the notorious Washington Consensus. China promotes the state-led gradualist reform agenda with remarkable social protection for mass of potential losers as opposed to Nigeria's type "shock-therapy" reform in which few winners are indulged while the mass of losers are left bare. China did not pursue doctrinaire privatization policy but encouraged state enterprises side by side with private enterprises with the eye on value adding activities, employment creation and inclusive development.

Sino-Nigeria relations have been characterized by robust exchange of leaders from 1978 when Vice-Premier Geng Biao first visited Nigeria and Vice-President Dr. Alex Ekweme visited China in March, 1983. This week's visit of the Chinese President is one visit quite remarkable. But the critical question is that beyond trade agreements and protocols Nigerian leaders must learn about the great transformation of China than anywhere (included the taunted Singapore) and turn the existing disadvantages in relations to opportunities for development.

NES 12: Policy Dogma or Policy Balance?*

If the Nigerian Economic Summit (NES) had not been an annual summit, it would have been desirable to have invented one this year! Never before has a gathering of stakeholders on the economy assumed special importance. Refreshingly the organizers of this year's summit are also conscious of the special context of next week summit. In apparent reference to the political calendar, we are reminded that NES 12 "will provide an auspicious opportunity for Nigerians and our development partners to initiate and set the tone for the impending political debate, at least with regards to the direction of our economic policy." The truth is that Nigeria is not short of "political debate", as such. Indeed any political observer will readily agree that the "impending" political debate NES is eager "to set the tone" for will be one too many. In the past six months, for instance, the country could very well be mistaken for one huge (political) debating society, no thanks to term-elongation in particular and the notorious constitutional amendments in general. Globally politics is a continuation of economics by other means. In Nigeria, pray what is the economic content of the last six months with its legacy of tons of arguments for and arguments against you-remember-what? The buzz-words thrown up were familiar: "rotational presidency", "power shift", "North-South", etc. Nothing about "Gross Domestic Product (GDP)", "Value addition", "Employment", "Industrialization", "Production and "Income-Distribution", "Poverty Eradication", etc. In fact of the proposed

---

* *The Daily Trust*, 5th June 2006

114 amendments, beyond formula to share oil revenue no proposal on economic empowerment and social transformation. Thus the imperatives of NES 12 in terms of economic agenda setting for the politicians in 2007 cannot be overemphasised.

But even at that, critical observers would insist that economic agenda setting is not new. As a matter of fact, since 1996, NES has been setting the agenda for the polity. NES accepts as much that substantial parts of the federal government policies in the past ten years regardless of regime type were logical fall out of NES recommendations. The question is; what is the impact of NES' policy thrust on the country's growth and development? Despite the rhetoric about diversification, crude oil predominance is still crudely predominant. The recent damning report of Manufacturers Association of Nigeria (MAN) that Nigeria is back to the pre-independence era of de-industrialization of the 1950s because of massive factory closures caused by energy cost and prohibitive production costs points to the widening gap between policy dogma and policy reality. It is remarkable that for once, NESG is increasingly conscious of the fact that with respect to the economy and just like politics, it has been motions without real movement. Read NESG's website confession:

> "Unfortunately implementation has fallen short of expectation and so the impact on the economy has been less than desirable. In essence, while the concepts produced (by NES) have been clearly articulated, the implementation has left much to be desired, particularly with respect to the co-ordination of all the elements in the planning process. These shortcomings have meant that the average Nigerian has seen little meaningful benefit from the sacrifices they have been asked to make."

True to expectation, NESG blames abysmal non-economic performance on non-implementation of its annual recommendations. But at another breadth, NESG taunts achievements that included economic liberalization, deregulation and privatization, improved investment climate, public sector reforms. The real truth is certainly in between the contradictory claims of NESG. There is certainly no doubt that a departure from the command economy and the attendant inherent wastage therein to private sector growth process has elicited some economic activism of late, especially in telecom and oil and gas. Many thanks to NESG, for its gospel of liberalization and deregulation. Every public sector official had been converted to this dogma, which was uncritically implemented to the point of pitching the public versus the private sector and at worse undermining the capacity of public sector as a whole. The new thinking about Public-private partnership (which significantly is central to this year's theme) comes too late too token. The result is that Nigeria privatizes without strong regulatory agencies, liberalizes without strong governance (in fact with preferred weak governments!) and promotes private sector growth without appropriate corporate governance. The problem therefore is not lack of implementation of policy but wholesale uncritical implementation of NES policy dogma that weakens governance while it privileges private sector operators. The challenge lies in looking for a paradigm (sorry, dogma) balance in which there must be a remarkable policy mix to strengthen the institutions of the market and the state. The recent total and abysmal collapse of energy sector shows the limit of liberalization mantra. It is the government that must build more power stations; it is the government that will halt "vandalization" of installations, it is the government that will create enabling environment for private sector participation. Thus the country needs strong governance not less as economic liberalization dictionary has long wrongly promoted. The serial disasters in the aviation sector shows that if there is no policy balance, we may replace public monopoly with competitive chaos (read-cutting corners) which in their trail they leave behind deaths and poor service delivery.

Economic Crimes, Be Damned!*

As much as $5billion (₦650 billion) had been recovered from various private-public sector economic criminals in the past three years. And that was official! According to the Chairman of the Economic and Financial Crimes Commission (EFCC), Mallam Nuhu Ribadu, the unprecedented pay back and recovery was the fall out of the commission's war against financial scams and corruption of different types in the country. In addition, the Commission has recorded whopping 76 convictions arising from various financial crimes. The cumulative impact of the EFCC's efforts is the de-listing of Nigeria from the 2001 non-compliance list of the global Financial Action Task Force (FATF). FATF monitors and evaluates each country's performance in terms of its resolve to combat financial crimes and terror-financing. The weekend EFCC's success stories are refreshing developmentalist news of the year! Critics of EFCC were eager to point to alleged selectivity of investigations and prosecution. EFCC's recent score-board belies the critics' allegation. In fact the emerging picture is that EFCC's relentless war against graft has gone a long way to redeem Nigeria's image as well as restore confidence in business relations. Economic crimes are economic crimes which ordinarily should be punishable but it took the bold steps of Ribadu's EFCC to drum this point home such that international community could not ignore its remarkable success in such a short period. The de-listing of Nigeria from the smear list of FAFT is a remarkable cost-effective image-cleansing for Nigeria and Nigerians just as the previous listing did far reaching damage to our collective efforts for growth and development. The lesson here is that rather than being

* *The Daily Trust,* 3rd July 2006

cynical at every official step to punish economic leeches and restore the great lost glory of Nigeria we should rather own the process EFCC sets in motion by collectively elect to damn economic crimes of various hues.

Corruption is a world-wide phenomenon. But according to Vision 2010 report it assumes notoriety in Nigeria such that "Corruption appears to have become a way of doing things, though it is resented by a significant number of people who are helpless in the face of weak and selective application of sanctions." At inauguration in 1999, President Obasanjo rightly observed that:

"Government officials became progressively indifferent to propriety of conduct and showed little commitment to promoting the general welfare of the people and the public good. Government and all its agencies became thoroughly corrupt and reckless. Members of the public had to bribe their way through in Ministries to get attention and one government agency had to bribe another government agency to obtain the release of the statutory allocation of funds."

Economic crimes erode the moral fabric of every society, violates the social and economic rights of the poor and the vulnerable. For instance, but for the efforts of EFCC that compelled recovery and returned stolen money to Ministry of Education, Universal Basic Education (UBE), among other programmes, for the poor would have been denied scarce financial resources. The truth is that what is stolen by few rogues cannot be made available for the mass need of the desperate poor multitude. Dangerously too, economic crimes undermine democracy and subvert the rule of law which is the basis of every civilized society. Economic crimes in turn retard development. Imagine recovered $5 billion still in the coffer of criminals, they would not only be able to buy votes, the press ahead of 2007 but would dare to buy off justice.

In damning economic crimes therefore the issue is not to hail and commend EFCC for well done jobs so far but to show that sustainable anti-economic crimes is indispensable for our collective survival. We dare not politicise what is clearly a developmental challenge.

Back To Basics[*]

"We want Nigeria to be one of the 20 largest economies by the year 2020. All other things must lead to that mission" – President Olusegun Obasanjo

Last week, (24th to 26th of January), event of developmental and continental significance held in the city of Minna, Niger State. The Directorate of Technical Cooperation in Africa (DTCA) an agency under the defunct Ministry of Cooperation and Integration in Africa organized a West African sub-regional Forum theme on the 'Frame work for Promoting Technological Development of Africa through Strategic Technological Co-operation'. After decades of trails and errors (wholesome errors indeed!) with poisonous and ruinous received wisdoms like "Structural Adjustment Programmes SAPS" and Reforms" this Forum brought *development* back to public discourse in Africa. It was a week of *back-to basics* for Africa with respect to technological development, which is the basis of development in general. For three days, basic critical developmental success factors such as *innovations, technology, human capital, industry and industrialization, entrepreneurship,* captured imagination. This was a liberating departure from polluted environment of corruption (is it anti-corruption?) hullabaloos and unhelpful poverty discourse, acrimonious politics of oil sharing and shock-therapeutic disjointed and un-informed reform agenda. In the age of Africa's unconsciousness yours sincerely (being a privileged participant) could bet that few of the robust participants at this historic forum were conscious of the big-bang impact of their developmental initiative!

---

[*] *Daily Trust,* 29th January 2007

The Ag DG DTCA, Dr Sule Bassi the forum's key driver was certainly clear in articulation that meaningful and sustainable development eludes Africa until the continent looks inward in the areas of science, engineering and technology capacity building. According to him, the imperatives of globalization demand that African countries strengthen solidarity and cooperation in research and development, innovations and technological development. These insights constituted a refreshing departure from the past decades of futile efforts at macro-economic stability and annul ritualistic annual budget-cut and budget diversion aimed at debt-repayment to Paris and London clubs at the expense of education, funding for research and development. The sessions witnessed new thinking on data-banking, country experiences in innovations and inventions and their commercialization, promotion of networking and collaboration among research institutions/ universities, industries and investors. The information overload at this conference was one thought for food for West African policy makers, (assuming they do not still prefer down-loaded handouts of donor agencies and multilateral institutions!). The most remarkable was the presentation on 'Technological Innovations and Development: Ghana's Experience' by Professor Kwesi Andem, Chairman Governing Council, African Network of Scientific and Technological Institutions, UNESCO, Nairobi. The other was "The Demands of Manpower in the Manufacturing Sector in Nigeria: the Dynamics, Trends and Prospects" by Professor Longmas Sambo Wapmuk of Industrial Training Fund (ITF). The damning statistics in these papers explain West African technological arrest occasioned by low school enrolment, intolerable bias for commerce and trade-related subjects, primitive technologies and official assault on science and technology via endless mutually destructive "educational reform" informed by cost-saving objective as distinct from developmental objective. According to ITF shows that:

"the largest single enrolment into any programme in the nation's 50 polytechnics and 38 monotechnics is Accountancy, with 32,963, followed by Business Administration and Management, 19,718, Business Studies 16,191, Banking and Finance 14,520, Marketing 10,097, and Secretariat Studies 9,325, whereas Ceramic Technology had a total enrolment of 23, Wood and Paper Technology 34, Textile Design 24, Water Resources/Public Health 45, Geological Engineering Technology 16, and Mineral Processing Engineering had only 14."

Any further evidence that Nigeria is a trading, as opposed to productive and manufacturing country? Both Professors Sheikh Lemu DG of ASCON and Kwesi Andam were the star-discussants whose critical commentaries provoked far reaching conclusions for research and development. Professor Kwesi who until this year was the Vice Chancellor Kwame Nkrumah University of Science and Technology Kumasi, Ghana was so passionate about girl child education and science and technology such that he declared that his bagful of degrees and academic awards which deservedly numbered scores were meaningless for Africa until Africa's primitive technologies were transformed. Professor Kwesi repeatedly celebrated the technological feat of Bida Baasam brass work site for its innovations and attended all sessions compared to his host counterpart, Vice Chancellor, Federal University of Science and technology, Minna, Haman Tukur Saad who acted as an on-looker in a programme he hosted. Professor Kwesi umpteenth time observed with outrage that any public officer determined to kill polytechnics as being crudely pushed by Education Minister Oby Ezekwesili was criminal and punishable. He took exception to unthinking copycats masquerading as African Ministers. He noted with disdain Africans' penchant for crude mechanical application UK model of merger of its polytechnics with universities adding that the homes of modern innovations are China and India, not technological under-developing UK.

The high point of the forum was the session on textile industry. The session exposes the disarticulation between resource endowment (cotton, fibres, yarn, huge human labour, etc.) institutional development frameworks - Raw Materials Research and Development Council (RMRDC) and Small and Medium Enterprises Development Agency of Nigeria (SMEDAN)- huge domestic market and abysmal collapse of a labour intensive industry like textile. The consensus is that the revival of textile industry is an acid test to institutions charged with the responsibility for innovations and development.

The missing link in this historic conference of is the official vision and mission to halt the technological arrest and unleash development. For one NEEDS lacks any vision on innovations and inventions compared to Vision 2010 which ably and competently identifies science and technology as one of the critical success factors for development and even laid bare proposals towards realisation. The only ray of hope is that after muddling through for 8 years with reform, President Obasanjo himself has returned to basics of development. He recently inaugurated Nigeria Development (note: development, not reform!). He tasked all inclusive participants (not some select economic team!) with the developmental challenge of making Nigeria one of the largest twenty economies by 2020, meaning we are officially ten years behind Vision 2010. Better late than never when it comes to development! Late developers sorry, "economic drivers" and "bridge builders" certainly must find useful the original ideas and policy options from Minna forum.

Fuel: may your days be rough[*]

Obasanjo government inherited persistent long queues at the pump station in 1999. Eight years after, the administration is not unhappy (at least no official regret so far!) it is bequeathing to its successor the miserable image of scavenging buyers of petrol at filing stations. It is a classical case of sustainable underdevelopment or better still discontinuity of reforms and worse still continuity of deforms. And that is official. Notwithstanding, the belated denial of fuel price increases (as if there had not been wholesome increases of products prices in many instances!) credited to him, Energy Minister Edmond Daukoru said it loud and clear that fuel shortage has come to stay until June assuming all things being equal (just as all thing have never been equal with this administration).

At the end of the Federal Executive Council (FEC) last week, Minister Daukoru reportedly said the obvious: products supply remains a function of repair of vandalized pipelines and rehabilitation of Kaduna and Warri refineries. According to him *no single drop of crude* has been processed in both Kaduna and Warri in the past one year as a result of vandalized pipelines. The vandalization of Mosimi pipeline has further worsened the shortage crisis as stock reserve had been exhausted. For those who care to task the Minister about the option of bridging to resolve the seemingly intractable problem of fuel supply especially to the up-land (defined as the North and the Creek areas of Niger Delta where paradoxically the black oil comes from) Dr Daukoru warned us to perish the thought. In his words: "As you are aware, it you send 80 trucks and 40 get there you are lucky due to massive diversion." So, either way we are inadvertently confronted

---

[*] *Daily Trust*, 12th February 2007

with Hobson choice: the more you are officially told the less you are officially salvaged from the scourge of products' scarcity. Earlier in the week, NNPC group MD Funsho Kupolokun had warned the nation that the "strategic" products reserve had been depleted. Lame and silly official excuses as distinct from direct actions have become substitutes for products supply. The most unacceptable of Daukoru's least resistance defined as "frank talk" was that the ongoing shameless grounding of the downstream sector was "*self-inflicted*". The critical question here is that whose self affliction is this singular affliction? Who constitute the "self"? Are they the fathers and mothers finding new abodes at filling stations rather than homes and workplaces willing to pay for products not available? Or are they the sit-in administrators like Daukorus and Kupolokuns and their multinational sponsors who rather than engaging in self-critical analysis of a failed policy of deregulation and accept their gross incompetence and therefore resign? The recent fuel scarcity and official explanations are simply untenable. For whatever reason, products' supply crises underscore governance crises of a sit-in government that is leaving us worse than it met us: no functioning refineries, 100 per cent import of products and gross incompetence in products' distribution! Without saying so Minister Daukoru's blame game was in the direction of so-called pipelines vandals well known but never arrested or prevented.

The issue however is that vandals cannot hold the country to ransom if truly governments at all levels perform their function of security and service delivery. Government that launched SERVICOM with fanfare cannot and should not insult the citizens with excuses for shameful products scarcity. The least the citizens deserve is mass resignation of those who accept public service but could not deliver not silly blame game. Why would there be no processing of a single drop of crude in the past one year while within the past few months we have shamelessly stressed the import reception facilities with dumped products from abroad? Even when drops of crude were being processed at what capacity utilization was it? It is simply unacceptable for paid government officials to talk to us about their self-inflicted helplessness when what is expected of them is performance and product delivery in spite of odds that are surmountable. To read from a serving Minister that it was a stroke of luck if 40 out of 80 trucks got to destination was an admittance of ministerial failure and ministerial accomplice since he knew so much and doe nothing? No economic crime is more heinous than the diversion of products critical for production in an economy with huge idle capacity and sickening poverty. For the Minister of the Federal Republic to know so much economic criminality and heap the blame on imaginary "inefficiencies" smack of criminal conspiracy to push the citizens to the abyss of permanent product diversions, price extortions and pump station misery. Government should urgently accept failure of deregulation policy and move to fix the refineries, repair the pipelines and announce a time-table for self-reliance in oil refinery and distribution. Nigeria cannot be counted among the twenty leading economies by 2020 when in the first quarter of the year, enterprises and working people are grounded due to lack of basic inputs like fuel. One thing is clear: certainly Nigeria would be counted among *the poorest of the poorest* if product shortage in the sixth producer of oil lasts till June.

Naira - dictatorship of CBN[*]

It seems the only thing constant with the CBN governor is *change, change and change*! He indeed said what Nigeria needs *"is Revolution"* not just reform! He is truly the last standing *comrade* contrary to the false claim of his former boss, President Olusegun Obasanjo according to which the last comrade was long buried with China's Chairman Mao. Late last year or thereabout, CBN governor actually revolutionized his name (for those that listen) to Chukwuma Soludo from Charles Soludo. The quality of his suit might however not differentiate him as such from Prince Charles of Wales. But what you dare not take from Charles, sorry, Chukwuma Soludo was the bold leap at name renaissance. In the age globalization in which every body Americanizes his or her name and even reasoning it was quite unorthodox to return to root name or give root name precedence before the foreign one! Yours sincerely is still at a loss to phantom the strategy of name renaissance at the CBN. However after reading Soludo's *long long* lecture trite on "Naira reform agenda" (does not have the brevity of a policy statement) I have come to realise that for this professor of economics, strategy is to be mouthed from the rooftop of the Bank than to be respected in action. CBN governor's last Tuesday's "Naira big-bang" was dubbed *"Strategic agenda for the Naira"*. But a critical reading exposes lack of strategy in policy pronouncement and policy formulation on the part of the CBN that has paradoxically launched a *Financial System strategy*, FSS 2020 with such international fanfare. Soludo, draws inspiration from the provision of 2007 CBN Act that accords autonomy to the bank on monetary matters. This is fine enough! The critical question however

[*] *Daily Trust*, 20th August 2007

is; does autonomy mean serial dictatorship of far reaching monetary policy measures on the country or does independence of the bank tasks the imagination of the central bankers to build groundswell of national consensus on policies that impact on all? What kind of strategy is presented with such finality of benchmarks and dates, only to instantly turn a subject of a review by the economic management team that ought to have announced it in the first instance? What kind of autonomy stretched to the point of isolation and alienation? The bane of Soludo's solutions is that they are presented in isolation of the broad context of the national economy. The hyper-activity of the financial sector contrasts sharply with inactivity and passivity of the other sectors. Can there really truly be sustainable Financial System Strategy, FSS without national development strategy? Soludo's naira agenda was cast within the context of the Bank's 13-point reform agenda? Good! But a policy text with such critical information overload about currency denomination, inflation targeting, dollarisation of state government accounts and current accounts liberalization, should have made reference to the seven-point agenda of President Musa Yar'Adua. Scandalously Soludo's speech that proudly links current account liberalization to Article VIII of the IMF is loudly silent on seven-point agenda and pretends that the legitimization of national assembly is not needed for such far reaching measures as Naira re-denomination. In his book, *The International Money Game,* Robert Aliber advices central bankers to read election results and not *balance sheets*! The tragedy of Nigeria's central bankers is that they neither read election results (no thanks to INEC's poor service delivery!) nor read balance sheets (by the way when last did you see CBN's audited accounts?) The question is to what extent is Naira as a sub-regional "reference currency" addresses the energy crisis? What is the relevance of dollarisation of states accounts to wealth generation, diversification of the economy, worsening insecurity of lives and property and anti-corruption campaign? This is not the first time CBN under Soludo hit the nation with a big-bang. We already had the big bang of bank consolidation. But of what relevance is the consolidation big bang to factory closures and increasing idle capacity and mass unemployment? There is certainly nothing strategic about the new "strategic" agenda for the naira? By singling out the acceleration of the process of naira convertibility as a priority in FSS, the CBN has further confirmed its mediocre orientation and preoccupation as a glorified Bureau de change, so called by the Minister of Finance during the ministerial screening. Who wants currency convertibility and why? The undercurrent assumptions of CBN are arrogant and self-serving. To further encourage state governors to turn from non-performers to instant money changers which most of them are already anyway under the least resistance of diversifying the funding of foreign exchange market is to compound more the problems of accounting and accountability at the state levels. There are more robust ideas in the FSS with all its limitations, than empty big bang grandstanding on Naira convertibility? The big-bang Nigerians ask for is a bold attempt by CBN to unlock huge pool of funds currently with the banks meant for SIMEs and quickly formalise the informal sector. The revolution we need in the financial sector is to "revolutionise access" to finance by the multitude of the increasing poor in the informal Nigeria that calls for true road shows by central bankers rather than grandstanding about Naira convertibility. CBN must urgently return to central banking and stop being a huge laboratory for pet and unhelpful ideas about foreign exchange management.

If the CBN officials insist they know about strategy, then they must disclose which school certify them on strategy and management. Last year Monusieur Soludo re-denominated the naira in an expensive grandstanding campaign that witnessed the introduction of new ₦1000 notes. Alluring arguments for that singular "revolution" made the citizens to ignore the costs of notes printing. A year after we are back to a new campaign for new notes that made ₦20 the highest denomination. Some strategy indeed! With CBN strategists and their strategy that changes every year and the attendant prohibitive costs without regrets we can as well close all schools of strategic planning. But somebody has to call the CBN to order that policy change for a nation is not the same as changing a name. For a nation all previous documents may not remain as valid!

UNTL closure and the End of History[*]

"The top management of the United Nigeria Textile Company (UNTL) last week informed me during a visit that the company will be closed down next week," so declared as a matter-of-fact by Kaduna state deputy Governor, Patrick Yakowa last week while receiving the visiting Minister of Energy, Henry Ajimogobia. Mr Yakowa disclosed further that all the textile mills in Kaduna, the cradle of textiles, had closed down except one. However, the official frustration the deputy governor buried under the sand was also the painful truth that a week before, his government had received the report on the Special Committee for the revival of textile and cotton industries in the state. The Committee of which yours truly was a member and the deputy governor, chaired was among other things tasked with the responsibility to examine the problems of the industries and recommend measures for revival. No industry had been considerably "panel beaten" like textile with tons of ideas for its revival but little actions that often come pretty late and miserably token for revival. If the latest news of UNTL closure and summary pay- off of 5000 workers could not shock the entire national economic team perhaps nothing else economically and industrially would.

When UNTL suspended production early this year because of non-availability of basic industrial input like LPFO (black oil), yours sincerely was quick to proclaim "End of Industry". With complete closure of the largest textile mill in the continent, with direct 5000 job losses and indirect 30,000 (suppliers, traders, cotton growers etc) jobs losses we can as well proclaim from the rooftops the end of history

---

[*] *Daily Trust*, 8th October 2007

of manufacturing in Nigeria! UNTL's history is about industry, productivity and quality prints, investment, positive economic climate, industrial policy consistency, mass employment, training and skills acquisition, research and development, market, consumption, communities (Kakuri, Trikania and Nasarawa) and value adding activities in general. An end to that robust industrial history means an end to history of enterprise in Nigeria. Beckman and Andre (1999), two Swedish political economists did extensive survey of textile industry in Nigeria. They singled out UNTL among other mills as the most "*successful adjuster*" that has weathered the storms of booms and busts of Nigeria's industrial development. With 10,000-strong union presence, UNTL is celebrated as a success case study in "large, integrated, multinational conglomerate." Established in Kaduna in 1965, UNTL was a product of developmentalist post-colonial Nigeria. Before British colonialism, there was a considerable dispersal of cloth manufacturing among the diverse peoples of Nigeria and West Africa, namely the Yoruba, the Nupe and the Bini of modern Nigeria; the Ashanti of modern Ghana; and peoples of modern Gabon, among others. Weaving technology was also widely shared. Remarkably too, gender participation in textile production was equitable. There was specialization along gender line with women's looms being vertical while that of men's were horizontal in both Nupeland and Yoruba-land with cotton spinning done mainly by women in Nupeland and Yoruba-land. The century of British imperialism killed this local enterprise that turned the colony to cargo economy which only supplied raw cotton to Europe in return for finished manufactured clothing. British colonialists never established a single textile mill. The Northern Regional Government led by the late Premier, Ahmadu Bello, established first textile industries in Kano and Kaduna to take the advantage of available raw materials like cotton and surplus labour in the region in late 1950s. During the competitive Federalism period of 1954-1966, regions engaged in healthy competition for development that included establishment and promotion of industries such as textile mills as part of the import substitution industrialization strategy. Hence, there were the Nigeria Textile Mill in Lagos and Aba and Asaba Textile Mills in the old Western, Eastern and Mid-Western regions respectively.

UNTL was established against this historic underdevelopment - development background. Its Chinese owners are part of a group of companies with affiliates in other countries in West Africa, in Hong Kong and "overseas" with the main owners being Cha family of Hong Kong Chinese origin. Mr Cha, a national honour holder, died last year! At the peak of its production in 1979, UNTL in Kaduna being one of the largest companies in Nigeria employed as many as 8,000 workers. When we combined the employment figure of its Lagos subsidiary, Nichemtex, as many as 20,000 workers were employed. Its installed capacity by 1980 was about 33,000 spindles including 360 modern rotor spindles and 2,300 looms, all shuttle-less.

UNTL is not the only integrated mill with spinning, weaving and printing activities. The moribund Kaduna Textile (KTL) was also an integrated mill. But it was the management style of UNTL that distinguished it from others and made it to be the last standing mill until this week. The closure of UNTL showed that the problem of the industry is not mismanagement but hostile investment climate. Where others were crippled with indebtedness and operational crisis, UNTL, opted for proactive measures of more labour discipline and work-load, backward integration "into spinning to replace the previously imported yarn, investing in associated spinning factories" (Supertex and Unitex), promoted a cotton trading company established under joint industry auspices making the company less vulnerable to raw material crisis. At a time outward orientation was not popular, UNTL was deep into export drive selling some of its produce to the US and by 1990 was said to "be exporting up to 25 per cent of its product". About ten years ago, the company had planned massive investment in garment production with an eye on huge domestic demand as well as export.

It is certainly not a good commentary that the above acknowledged enterprise comes to naught with the avoidable closure of UNTL. UNT closure only adds to the deafening noise level of the state of industry in general. Many textile mills have actually closed in avoidable quick successions. They included Afprint, Five Star, Aswani, Nigeria Textile Mill, and Enpee, all in Lagos. In the East, Aba and Asaba textile mills were long closed. Being in the North, the closure will further push the region into abyss of income poverty and human de-capitalization.

One of the seven-point agenda of Yar'Adua government is wealth generation. The key to wealth generation and economy is industrialization with basic labour intensive industries like textile as the key driver. In the absence of intermediate and secondary industries, total collapse of basic industries like textile means an intolerable return to wholesale de-industrialization of colonial era. President Musa Yar'Adua has said his priority is *economy, economy and economy*. He must however come to terms with the truism according to John Ralston Saul that *"Economies are created and they in turn create jobs-*. Textiles, just as closed Dunlop were among industries created by developmentalist Nigeria via import substitution industrialization strategy. These factories now groan under the weight of unwritten strategy of wholesale importation and trade liberalization.

The immediate threat factor to UNTL and industry in general is wholesale smuggling and domination of Northern textile market by smuggled textiles through land borders with Niger Republic as well as ports in especially in the last six months. At the peak of Sallah season, when domestic mills make sales, major markets at Balogun Lagos, Kantin Kwari Kano and Onitsha are full of smuggled goods occupying over 80% of market share. Most of these illegal imports are even fakes of the trade marks of Nigerian textiles by Chinese manufacturers. Nigeria loses annually USD 1.3 billion on illegal textile imports due to revenue loss on evasion of customs duty and VAT of 700 million naira. Smuggled goods are open-ended waivers. Apart from the limitation of the Customs service, the issue is the re-emergence of cargo/container economy in which there is official preference for imports from tooth picks to policy advice! The challenge is to immediately overcome and drop the official mindset of import dependency to real sector domestic value adding activities. It is this radical paradigm shift that will make the government deliver power for industry, make basic inputs like black oil available, encourage banks to move from double digit to single digit interest rate and make industry competitive as well as protect the domestic market. It is commendable that Yar'Adua's priority is triplicate; *economy, economy and economy*. He must add another critical success factor-triplicate; *industry, industry and industry*. Economy as it were has to be created and not assumed precisely because real economy, defined as value-adding activities either in oil and gas or manufacturing is currently dead. Vision 2020 is blurred and even imperilled when domestic investment casually winds up. No foreign real sector investor would come when they read about retrenchment of the existing ones. President Yar'Adua must urgently come to terms with the challenge of China unlike his predecessor, President Obasanjo who opportunistically muddled through with China. In fact the real industrial challenge for Nigeria is *China, China and China*. We must be romantic as well as strategic about China. Romantic in the sense that we should copy China's industrial strategy; huge protected domestic demand, job-led growth, single digit interest rate (in most cases, grants for industry), labour intensive basic industries like textile, food and beverages and aggressive state backed export drive. The other form of unhelpful romanticism is to continue buying China, fake or real, from drugs to textiles, toys to *chen-chen* motor cycles and in the process, kill domestic jobs and importing unemployment! With 41 real wax factories already established in China today, 40 million meters of African prints monthly targeted towards Nigerian markets, via unofficial import channels, it is doubtful if Nigeria's industry can be saved with the existing uncritical relationship with China. We must be strategic with China if we must partner with China. China should be encouraged to invest here rather than seeing Nigeria as a trading post. Nigeria needs Chinese factories NOT "China Towns" selling China-made products via Nigerian traders.

DAVOS Declaration[*]

"The question we ask is what makes people commit corrupt acts? And when we looked, we found that really, the system itself is weak and when you have a weak system, you have a problem of giving opportunities to people to commit corruption". President Umaru Musa Yar'Adua, in Davos, Switzerland

The President's backing for the removal of immunity clause for serving President and governors understandably hits the headlines from Davos, Switzerland. But a critical reading of the reported remarks of President Yar'Adua at the dinner organized by Partnership Against Corruption Initiative (PACI) at the World Economic Forum reveals that it was more than a flash on the controversial immunity clause. The remarks are the most extensive on the recurring spectre of corruption so far from new (?) Yar'Adua administration. Coming against the global anxiety about the future of anti-corruption war in the wake of recent development at EFCC, Davos remarks pass for a definitive and unambiguous declaration on corruption war by the administration. For one, it was refreshing that the President shared the perspective that corruption is a "de-humanizing" affair that involves not just public officials but also the multinational companies. It was remarkable that the President point-blankly indicates that the multinationals are beneficiaries of the scourge even if they hardly capture public imagination. According to him "...the truth is that some companies have benefited materially from corruption, while we the governments and the nations are usually at the receiving end..." The legendary one finger of the Transparency International (TI) had repeatedly pointed at the

---

[*] *Daily Trust* (Monday, January 28, 2008)

131

government and government alone while the other four pointed at those who are eager to do business at all costs including buying off the civil servants and public office holders alike. The recent examples of money-for-contracts involving Siemens and Wilbros, two notable multinationals in Nigeria justify why the heat should be on the companies as much as on the public officials. However significant is the President's straight talks at the multinationals are, beyond naming the companies as beneficiaries of corruption, it would have been helpful if the President used the platform of the World economic forum to press for a global demand for index of Multinationals based on perception of their corruption traits. The ranking of corrupt companies is as desirable as the ranking of corrupt nations.

It was also significant that President Yar'Adua celebrated the achievements of the anti-corruption agencies, namely the EFCC, ICPC and Code of Conduct Bureau putting paid to the emerging perception that the agencies, at least the EFCC might soon be "on leave" as its chief executive. There is no doubt that like any agency operating in a polluted political environment, the anti-corruption agencies could not have been immune from numerous partisan viruses. But nothing could be more reassuring for the critics and cynics alike than to read the President that:

> "The activities of the anti-corruption agencies have raised the level of consciousness against corruption in Nigeria and it is quite high. What the agencies are doing has the backing of the whole nation and for the first time in Nigeria, within the last four years, highly placed public officials are being investigated, arrested and prosecuted "people that were considered before to be above the law."

The task of government is to play up the strengths of anti-Corruption agencies however insignificant, while minimizing their shortcomings however obvious they are. Political observers noted that the President's remarks would have been better appreciated if made on the floor of National Assembly rather than select audience at Davos. So much for local content! With this singular remark nonetheless, the President has exonerated self from the accusation that he is the unofficial patron of the union of ex-corrupt governors (no affiliation to NLC pls!). Thus what is expected is further strengthening of the anti-graft agencies, more funding and capacity building and less of subterfuge. Davos should not be another global public relations. It is certainly gratifying to read that corruption monitors are being recruited to help at prevention rather than cure of a seemingly protracted problem.

Another strong point of Davos is that the President went beyond the ordinary to look at the cause of corruption. For one, we are witnessing a move at official conceptualization of corruption which yours sincerely has repeatedly demanded for in this column. What are the causes of corruptions, how do we prevent it are some of the critical questions President posed in Davos. For one, the President answered in the affirmative that what we have at hand is systemic corruption and not just individuals' malfeasance. And that it's desirable that we tackle the problem at source than at the damaging end. According to him:

> "What we are doing now is looking at measures we are going to put in lace to ensure that opportunities to commit corruption are reduced to the barest minimum so that anybody, any public official who commits an act of corruption will know he has done it as a deliberate attempt, not because he has an opportunity to commit corruption. And that is in the long run, what is going to sort out this problem and make it a corruption free system."

Well said but it is debatable if Yar'Adua government is actually reducing the opportunities for public theft and grafts. On the contrary there is evidence to show that this government unintentionally might be expanding the notorious space for theft. What with dollarisation of state accounts? What with sharing of "excess crude" receipts without challenging the governors to meet basic obligations for their citizens in the states? How can there be talk at all about excess monies at all with this sea of deprivations? It can only be "excess" for few select governors and their limitless indulgencies.

The President posed the right question:

> "The question we ask is what makes people commit corrupt acts? And when we looked, we found that really, the system itself is weak and

when you have a weak system, you have a problem of giving opportunities to people to commit corruption."

But his answer is not as strong as his question. Witness this:

"That is why today in Nigeria I have told those I work with that we have to look at corruption and give it a basic definition that is more comprehensive. We have to look at the system by ensuring we have regulations and procedures to ensure that only the criminal can commit an act of corruption. It's just like in your house, you have $100 and you place it anywhere. It takes great discipline on the part of the house-maid, your own child and other people not to be tempted because they already have the opportunity, with someone probably thinking that if he takes $10 out of the $100, he may not be caught. But if you put the money in a locker and lock it and go with the key, then somebody has to make a deliberate decision to break the locker and take the money. That is the responsibility of leadership; you must not have a situation like the first one, you must provide the second scenario, where for people to commit acts of corruption, they have to go out of their way knowing fully that if I do this, the system is such that I am going to be detected. But if the system is so loose that detection is not easy, then more and more people are tempted to commit acts of corruption".

As novel as Yar'Adua's insight on causes and solutions to corruption are compared with OBJ's partisan and muddling through approach, it is still grossly defective. Davos declaration operates within the same unhelpful corruption paradigm. Yar'Adua and his handlers should know that Davos is about economic development. It is indeed an economic forum defined here as anything about GDP, national income, employment, growth and development among other critical economic factors. For Nigeria to hit the headline via corruption from Davos is certainly not a strong point. Yar'Adua prides himself with seven-point agenda for development not corruption fighting alone. Davos offers the opportunity to replace corruption agenda with development agenda. It is the absence of the latter that makes the former thrives. The point here is that Yar'Adua can keep trillions of dollars in "safe-keeping", in the absence of genuine development agenda, the money will still be stolen or wasted anyway. There cannot be talk about excess crude money when millions are working poor on account of low wages, when many millions live bellow a dollar per day and we are confronted with intolerable multitude of human destitution the major one being unemployment. The key to anti-corruption is not in catching thieves and preventing their emergence but in putting development agenda on the table at relatively warmer home *not* in faraway, colder Davos. Let us replace "corruption agenda" with "development agenda", we will discover that there is nothing to be stolen precisely because what we have now is far enough to meet basic needs not to talk of the "needs" of few thieves however defined.

Non-Oil Sector: 50 Years of Neglect[*]

With all the acknowledged strength of historic reflections, the bane of the 50th anniversary discourse of oil discovery in Nigeria (tons of such commentaries in recent times could fill some barrels of oil!) is that it is largely located within the oil and gas paradigm, (paradoxically so much decried as a curse rather than blessing). But simple dialectic of development (or is it underdevelopment?) dictates that you cannot appreciate whether some $600 billion oil receipts over the last five decades constitute some blessings or not unless we encourage relative analysis of the impact assessment of oil on the economy as a whole. As informative as it could be, in terms of policy advancement, it is still meaningless to discuss part (in this case oil and gas) only in relations to the very part (looted oil money, wasteland oil fields, Niger Delta woes, etc.). We must think outside the oil and gas box. Therefore, it is more meaningful to critically examine the part in relations to the whole (in this case, Nigerian economy with specific references to real manufacturing, agriculture sectors and indeed social sectors like education and health). It is far more helpful to turn the heat on the collapse of value-adding non-oil sector rather than the overheated value-subtracting oil and gas sector. Indeed 50th anniversary of oil for all it worth (either 600 billions, or hostage takings) tasks our imagination to focus and reinvent the non-oil sector, namely industry and agriculture, long neglected with oil discovery.

Today international comparison is fashionable. Expectedly Nigeria is put at the lowest rug of development ladder with miserable per capital income, poor competitiveness, and low Gross Domestic

---

[*] *Daily Trust* (Monday, February 25, 2008)

136

Product. But this has always not been the case. Indeed, when Nigeria stood on the two pillars of industry and agriculture and *not* oil and gas extraction, Nigeria displayed impressive performance indicators. For instance according to Vision 2010 report, in 1965 Nigeria's GDP was $5.8 billion, (driven by agriculture and manufacturing), compared with $3.8 billion for Indonesia, $3.1 billion for Malaysia and $9.8 billion for Venezuela. Thirty year later, in 1995, Nigeria's GDP had increased to $26.8 billion (3.6 fold increase, propelled by oil and gas), but relatively low compared with Malaysia's $85 billion (27 fold increase), Indonesia's $198 billion (52 fold increase) and Venezuela $75 billion (20 fold increase). The implication is that the countries hitherto led by Nigerian economy (driven by agriculture and industry) have left oil-driven Nigeria far behind "in terms of productivity, income generation and general economic development". Between, 1960 -1980, the manufacturing share of Gross Domestic product (GDP) was on the upswing; increased from 5 per cent to 8 per cent. The strong point of Nigeria's industrialization efforts in the 50s and 60s was its articulation within the development plan of Import Substitution Industrialisation (ISI). The idea was to industrialise the country and to produce what was being imported, thereby conserving scarce foreign exchange. Local industries were to be protected from foreign competition by high import barriers. Consequently, government and private sector invested in heavy industries including steel rolling mills, machine tools, vehicle assembly, fertilizer manufacture, sugar mills, aluminium plants, paper mills, development banks, and textiles, insurance.

A developmentalist state also put measures to assist Nigerian enterprises as a process of translating political independence to greater participation in the economy by Nigerians. Witness Indigenization policy which tended to reverse the dominance of foreigners in oil, banking and finance industries and significant sections of the retail trading business. Sadly the surging contribution of manufacturing to GDP has miserably nose-dived by 2001. Manufacturing value-added as a percentage of GDP was about five per cent in 2000 (less than the proportion at independence in 1960), making Nigeria one of the 20 least industrialized countries in the world even with billions of naira oil revenue. The basic problems are rapid de-industrialization, continuing loss of market shares in traditional export markets and increasing import dependence, all occasioned by relatively cheap oil revenue even when proven to be expensive for the environment for the peoples of Niger-Delta.

Same applied to agriculture:

> "In the 1960s, primary agricultural exports accounted for an average of 62 per cent of total export earnings and a similar proportion of GDP. As oil output and prices increased during the 1970s, the share and role of agriculture in the Nigerian economy declined considerably. Windfall earnings from the oil sector encouraged the neglect of the nation's agricultural export potential. This led to a sharp decline in agricultural output during the 1970s. Ineffective government support has prevented agriculture from playing the dynamic role it could have played in the development of the country, neither has it provided a source of rising income for most Nigerians."

There is an urgent need for Nigeria to reinvent industry and agriculture within the context of rapid industrialization efforts. There is a direct relationship between industrialization, employment and poverty eradication. In fact there is no way Nigeria can meaningfully address the problem of poverty without addressing the production issues. As important as oil and gas industry and solid mineral resources may be, they are exhaustible. In any case there are abundant evidences to show that extractive industries are the curse rather than blessings for sustainable development in developing countries. As we lament $600 billions oil revenue wasted in the past 50 years, let's reflect on trillions of naira potentially denied due to intolerable neglect of industry and agriculture. Even oil and gas sector is not run as a value-adding manufacturing venture, no thanks to crude extraction and crude exports and imports of refined products. Employment is a derived factor. The challenge therefore is to revive the real productive sectors of the economy and creatively engage the unemployed in value-adding activities. We must alter the existing image of a mono-cultural economy with oil dominating its export while agriculture and manufacturing have gradually stagnated. The basic problems facing the industry include policy inconsistency, trade liberalization, high cost of production due to the identified problems are in the long run mainly governance issues. These problems call for more activist roles of the state in the economy and not the passive role being recommended by neo-liberal advocates. The issue is not that the government sets up new industry. The abysmal performance of state run mills and public enterprises in general shows that this is better left for private sector entrepreneurs. However government has the responsibility to protect the existing industries through appropriate policies. For one Nigeria must relook at its new development strategy which puts the prospects of growth on the recommendation of IMF/World Bank/WTO with respect to trade liberalization, and lowering of tariff for *"infant industry"*. While import-substitution industries such as textile had a mixed record of performance, these industries certainly faired better in terms of capacity utilization and employment during the period of protection than the period of wholesale trade liberalization. Government should therefore be encouraged not to pursue trade liberalization as an end but a means with critical assessment of its costs and benefits. As we see with respect to textile the *"transitional cost of trade liberalization"* in terms of employment and income losses including outright destruction of industries outweigh the envisaged benefits of exports which in Nigeria setting has been undermined by high cost of production and non-competitive environment in general. Government must therefore exercise caution in uncritically getting committed to whole trade liberalization within the WTO, when critical issues of strengthening local industrial base, human resource and technological development had not been addressed at home.

How CBN Under-develops Nigeria*

This writer has always been an enthusiastic supporter of the governor of the Central Bank, Professor Charles Soludo. The enthusiasm was far from being personal no less than it flew from the conviction that as a professor of economics, (and one time economic adviser to the President), Mr. Charles Soludo, as the new governor of CBN would make a difference in the administration of the bank. The apex bank had hitherto been under the heel of an accountant. For a considerable part of Chief Joseph Sanusi's tenure, (true to the callings of an accountant), he successfully tried hard to balance the books but not without ignoring the development objectives the bank was set up to achieve. The sanitisation of banks from the dirt of foreign exchange round tripping, his drastic albeit controversial measures such as closure of some non-performing banks and forced resignation and persecution of some bank's executives are part of the commendable legacy of the outgoing governor with respect to bank supervision. But Central banking worldwide has been likened to a good (economic) driver, which must keep an eye on the road and maintain steady hands on the wheel for a good (economic) ride.

Countries preoccupied with issues in development use their Central Banks to keep the economy on course through activist macro economics with respect to pricing, (inflation), exchange rates, interest rates, capacity utilisation, employment, debt management etc. Sanusi's CBN failed woefully with respect to macro economics. It offered endless excuses and buck passing rather than answers to depressing economic situation. The naira had a free fall from 85 naira at Sanusi ascendancy to 138 naira to a dollar. Do nothing approach

* *Daily Trust* Monday, April 14, 2008

to interest rate management brought rate to all time high level of between 25 to 30 per cent. In fact the battle to lower interest rate was left to President Obasanjo (always a lone-ranger anyway) who more than once had to exchange hot words with bankers for them to appreciate the imperatives of investment-friendly interest rate.

The return of an economist (certainly a man with an eye on the bigger picture) as distinct from the limited horizon of an accountant raised legitimate expectations.

True to expectations, Soludo for some brief spell kept eyes on the big pictures that saw unprecedented bank recapitalisation and consolidation. CBN, true to its promise, released comprehensive, (albeit controversial) guide-lines and incentives on consolidation in the banking industry. CBN governor served notice of banking reforms. The speed, the passion and the intensity of banking reform underscored the fact of a new purposeful driver of the apex bank. Yours sincerely favoured capital control rather than capital base-build up, but it is nonetheless agreeable that recapitalization is indispensable to genuine capital control.

Thus CBN's bank consolidation efforts under Soludo had been adjudged a singular progressive monetary policy in recent times. For a significant take-off period, we witnessed return of macro-economic management that marked a return of single digit inflation, fall in interest rate, up-ward surge of external reserves and even naira appreciation. Soludo's CBN for once read "elections results" (certainly not as declared by "spineless body", apology to Justice Belgore, like INEC but as preferred by electorate). "Election results" in this sense are all about macro-economics, namely stable price, stable exchange rates, full employment, improved capacity utilisation, external reserves and debt management. Indeed Vision 2020 which aims at making Nigeria one of the 20 leading economies by 2020 emerged against the background of the dividends of new activist CBN compared to the discredited regime of SAP era.

Alas all these significant achievements are being undermined by the same very Soludo's CBN inconsistent policy of- one- step-forward and two- steps backward with respect to fiscal and monetary policies. Indeed far from propelling Nigeria on the path of steady growth of late, CBN is fast *under- developing Nigeria* through its periodic unhelpful whimsical policy interventions (or are they policy summersaults?) That in turn calls to question the Bank's capacity to mange its new found autonomy.

Change is certainly desirable and at a point many agreed with the governor that what Nigeria needs *"is Revolution"* not just reform! But when changes are putting the economy on the reverse and the changes become addictive, the thing line between revolution and counter-revolution is not clear. CBN governor's, "Naira big-bang" redenomination policy dubbed *"Strategic agenda for the Naira"* was one of such disasters that are now part of history of non-strategic management. The bane of Soludo's solutions in that agenda is that they were presented in isolation of the broad context of the national economy. The hyper activity of the financial sector contrasts sharply with inactivity and passivity of the other sectors. Then came the Dollarisation of state government accounts which ran into the brick wall of seven-point agenda of President Musa Yar'Adua that include war on graft. To further encourage state governors to turn from non-performers to instant money changers which most of them are already anyway under the least resistance of diversifying the funding of foreign exchange market is to compound more the problems of accounting and accountability at the state levels. The latest big-bang is the unnecessary increase in Monetary Policy Rate to 10.0 per cent ostensibly to tame inflation which reportedly jumped to 8 per cent in February under its nose. Increase in MPR will further reverse the gains recorded in interest-rate management that has witnessed some token increase in private sector leading. It is another arrogant class-bias policy to privilege the already over-privileged banks at the expense of the real value-adding sector of the economy. At a time the Executive has come out with creative intervention fund with single-digit interest rate like Textile Revival Fund, CBN's MPR which would push lending rate up is subversive of wealth generation component of seven-point agenda of Yar'Adua government. The neo-liberal least resistance policy of managing inflation through hike in interest rate is also at variance with current thinking in emerging economies that down ward push in interest rate is indispensable to economic recovery, economic competitiveness and employment generation. It is also a return to the notorious TINA (There is No Alternative) policy which Nigeria has abandoned for better in recent times. We already had the big bang of bank consolidation. But of what relevance is the consolidation big bang to factory closures and increasing idle capacity and mass unemployment when interest rates remain double digit? CNB dares not hold Nigerians hostage on account of its neglect of the economic fundamentals that call for creative monetary policies that would impact on supply side such as unlocking huge pool of funds currently with the banks meant for SIMEs and quickly formalise the informal sector, "revolutionise access" to finance by the multitude of the increasing poor in the informal Nigeria that calls for true road shows by central bankers rather than lazily grandstanding with MPR adjustment. What Nigeria needs urgently is *Development Policy Rate Not Monetary Policy Rate* that further enhances the profit profiles of bankers and pushes many factories into early closures and many into income poverty. CBN must urgently return to central banking and stop being a huge laboratory for pet and unhelpful ideas about interest rate exchange management and dubious inflation management.

The current lending rates of between 17 to 25 per cent, inadvertently lock up scarce financial capital in financial markets (banks) rather than in productive investments (industries - small and medium scale alike). Nigerian economy has been in recession for the past two decades. It is an irony that Nigeria's CBN still requires presidential prodding before seeing interest rate management as instrument for recovery, and mass employment.

Return of Development Politics[*]

"A single bracelet does not jingle"- A proverb from DRC

"After a long deliberation, the states supported   the proposal that funds from our excess crude will go towards this project (power supply) as part of our national efforts to address this problem that we see as key to the development of our great country"- Governor Bukola Saraki of Kwara State.

The Devil, (just like the seemingly intractable national darkness and power melt down), is in some details. But so of course Godliness, (which is the desired uninterrupted national power supply and national lightening), is also in bagful of (megawatt) details. The details of the weekend $5.3 billion power supply finance deal between the Federal government and the thirty-six states of the federation are still sketchy. Whatever the details turn out to be (assuming there will be freedom to information!) what is crystal clear is that with this stroke of unprecedented cooperative deal between the tripartite federal, state and local government, we are commendably reinventing *development politics* of the greater years of 1960s and 1970s rudely terminated by decades of anti-developmentalist military dictatorship and eight years of *para-military* regime of OBJ. Former President Olusegun Obasanjo, for all you care to remember, also engaged the state governors and local government councils. But it was largely the engagement of an imperial overlord over his vassals and many an instance, an engagement of some rogue leader with his victims than sincere development constructive partner the constitution envisages.

---

[*] *Daily Trust*, 23rd June 2008

Between 1999 and 2008, at the best of times, the states were engaged in wars of attrition (witness Lagos' criminally withheld local government funds) Bayelsa and Ekiti (impeached Governors) and Anambra and Plateau (with periodic politically motivated mayhems). States not so destructively engaged were transfigured into some federal parastatals and agencies hosting serial weddings of Monsieur Le President's sons and daughters' weddings (Rivers and Ogun states), competing to occupy the frontline chairs at Owu day (Ogun and many others) or shamelessly financing illegalities like Presidential Library (virtually all states) Third term agenda (Jigawa and Delta among others). At worse of times the states were randomly patronized through unsolicited wasteful visits of a Federal Garrison commander commissioning "projects" which the Federal government did not finance nor initiate. All states were routinely talked at through ad hoc unplanned stakeholders' forums on such clumsy open-ended subjects ranging from cassava, malaria, Avian flu, census, Niger Delta to banking sector reform with disastrous marching orders packaged as stakeholders' resolutions by the Villa courtiers. For instance, the take-off crisis which characterized 2006 census was attributed to the fact that the governors and other relevant stakeholders who should be working for proper head count at state and local levels were receiving Presidential lecture at an Abuja town hall. The result was a decade long governance crisis that leaves in its trail power outages of national embarrassment, high profile corruption, jobless growth, worsening poverty and massive job-losses.

It is certainly significant that through knowledge, some planning and painstaking consultations, President Yar'Adua has cultivated the needed cooperation of the states governments for great battle for urgent re-electrification of the country. This raises the nostalgia of the immediate post colonial Nigeria in which development politics by development politicians cooperated to combat the scourge of underdevelopment left behind by colonialism. The point cannot be overstated that the large scale power plants development started in the 60s of democratic Nigeria. Kainji power stations, Afam, Delta, Ijora, Egbin and Shiroro stations were conceived, built and expanded during this development decade. What Yar'Adua shows is that that once there is development will, there will be some ways to cope with the challenges of development without alienating all the stakeholders.

The debate on the constitutionality of the financing deal is here nor there. The debate is clearly unhelpful. The issue is not what sections 80 and 81 of the constitution say with respect to revenue allocation. We all know that the constitution says all monies should go to the consolidated fund to be shared and never provides for an excess crude account. The constitution should not be learnt by route but by well-thought reasoning. Our preoccupation should be what the constitution does not say. The Constitution does not say all should be spent or that some cannot be saved either or that that there cannot be joint-financing. On the contrary, given that the constitution rests on the premises that governance is about the welfare and security of Nigerians, a financing deal between the Federal and the state not to finance another presidential library but to build power plants is in line with the sprit and content of the Constitution.

By this deal, Yar'Adua administration has dealt a constructive blow at the notorious concept of excess crude without much grandstanding and wasteful litigations. By soliciting the states equity investment to raise $5 billion for the take off of the power emergency, Yar'Adua government is saying that contrary to make belief of surplus fund to be routinely shared, given the financing gap in the country, there is nothing like excess crude when we are unable to fix power, water and education among others. By the time we apply same cooperative approach to education, Niger Delta, road and rail development, as we must urgently do it will be self evident that excess crude is more nominal than real. Indeed with respect to power alone to move from 10,000 MW to 30,000MW as much as $30 billion dollars are required which makes the raised $5 billion a token. The entire federal government share of national budgets in foreseeable future is one "single bracelet" that cannot "jingle" power megawatts. As a matter of fact the federal/state partnership can only help but cannot salvage the power sector. We need multiple "bracelets" as it were. There is the need for public/private partnership not through a doctrinaire privatiztion plan (of what is not there) but through same engagement that will induce private equity investment to lift Nigeria from the sickening age of darkness and non-production to electricity and wealth generation. Lastly, all inclusive development process will engender automatic accountability. It is now an open knowledge that we know the exact figure of $5.3 billion for power emergency compared to the guess figures of OBJ's top-down releases to bottomless/powerless pits/poles. The states who are also investors in this worthy venture will certainly not be on-lookers to see scarce resources going down the pits. We may not need future public hearings/hirelings of the House when we can routinely demand for accountability of the all-inclusive steering/implementation of the committee of the new project.

What about the National Economic Plan?*

According to Dr Ayodeji Omotosho, the co-ordinator of the Economic Analysis unit of the Planning Commission, Nigeria witnesses a new Economic plan in October this year. The Plan is reported to be the outcome of "harmonization" of National Economic Empowerment and Development Strategy (NEEDS-2) and the Seven-point Agenda. The new Plan is expected to run in three trenches run up to the magical year 2020 when Nigeria is envisioned to be part of the 20 leading economies. The time table reads as follows: 2008 (which is certainly over) to 2011 (first Plan), 2011 to 2015 (second Plan) and 2016 to 2020 (third Plan).

The return to national development Plan is certainly news worthy decades after "Planning" was rudely abandoned for muddling through disastrous contraptions which included "Austerity regime", "Structural Adjustment Programmes" (SAPs), "Poverty Alleviation", "Reform agenda" etc. There is certainly a paradigm shift of a kind given that Yar'Adua administration returns endangered concepts namely "Development" and "Planning" to official discourse. However the way this administration is going about its new found Planning points to the possibility of its acknowledged strength turning into abysmal weakness. For one, until the new Plan is unveiled, little information available betrays Development and Planning as known to undergraduate students of social sciences not to talk of serious Development planners who have delivered prosperity in emerging nations like India and China. Nigeria was a once Planned Republic. To this extent, we can learn from our past promising development experience no less we can draw from the

---

* *Daily Trust*, 4th August 2008

experiences of other nineteen countries in the envisaged club of developed 20 by 2020.

Since 1946 (and expect during the Civil War), Development Plans historically set the national agenda with amazing impressive outcomes. In fact, Nigeria was once one of the leading 10 newly independent economies by late 1960s. For instance, in 1965, Nigeria's GDP was $5.8 billion, compared with $3.8 billion for Indonesia, $3.1 billion for Malaysia and $9.8 billion for Venezuela. By mid-1990s, Nigeria's GDP had increased to $26.8 billion (3.6-fold increase), Malaysia's moved to $85 billion (27 fold increase), Indonesia's to $198 billion (52 folds) and Venezuela to $75 billion (20-fold increase). Latest figures would even reveal that while others held to planning with consistent GDP upward results, Nigeria's era of militaristic "adjustments" and "reforms" as distinct from development left it criminally far behind in terms of productivity, income generation and general economic development. Indeed three notable National Plans set Nigeria on the part of growth and development in the 60s up to 80s. They are the First Plan, (1962), Second Plan (1970) and Third Plan (1975).

The new Plan with all its taunted promises cannot be taken serious if it ignores past efforts at development and Planning. In fact the bane of the new disposition is its ahistorical orientation. What for instance are the objectives of the new Plan? Again the past provides a guide assuming the purpose is to move the country forward. The second National development Plan (1970-74) is perhaps the most far reaching in depth and objectives. Coming on the heel of the civil war, the Plan threw up Five objectives namely *(a) a united, strong and reliant nation, (b) a great and dynamic economy, (c) a just and egalitarian society, (d) a land of bright and full opportunities for all citizens and (e) a free and democratic society.* We may interrogate the above expressed objectives but what cannot be faulted is that the objectives were profound enough to move a nation and its citizens to greater prosperity. New mantra of the vision of making Nigeria one of the leading 20 economies as alluring as any Nigerian new rap song cannot be substitute for clear cut development objectives as enunciated in second Plan.

It is a misplaced thinking to reduce national development plan to some efforts at meeting Millennium Development Goals (MDGs), which some 189 Heads of States and governments (including Nigeria's government) signed into in 2000. Are we saying without MDGs, we are not committed to totally eradicating poverty? Let's get it clear, MDGs are global distributive guideposts and not productive/development goals. A non-performing economy with scandalous constant power melt down and massive unemployment like Nigeria desperately needs serious development agenda beyond some eighth goals that hardly reflect national priorities. Indeed MDGs assume that development has taken place and all needed is to share the dividends. This assumption might be valid for G-8 but certainly not bottom-of-the-ladder economies like Nigeria's which could not even meet extractive oil production quota due to conflict in Niger Delta. The point here is that in the light of our current realities, the new national development plan should look for inspiring objectives beyond meeting MDGs (the target date of which is just few years to go). Recognising that the dramatic growth and development of the 20th century had not translated into prosperity for many, world leaders signed on to a Millennium Declaration. Nigeria has not generated enough prosperity that will eradicating poverty, promote human dignity, achieve peace, democracy and environmental sustainability in the twenty-first century. Indeed, Millennium declaration brings home the great expectations of the late 70s during which international community and countries promised among others "health-for-all", "education-for-all" and "eliminating-hunger-by-2000". We all know Nigeria did not meet any of the above high sounding sign posts. What is needed is fundamental stock-taking within the context of the new Plan.

The last critical question however is: how new is the new Plan? If a Plan harmonizes controversial NEEDS and seven-point agenda then what we have is some hybrid of some ill-digested proposals rather than serious plan agenda. Take NEEDS for instance. With its controversial policy instruments of liberalization, privatization, right sizing the public sector, redefining the relationship between the government and the people; diversification of the economy away from oil, eight years after, NEEDS 1 left Nigeria poorer in power supply and employment generation while Nigeria is still oil dependent. How harmonized NEEDS2 would make a difference when the two NEEDs are not development strategies beat imagination. Seven-point agenda for all its raised expectations about Niger Delta, food security, human capital development, wealth generation and infrastructural development among others still remain a promissory note. Some critics even say that with abysmal incompetent handling of Niger Delta so far (a summit could not even hold!) and the protracted teachers' strike, that what we have is 5-point agenda and not seven-point agenda. A new national development planning should be more than harmonized NEEDS and seven-point agenda. What is the economic philosophy of the new Plan for instance? Is it the same dogma of liberalization, private sector-led economy even when private sector is undermined by massive smuggling and factories closures? Or are we returning to mix bag of pragmatic policies that must urgently break the supply bottlenecks, generate wealth and offer sustainable jobs for the multitudes that are dying on recruitment queues across the nation?

Olympics or China Challenge?[*]

"I am so proud to be Chinese tonight"- Ju Ke a 19-year old animation student who got a front row seat on the grass of Ditan Park before two giant monitors covering Beijing Olympic.

The most politicised Olympics on earth after the end of Cold War (no thanks to Western mis-information) turned to be the most spectacular sporting extravaganza ever! A week before, a visitor from outer space watching and listening to the Olympic serial previews by the CNN and allied Western media would have thought that Beijing Olympic was another disaster in waiting as they unfairly promoted stereotypes about a "command system" (as distinct from a democracy) striving to host the world sporting activity. We recall how Olympic touch was reported in relations to Tibetan "human rights" situation than the spirit of sportsmanship Olympic was formed to promote. It is to the eternal credit of the Chinese that they confounded cynics and showed that it could host humanity in a remarkable way that completely shattered into smithereens all stereotypes of the cold war mentality of the West.

With unprecedented imaginative and colourful opening ceremony which dazzled audience of 91,000, and 4 billion viewers world wide, the Chinese had established a powerful link between the ancient and modern achievements. Whatever the harvest of medals, eventually looks likes, what cannot be disputed is the fact China has made remarkable progress in productivity, human capital development and technology that put it at par if not more than many so-called developed countries of the world. Instead of insecurity

---

[*] *Daily Trust,* 11th August 2008

smear campaign of the global media, we witnessed serenity that accommodated as many as 80 heads of states including America's George Bush. He even did Sunday service in Beijing with unsolicited sermon about virtues of religion to people who in the first instance hosted him in their Church. Instead of heat ostensibly occasioned by pollution, we witnessed a spectacular touch of 2008 Beijing Olympic lit in multi colours. Certainly what we witnessed by the weekend was more than the opening ceremony of a great sporting event. What we witnessed was the great challenge of China especially for a developing nation like Nigeria.

Development observers agree (and Olympic has further confirmed this!) that there are three global development challenges in the new millennium. The number one development challenge is *China*. The second development challenge is *China*. And the third development challenge is *China*. No country has recorded remarkable rapid economic ascendancy in the past 25 years like China. With 1.5 billion population and consistent 12% growth rate in the past 3 decades, China has shown that huge quality human resource is indeed an asset and not a liability. The opening ceremony of this game showed how China proved that human multitude is indeed a blessing for ancient and modern Operas.

China shows that development process is *not* a zero-sum game in which growth is traded off for jobs and in which few *are well-having* and many lack *basic well being*. China shows that the issue is not extractive resources (China not an OPEC member) but value additions and manufacturing (China has more functioning oil refineries than Nigeria!). China shows that growing the GDP does not mean pushing mass of people into the margin of mass poverty. On the contrary, China is perhaps the only country since the great Industrial Revolution that has combined consistent aggressive industrialisation drive with high growth rate side by side with full employment. China makes nonsense of neo-liberal/textbook received wisdom about jobless growth. We can indeed have job-led growth, China proves that. China has shown that addressing production issues is not mutually exclusive from confronting poverty and coming to terms with distributional issues. While many sub-Saharan African countries, including Nigeria have pushed millions into poverty due to

IMF-inspired "reform" process, (SAP) China is the only country that has recorded the largest reduction in poverty in history in recent time. Indeed it has lifted as many as 250 million people (twice the population of Nigeria!) out of poverty. In international trade, China's goods and services rule the world such that the new America's Cold War with China is about articles of trade rather than weapons of mass destruction.

Can we truly copy China and achieve similar feat? When will Nigeria host Olympic and achieve similar spectacular achievements? Notwithstanding development gap, Nigeria has a lot in common with China and indeed could be another China, just as China used to be like Nigeria. Nigeria is the most populated country in Africa just as China is most populous country in Asia as well as in the world. In development parlance we are talking of two largest markets in the world. But while China is one huge working and productive house, Nigeria is yet to be unbundled to realise its potentials as it is weighed down by consumption and idle capacity.

Paradoxically the two countries are undergoing reforms. But while China's reforms are delivering on promise, Nigeria's reforms are far from the expectations. This is where Nigeria can creatively copy China. Stiglitz, the Nobel Prize Winner in Economics shows that the strength of China lies in its home grown policy initiatives. Even President Hu Jintao spoke his language in delivering the opening address.

China just like Poland ignored the so-called Washington Consensus (devaluation, uncritical privatization, trade liberalization, removal of subsidy etc) as promoted by IMF and the World Bank and went for creative alternative local policies that reflect national priorities. China employs "*gradualist approach*" to reforms compared to "*shock therapy approach*" of Russia which uncritically privatised public enterprises without addressing fundamental issues of goods and service delivery. China built democratic mass support for reform agenda not through election riggings, political thuggery and mass unemployment as in Nigeria OBJ's era. On the contrary China shows that stability, political unity of purpose and common wealth (as distinct from private aggrandisement and corruption) are indispensable to reform agenda. China also has negative (not just zero) tolerance to corruption (it engenders capital punishment in many instances). Lastly the point cannot be overstated that China appreciates the imperatives of labour-intensive industries for a populous nation. Nigeria is boastful with enclave sectors like Telecoms, banks and oil and gas but the labour absorption is therein insignificant. On the contrary China holds on to textile and agricultures where millions are employed. What is good for China is good for Nigeria; macro economic stability and protection of domestic market. The issue is not to be romantic with China but to be "strategic" with China just as China has been strategic in its dealings with Africa and the world, moving at its own pace, closed up when it wanted, opened up when desirable and confounded the world with the most acknowledged successful Olympic opening ceremony. When will Nigeria hosts the Olympic? When will a 19-year old be so proud to be Nigerian as 19-year old Ju Ke Chinese?

Q & A on Niger-Delta Ministry[*]

"The final decision concerning the home stead is the prerogative of the head of the home stead"- *A Gikuyu proverb*

Q: What then about the new Ministry of Niger Delta?

A: Better late than never! The new initiative constitutes both radical theoretical and practical paradigm shift from the hitherto seemingly national muddling through approach to Niger Delta Mess (NDM). By dint of unorthodox official thinking, Yar'Adua administration has happily put paid to the unhelpful regionalization of Niger-Delta discourse (remember divisive Arewa Consultative Forum/ South-South heat without light!). A federal portfolio on the scar of the nation (which Niger Delta represents is) puts NDM squarely on the Federal exclusive list that it truly belongs. The point cannot be overstated. Niger-Delta issues are Nigerian (and indeed global issues!) which require concerted collective actions of all the change agents, the main driver being the Federal government. It is refreshing that for the first time in recent times, the Federal government sets to claim ownership of the neglect it has nurtured into some intractable monster over the years. Thank God too; what we are being served is ministry *of* NOT Ministry *for* Niger Delta. For once, the official rhetoric must change from us versus them to our collective national resolve to salvage a depressed and neglected region that in turn is under developing the entire federation.

Q: But given the history of failure of bureaucracy in general, don't you think Ministry of Niger Delta is another deafening failure waiting to happen?

---

[*] *Daily Trust*, 15th September 2008

A: The fact that we are even discussing about failure or success of the new initiative shows that there is a new initiative on the table to be discussed. Nobody could have debated the strength and weaknesses of the current vicious circle of violence, oil field short downs, divestment, kidnappings and abysmal neglect in Niger-Delta precisely because all are manifestations of failure anyway. Even given that we are saying that a ministry may not perform indicates that it has a potential to perform, the same expectation that we can not accord the current wholesome vicious circles of kidnapping and violence in the region. The challenge therefore is for all stake-holders to make sure that this ministry delivers on promise, not asking if it will work or not.

Q: Are we then to close the debate on Niger Delta Ministry altogether?
A: Far from that. But the point cannot be over stated that there is nothing inherently bad in a bureaucracy. Bureaucracy rules the world for better for worse. United Nations Organization is one bureaucracy suffocating the world but the world is yet to invent an alternative to web of men and women pushing papers to get service delivered. All we need to do with respect to Niger Delta is to make sure that the bureaucracy which that has proved successful world wide and performed for the better in other parts of the world also works here for better.

Take the singular event of September 11 terror attack on New York, seven years ago, the United State of America, (a "free-market economy") established series of bureaucracies which included an enlarge open-ended Home Land Security Ministry which employs hundreds of thousands of American workers and million of indirect workers world wide with the aim of making sure that terrorists will never take America for granted as they did during September 11. For us here, Niger Delta is more than a singular event. Niger Delta crisis is a historic systemic malaise dated back to the 1950s. Indeed a Ministry is coming better late to manage this mess and if I dare to say too token to clear the underdevelopment rot! The ministry must just be seen to deliver on promise.

In summary therefore, the point here is that it is a wrong question to ask as to how the Ministry will work, precisely because this Ministry must just work as our last bold step to stem the slide into *politicide* in Niger Delta. We have seen the consequences of failure such that what will must *work and worship* for is success of this new initiative. Coming on the heel of renewed heat in the region, it must definitely raise the noise level of Niger Delta problem. But beyond analysis what is needed are the solutions to the seemingly intractable problems of the region.

Q: But in concrete terms how will this Ministry deliver much needed bridges, water, light and above all decent jobs for the boys in the creeks of Niger Delta?

A: Again this is clearly an unhelpful question. For one, Niger Delta question is long dated and long asked. What the nation needs urgently now is *answer, answer and answer*. We've questions too many and any additional one is one question too many. President Yar'Adua must have realised the futility of endless Niger Delta questions through panel beaten and feverish summits before he came out with a creative original proposal like a new Ministry of Niger Delta. Questions, doubt and cynicisms about how to make Niger Delta work again reinforce the unhelpful and discredited Niger-pessimism syndrome. The only way to truly claim the ownership of Niger Delta crisis is to stop endless questions but proffer concrete solutions that will make worthy initiatives like the new Ministry to work.

Q: *What then are the possible measures to make the new Ministry work, where other Ministries have failed?*

A: The Federal Capital Development Authority (FCTD) is a Ministry in charge of the new capital. With all its limitations that include so far land grabbing has worked, then our solution to the success of new Niger Delta Ministry will not be far fetch. If FCTD can build bridges where there is no river, why should new Niger Delta Ministry fail on building bridges where there is globally acclaim flooding. If Lagos right from its status as Lagos Colony up to the time that it became Federal Capital had and still has functioning bridges on waters including Atlantic, why will similar infrastructure elude Niger Delta for whatever reason? Or bluntly put, if Abuja, which is a parasitic capital territory with insignificant or no contribution of value added tax and without generating any royalties to national revenue, parades the best of modern roads and street light why not Port Harcourt, Asaba, Warri and Benin and other value adding communities of Niger Delta? If there is the will there will always be the ways that are not far fetch. All we need to do is to see how we have developed other areas namely Lagos and Abuja.

Q: Who then should herd the Ministry?
A: Judging that this is not a normal routine Ministry, this is historic Ministry requires a unique historic supervision and management. Niger Delta master plan is to masterly and challenging to be left to the interplay of the forces of Nigerians regional and interest balancing. The new Ministry is out of the high sense of urgency to fix a broken territory. Only the President has the historic responsibility to herd and direct this Ministry to deliver. If the president had for whatever reason held on to the Federal Ministry of Petroleum Resources before, just like his predecessor OBJ ostensibly because of the strategic' importance of that sector, then there is no reason why the president cannot preside over the Ministry of a territory whose fate is inextricably linked to the fate of the country.

****

This makes the second recommended agenda of effective local governance and responsiveness to people's needs useful. There is no doubt that the region can make do with more revenues derivable from oil. But the critical question is that what has the region done with the relatively improved allocations since 1999? The region just like the whole country desperately begs for accountability and transparency. It is a scandal that a region that miserably falls bellow in virtually all development indicators also features merry-go round governors the most notorious of which was the former governor of Bayelsa who was caught not in the creek of Niger Delta certainly not rooting for development but in London with cash on a tummy-duck trip.
The third agenda dealing with improvement and diversification of Niger Delta economy is by far the most significant. The only limitation of this agenda is UNDP's flawed assumption that oil and

gas potentials have all been exhausted and that all that is needed is a flight to new industry and agriculture to engage the huge army of the unemployed in the region. The issue is that diversification must start in the oil industry itself that must include value-adding activities beyond crude lifting and crude theft by the predatory forces of oil companies and the new militants. With scores of derivatives from oil and gas developmentalist states in Niger Delta will not only guarantee full employment for the youths in the region but start as catalyst for the transformation of Nigeria as a whole. In fact the seven-point agenda is as good for Niger-Delta as it is good for Nigeria as whole. The report comes out with seven-point agenda for the region. The first deals with the necessity for peace as foundation for development. "There cannot be any meaningful human development without peace". The hope is that both the militants and the federal government currently locked in operation fire for fire appreciate the import of this dictum. Even at that, it requires practical developmental agenda to win more souls for peace in the traumatised region. The truth is that past decades of peace have not ushered in development. On the contrary we have witnessed peace of the graveyards, peace of pot-holes, peace of ruined schools, peace of failed airport, peace of failed and murderous leaders, peace of judicial murders (remember Ken Saro Wiwa!) and peace of widespread poverty.

Wealth in the North, (Sorry), Nigeria*

"Work and Worship" - late Ahmadu Bello, *Sardauna* of Sokoto

The Conference of Northern States Chambers of Commerce, Industry, Mines and Agriculture (CONSCCIMA) commences its *Northern Nigeria Economic and Investment Summit (NEIS 2008)* in Abuja today. This conference assumes a special significance. For one in recent times, it represents a paradigm shift from the poverty/corruption discourse that has characterized the development discourse in the region and indeed the country as a whole. Regionalization of discourse in the country is proving an entrenched habit rather than a passing fad. This is bad enough! But to diminish such discourse to poverty and some poverty alleviation or something related like corruption and anti-corruption as distinct from the much needed wealth generation and wealth distribution is an unworthy turn for the worse.

Paradoxically those paid to promote *development, development and development* (in that order of priority) are the most visible salesmen of poverty alleviation measures which in turn deepen poverty and legitimises poverty discourse. Since the controversial thesis of the CBN Governor, Professor Soludo according to which Poverty is a Northerner, (or something that sounds like that!) volumes of commentaries of printed words have added to the misrepresentation, distortion and the diversion. This is not saying that poverty and acute deprivations are not widespread in the North perhaps more than the other regions (where poverty exists nonetheless). On the contrary! The issue is that any differentiation of poverty in scale and

---

* *Daily Trust*, 6th October 2008

context is unhelpful in a country that is holistically begging for development and prosperity. The point cannot be overstated. Poverty in whatever dimension and in whatever region or state is a threat to prosperity anywhere. The truth is that the poverty of the North is no less worrisome than the notorious poverty in Niger Delta. In fact if we look everywhere there is plausible *Niger-Deltanization* of every where defined here as neglect amidst plenty, decay and idle capacity even when there is so much to be done, *okada*-riding amidst petro-dollars. The Sultan of Sokoto, His Eminence, Alhaji Muhammadu Saa'd Abubakar, *mni*, said as much recently when he rightly observed widespread poverty in the country and demanded for good governance.

The truth is that poverty might be more pronounced in some areas but sustainable prosperity as we know it in other parts of the world is lacking in any part of the country. It is therefore important that NEIS 2008 is set to move from poverty paradigm to wealth generation discourse. You cannot get out of poverty by lamenting and unconsciously legitimizing the very scourge. As an activist of the poor, I bear witness that the poor do not relish in differentiating the scale of their misery but want to jump out of poverty box. The motto of Nigeria Labour Congress (NLC) reads: *Labour Creates Wealth* not *Labour Laments Poverty* in the knowledge of the labour movement that it is only by creating wealth that we get rid of poverty anyway. Labour's view also tallies with global perspective about development. Adams Smith wrote about *Wealth of Nations* not *Poverty Differentiation of Nations*. Even Karl Marx who provided Communist Manifesto for transformation wrote about Capital and process of capital formation not about Lamentations of the Poor. It is therefore refreshing that in the next three days policy ideas would be generated to reinvent the region and indeed Nigeria back to the process of development.

I share the perspective of Mallam Muhammed Haruna (1st of October) in his article entitled "Time For More Actions..." that we must replace talk-shops with *real workshops* in meaning and content. All we need to do is to return to history as Mallam Muhammed demonstrated with the history of the NNDC which once built prosperity in the region. Let's urgently recapitalize the agency and demand for accountability. Interestingly the late Premier did not sit by and listen to empty sermons about poverty in the region before he moved into actions of historic significance to insist that the North must catch up in words and actions. The strength of the late Sardauna lies in the fact that he operated outside poverty box and mainstreamed prosperity awareness at a time it was a luxury to do so. Sardauna's vision for Kano for instance was to make the city Manchester of Nigeria (an euphemism for industrial revolution) not *okada riding* (or is it poverty alleviating?) city which we now shamelessly made the city. And the late Premier realised his vision given that Kano became a continental industrial power house followed by Kaduna. The question today is: if the old region with its less endowment compared to now, could engage in value addition and mass industrialization how can 2008 North presides over industrial obituaries with factory closures, mass unemployment and poverty and additional insult of being talked at? Happily the North does not have to look for "foreign" investors when all it needs is to revive the existing initial plants and assets being wasted. If Sardauna in the 50s could engage the British to build KTL in partnership and ensure the Chinese relocate to build UNTL the largest textile mill in the continent, the 19 governors have no excuse to preside over the collapse of this massive investment if they cannot add to it. We need a programmatic mix of public and private sector policies to reposition the region and indeed the country. If the most "private sector driven" economy in the world, USA could mobilize $700 billion to rescue the financial market, because of just one singular financial shock, then Nigerian government must return to duty of good governance given the abysmal level of current depression and lack of wealth generation. I recommend UNIDO report of 2003 on revival of textile industry for NEIS 2008. If the North can implement its side of this all inclusive report on reindustrialization of the country, then the next three days would show that we have moved from poverty paradigm to prosperity action. What is good for the North is probably better for Nigeria and indeed Africa! Prosperity not poverty should be a northerner and indeed an African.

The fall and fall of the Market[*]

With the so-called global financial crisis proving protracted despite feverish state (note: state!) interventions world wide via bail outs and unplanned budgets (a kind of bare-face "financial socialism" for the money and capital market) my interest here is purely academic. Understandably so, precisely because, it is now self-evident that raw corporative class power, state connections and social relationships (and not necessarily the market) govern our world anyway regardless of alluring rationalizations, arguments, logic and reasons to the contrary. Received wisdom, for times immemorial, had it that market transaction is a voluntary exchange (and subject to the rules of the market), every market actor agrees to the terms of the exchange for better for worse. In the last one month, however, exchange seems no more voluntary. Some of exchange's bad outcomes which include collapsed prices of stocks (as a result of mass speculative greed) are redefined to be "global crisis" that should be discouraged and totally contained. Financial and capital market has been redefined to be a regulated process with a view of protecting those who make wrong choices and the rescue comes in torrent via tax payers' monies. At home, following a dramatic 35 per cent crash in stock prices for which nobody has so far offered official causation explanation, safety (real and imagined) measures have been rolled out. No NSE/SEC chieftains have been urged to resign either. Even though, it is an open knowledge that their unofficial resignation, from their statutory regulatory functions, nurtured the current mess. Taunted "emerging" Nigeria's capital market altogether turned to be nothing but a mere notorious "frontier", apparently for cheap feverish hot/hedge

[*] *Daily Trust,* 13th October 2008

speculative funds as distinct from a market place for capital formation for an economy begging for development. It is instructive how "investment destination" of "400 per cent rate of return" (sounds like Mugabe's distortionist inflation percentage figures or what the late American economist John K Galbraith once called "mass insanity"!) came into smithereens or ground zero. But Nigeria's regulatory meddlesomeness is no more an exceptional "exuberance", judging from the recent global serial governmental bail outs of money and capital markets from Washington to London, Tokyo to Berlin, and Paris to Moscow. Governments are not only in active feverish business of saving businesses (although we have been told that government has no business in business!) but activist bail out for the market is the new mark of good governance. What hitherto was unthinkable or presented as the downside of socialism, namely overruling the market outcome, is now the rule rather than the exception. All of a sudden, central planning (witness G-7 meeting on the financial melt down!) of financial policies as opposed to market forces is the new economic model. Senator Obama, my obvious favoured candidate for the White House race who in his nomination acceptance speech observed that America "should ensure opportunity not just for those with money and influence but every America willing to work" almost pitched his tent with Wall Street (those with money and influence) well before those on the Main street (every American willing to work). No thanks to the levelling global financial turmoil! This shows that the difference between him and McCain is not as clear when it comes to "market fundamentalism" (read: saving the market from itself!). The duo compliment rather than contradict other in "fixing" the broken egg (the market) with an unprecedented (or is it exuberant?) $700 billion bail out. "Regulation" is now the new fashion than a passing fad. Deregulators, until recently were the most celebrated heroes of the market economies. No more! Paradoxically the new heroes are the "regulators" (with capital R) with financial socialism as their ideology defined here as some poverty alleviation measures for money and capital markets brothers (not yet collapsed sisters!) who have collapsed like pack of cards. Whatever this development portends for the binary ideological market/state debate, what is not in dispute is the new disrepute status of neo-liberalism or laissez-faire doctrine in which visible hands and heads of governments now rally round the market contrary to the invisible hands of some unidentified flying objects we hitherto made to believe to have ruled the markets. Not even at wars has there been such unprecedented feverish consensus building in the desperate carpet bombing of global economic crisis. Today's George Bush seeking global cooperative approach to market failure contrasts sharply to George Bush the bully who unilaterally bombed Iraq to Stone Age! It is almost a great conspiracy against the public that it is the latter that would save the market and not the other way round as we have been made to believe that nothing but the market was the engine of growth. The recent global sobriety contrasts sharply with the acrimony and sharp division about how to share the fruits of prosperity when the market bubbled as it used to bubble with trillions of dollars declared profits. Issues of dividends of global prosperity are not as settled (MDG in 2015!) and even discussed as the burdens of bust are being globalised today. London moved a step ahead and even shows that it is not yet the end of history contrary to the outlandish claim of Fakuyama by reverting to the discredited 21st nationalizations (a la North Korea's or Venezuela). Critical questions that task received wisdom of the old are: Whence on earth are the IMF chieftains and World Bank's mistresses (two of whom are my notable compatriots, namely Ngozi Okonjo-Iweala and Oby Ezekwesili!) in this entire spectacle televised rescue mission? Whence these celebrated sheriffs of international finance? Are they simply impotent in forecasting or managing the global financial climate change in Washington? Why their indifference compared to their frenzy diplomacy on Asian melt-down of two decades ago? Who really rules the international financial world: the American treasury, the US Congress or paid unaccountable and unelectable international civil servants in IMF and the World Bank? What happens to the Bank dogma of deregulation of capital and money markets dubiously rammed down the throats of developing countries? Not even Karl Marx would have envisaged that bottom-up socialism which collapsed into smithereens in former USSR, would manifest again some high wire Top-down communism or economic fundamentalism at the heartlands of capital, namely in

Washington and London as we have witnessed in recent times. As a partisan of activist state and development, this global frenzy for capital and capital alone beats my imagination and the open-endedness of the policy nepotism for capital makes imagination run riotous! However the issue is why this midnight measures are restricted to money and capital market and not extended to labour market (long distressed due to mass unemployment, slave labour, miserable pa, absence of social security) and even the entire global economy defined here as manufacturing and agriculture ? Why for instance no such rescue for the global food crisis?

Wither New Economic Hit Men (EHMs)*

The appointment of the governor of the Central Bank, Professor Chukwuemeka Soludo, years back generated some excitement. Yours sincerely was among the earlier callers of the professor of economics, (and one time economic adviser to the President) with words of encouragement. The expectation was that Soludo, as the governor of CBN would make a difference.

The apex bank under the heel of Chief Joseph Sanusi,, an accountant, for a considerable part of his tenure tried hard to balance the books but *not* the development objectives the bank was set up to achieve. Sanusi made modest impact in sanitisation of banks from the dirt of foreign exchange round tripping and some drastic albeit controversial measures such as closure of some non-performing banks and initiated forced resignation and persecution of some bank's executives. But on the whole his tenure was disaster so far Central banking was concerned.

Countries preoccupied with issues in development use their Central Banks to keep the economy on course through activist macro economics with respect to pricing, (inflation), exchange rates, interest rates, capacity utilisation, employment, debt management, etc. CBN under Sanusi failed woefully with respect to macro-economics.

Endless excuses and buck passing in place of activist monetary policies. The naira had a free fall from 85 naira at Sanusi ascendancy to 138 naira to a dollar. Interest rate (mis)management brought rate to all time high level of between 25 to 30 per cent. In fact the battle to lower interest rate was left to President Obasanjo (always a lone-ranger anyway) who more than once had to exchange hot words with

---

* *Daily Trust* (Monday, February 2, 2009)

bankers for them to appreciate the imperatives of investment-friendly interest rate.

The return of an economist Soludo raised the hope of a governor with an eye on the bigger picture as distinct from the limited horizon of an accountant!

True to expectations, Soludo moved into actions. We witnessed unprecedented, albeit controversial bank recapitalisation and consolidation. The speed, the passion and the intensity of banking reform underscored the fact of a new purposeful driver of the apex bank. Yours truly favours capital control rather than capital base-build up, but it was nonetheless agreeable that recapitalization is indispensable to genuine capital control.

Thus CBN's bank consolidation efforts under Soludo had been adjudged a singular progressive monetary policy in recent times. For a significant period, we witnessed return of macro-economic management that marked a return of single digit inflation, fall in interest rate, up-ward surge of external reserves (which hit $60 billion) early 2007 and even Naira appreciation and very well stable exchange rate indispensable for corporate planning.

Indeed Vision 2020 which aims at making Nigeria one of the 20 leading economies by 2020 emerged against the background of the dividends of new activist CBN

Alas all these significant achievements are today trampled underfoot by the same very Soludo's CBN inconsistent policy of- *one-step- forward and two- steps backward*. Indeed far from propelling Nigeria on the path of steady growth, of late CBN is fast *under- developing Nigeria* through its periodic unhelpful whimsical policy interventions and policy summersaults and of late, scandalous dubious and criminal policies which in turn call to question the Bank's capacity to mange an autonomy and independence.

Indeed Soludo is emerging as number One the New Economic Hit Man, (EHM), defined here as highly paid professional who wrecks Nigerian economy, kills real sector and fuels smuggling/container and speculative economy.

Soludo who once said what Nigeria needs *"is Revolution"* not just reform has now imposed a *counter Revolution* which has left in its trail, weak consolidated banks, criminally devalued naira,(almost by 50 per cent!) since December last year. At a time world wide Central Banks are strengthening national currencies to respond to global economic melt down, Soludo's policy whimsical changes putting the economy on the reverse, becoming dangerously addictive and destructive.

The promise of Bank consolidation includes stronger banks, credit surplus, more jobs and lower interest rate. With twenty-five mega-banks with paper mega profits side by side collapsed share prices, Soludo has not delivered on the promise! The hyper activity of the financial sector through huge paper profits contrasts sharply with inactivity and passivity of the other real sectors. Banks might be bigger but certainly not safe. They have not provided real lending to the real sector either which explains why we needed special intervention fund for Textile, current spate of factory closures and massive unemployment and under employment in the labour market!

CBN governor's, "Naira big-bang" redenomination policy dubbed *"Strategic agenda for the Naira"* SAN under the so-called Financial System Strategy (FSS) was one of Soludo's policy disasters. Soludo's CBN is increasingly disconnected from the broad context of the national economy. Take the so-called dollarization of state government accounts. It was a clever device to legitimise graft and corruption and rightly failed at conception.

Under Soludo, MPR has dramatically moved to double digit. Persistent increases in MPR have further reversed the gains recorded in interest-rate management of the recent past. Interest rate is now as high as 20 per cent taking us to the discredited Sanusi era. The interest rate is almost zero in Europe and America as part of the Economic Stimulus agenda in the wake of the economic melt down. Interest rate is indispensable to economic recovery, economic competitiveness and employment generation. Of what relevance is the consolidation big bang to factory closures and increasing idle capacity and mass unemployment when interest rates remain double digit? CBN must urgently return to central banking and stop being a huge laboratory for pet and unhelpful ideas about interest rate exchange management and dubious inflation management.

The current lending rates of between 17 to 25 per cent, inadvertently lock up scarce financial capital in financial markets (banks) rather than in productive investments (industries - small and medium scale alike).

Within two months alone naira has witnessed the worse devaluation of up to 50 per cent under Soludo. We are on the road to Mugabe's Harare, capital of devaluation that ruins an economy and working people reminiscent of the discredited era of SAP under Babangida. And Soludo was even cheeky and bold enough proclaiming from the roof top that devaluation was deliberate. External reserves run down by 10 billion fuel currency speculators and inflation! Who profits from this deliberate unilateralism?

No governor of Nigeria's CBN has abused naira than Soludo. He was recently on road shows promoting new notes and currencies printed with trillions of naira. Few moments, after he announced a failed re-denomination policy with observers wondering while printing huge bills like N1000 only to latch on redenomination. Without apology to tax payers and Nigerians as whole the same CBN Governor is now advertising for people to come and buy tons of valueless coins to recycle the coins into bangles, trinkets, copper pipe and wires or other! Soludo has sadly taken Nigeria down the road of Onitsha market.

No Governor of CBN engages in denials of obvious economic fundamentals like Soludo. In the face of mounting unemployment, persistent power failure, low capacity utilization, falling prices of crude oil, collapsed share prices, closures of factories, run-down external reserves and naira devaluation, CBN insists the global economic crisis does not affect Nigeria. Nigeria has been in crisis even before the current global down turn and that Nigeria would only be further made worse off. The reconstitution of the President's economic team and the admittance by the President that our crisis is real shows why Soludo is a lone ranger as an unelected and unaccountable Governor.

One is younger, another is older but they are united by the Age of their outdated ideas. Rilwan Lukman shares a lot with Soludo as EHM. Never in the history of ministerial appointment has so much heat, as distinct from light, been generated over a ministerial list as the most recent one.

At the centre of this heat was Dr. Rilwan Lukman, a multiple recycled chieftain spanning some decades. The 70-year old minister of a 40-year old Ministry of Petroleum made many observers to question the sincerity of purpose of Yar'Adua administration to bring about the new governance paradigm shift in the badly managed oil sector. Lukman had been part of the sector that has not delivered products regularly and at avoidable prices.

A cabinet of some oldies amidst idle youth under-representation constitute gross insensitivity in governance. Significantly too, an ageing cabinet departs sharply from the current global best governance democratic practices. The newly elected President of United States of America, USA Barrack Obama is forty something years old. This is not to say that age is a liability for good governance. Far from it! Indeed there is virtue in experience and Nigeria could very well make do with more experience and memory in governance. The issue is *not* age but the age of his ideas. Pray what are Lukman's fresh or original ideas that will help in reviving the depressed oil and gas sector? The current discordant voices over pricing of petroleum products, namely petrol, diesel and LPFO points to crisis of governance in that sector and the more reason why Lukman must resign.

Where is Lukman in the wake of the current controversy over the pricing of petroleum products? He is certainly *not* on duty. It was President Yar'Adua who after accepting that the global economic crisis impacts on Nigeria tasks the new Steering Committee on the economy to address the three issues of fuel price, Naira value

Pray how old is this idea and how has it delivered regular products for Nigeria?

Who then speaks for the Industry?*

Last Thursday, in Abuja, United Nations Industrial Development Organization (UNIDO) launched its Updated Report on Nigeria's textile industry. The report was as damning as it was in 2003; more factory closures, more job-losses (from some 60,000 in 2003 to 24,000 in 2008!) and indeed a complete slide towards de-industrialization. Alas, the Minister of Industry and Commerce, Chief Achike Udenwa was conspicuously absent at the UNIDO presentation. A week earlier, the Minister had assumed notoriety for his remark, according to which, in the age of globalization, Nigeria's industry needs no protection. Was that why he was absent at a function long dated and in which all stakeholders were long notified? If the industry, according to him, needs no protection (in a globalised world in which we see all leaders feverishly protecting their infant and adult industries), the industry also does not need to be heard?

Minister of State, Monsieur Humphrey Abah, in the same Ministry of Commerce and Industry was 'kind' enough to come over an hour late and notwithstanding, the sobering statistics pointing to imminent industry collapse, abruptly left without official response to or against the UNIDO report.

Who then speaks for Nigeria's industry in the wake of acknowledged massive illegal imports, counterfeiting, gross under-capacity utilization, collapse of industrial estates and mass job-losses? The managing director of Bank of Industry (BOI), Ms Evelyn Oputu and Director General of Standard Organization of Nigeria (SON), Dr Akayan who have critical responsibilities for industry financing and protection (against counterfeiting!) respectively spent more time

---

* *Daily Trust* (Monday, April 20, 2009)

during Q and A sessions in self-denials, self praise than showcasing their work plan to reverse the de-industrialization process.

For one, the MD of BOI was cheeky enough to announce that she was not aware of any ₦70 billion intervention fund for the industry. Pray what is she aware of then? It is an open knowledge that 2003 UNIDO report recommends an intervention long term fund at single digit interest. The Federal government under President Olusegun Obasanjo accepted this singular recommendation, announced ₦70 billion intervention fund with fanfare and even presented a dummy cheque to underscore some commitment. Two years after, if the BOI now challenged with the task of managing an intervention fund is *not* aware, pray who will? There is something inherently worrisome about service delivery of public officers under President Yar'Adua. They arrogantly boycott critical stakeholders' forums and where they attend; they proudly come late and leave earlier. The official mindset is not for problem solving but problem deflection and problem aversion, in the process we are faced with problem entrenchment as in the case of the textile industry. Given President Yar'Adua's commitment to wealth generation within the context of seven-point agenda, he (not by proxy!) should have personally received the UNIDO report. But even his Minister was not there while Minister of State left earlier even when he came so late. So much for wealth generation and Non-Oil sector/ diversification official rhetoric!

UNIDO report shows how various developed and developing countries have announced varying stimulus plans to reinvent industries. And these are countries without power failure and prohibitive interest rate regimes like Nigeria. Whence Nigeria's industrial recovery plan in the wake of global economic crisis?

Industrialization assumes a special importance in development given its importance in the transformation of the economy through production of goods and services, employment generation and poverty eradication.

Industrialization is at the heart of development discourse. Industrialization delineates between growth and development of nations. If goods produced are not broadly distributed, among the population, we can only talk of economic growth. However if the goods meet the basic human needs of a large percentage of the population, industrial growth can then be said to be accompanied by development. The advantages of industrialization include lessening of dependency on imports, thus saving scarce foreign exchange.

Where the economy is diversified, industrialization serves as a source of foreign exchange. It also serves as a source of employment for greater number of the population and invariably reduces income poverty.

The dispersal of industry and the emergence of new industrial centres are the most remarkable features of globalization. In the past two decades, for instance, Japan has emerged after USA as a leading industrial power in the world. There had been dispersal of industry away from Europe and America to the newly industrializing countries of South East Asia. Africa and indeed Nigeria cannot be indifferent.

The centrality of the transformational role of industry was widely shared by post-colonial states which informed the aggressive campaign of the post-colonial government on industrialization. Industrialization was part of the post-colonial development project. Colonialism had undermined the growth and development of domestic industry through a deliberate policy of import for a protected market and blatant indifference to local efforts to promote indigenous enterprises The Commission for Africa (2005), notes that "Africa is poor, ultimately, because its economy has not grown" and therefore urges for unleashing of entrepreneurship of African peoples through massive investment that create jobs and eradicate poverty.

UNIDO (2004) shows that manufacturing industry in sub-Saharan Africa (SSA) lags behind other developing regions in almost all measures of economic development, namely income per head, industrialization and agricultural productivity. The distribution of manufacturing activity in SSA, measured by the dollar value of manufacturing value added (MVA), is highly skewed. Only ten out of 45 countries have an MVA of one billion dollars or more, while just one country, South Africa, accounts for 27.3% of the subcontinent's total MVA. The top ten producers of manufactures (equivalent to 21 per cent of the total number of countries) account for 45 per cent of total MVA and the top 15 (equivalent to one-third of the total number of countries) are responsible for almost half.

With the exceptions of South Africa and Mauritius, MVA per head in the 15 most industrialized countries is very low. South Africa is the only country in which manufacturing plays a major role in both domestic output and exports, while Mauritius, an island with a population of only 1.2 million inhabitants, is best described as an export platform. Low levels of MVA per head reflect the underdevelopment of African manufacturing. Beyond the factors discussed UNIDO attributes the African low performance to small markets, and the failure, (with a few exceptions like Mauritius, South Africa and Lesotho), to break into export markets. The report reveals that top SSA countries ranked by share of manufacturing gross domestic product (GDP), as well as by MVA per capita, 40 out of the 48 countries (83 per cent of SSA countries for which data are available) have an MVA per capita below$250 (UNIDO 2005).

Vision 2010 had identified manufacturing and industrialization as one of the critical success factors that by year 2010 which "*should contribute about 24 per cent to the GDP and should be a major employer of labour.*" What is the role of manufacturing in the much talked about Vision 2020? The painful truth is that Nigeria, a country of 140 million is fast becoming a non-value adding, container-economy, exporting scarce jobs, importing everything plus unemployment. Somebody must just stop this avoidable industrial suicide.

Lamido Sanusi: player turned referee[*]

'Central Bankers Read Election Returns, Not Balance Sheets' - *Robert Z. Aliber*

Much heat (with little illumination!) has been generated over the federal character impact assessment of the appointment of Mr. Sanusi Lamido Sanusi as the new governor of the Central Bank of Nigeria (CBN). It is time for the needed searchlight on the socio-economic significance of the ascendancy of the former CEO of the First Bank as the new regulator. We are in the season of Soccer. It is part of the climate change therefore to see a transformation of a player as the new referee of CBN! Many thanks to President Umaru Musa Yar'Adua for ensuring generational continuum in the apex bank appointment. While we are unhelpfully inundated with their regional/ethnic profile, both Sanusi Lamido and his predecessor, Professor Soludo actually have a lot in common. For one, they are middle-age new Nigerian activist money market actors. For a nation long suffocated by failed grand fathers in public offices (read: Obasanjo, Rilwan Lukman and Joseph Sanusi,) it is refreshing that Yar'Adua challenges us with another accomplished and tested kicking appointee. Importantly, both have shared values in scholarship meaning we should further expect critical owned policies as distinct from general circulars. Importantly both are economists very well unlike accountant Chief Joseph Sanusi, (who true to the calling of accountancy), spent his tenure "balancing" books rather than balancing monetary policies.

---

[*] *Daily Trust* (Monday, June 8, 2009)

Central banking worldwide has been likened to a good (economic) driver, which must keep an eye on the road and maintain steady hands on the wheel for a good (economic) ride.

Countries preoccupied with issues in development use their Central Banks to keep the economy on course through activist macro economics with respect to pricing, (inflation), exchange rates, interest rates, capacity utilization, employment, debt management etc. This is the point the new CBN governor, Sanusi Lamido Sanusi, has commendably brought to the fore on the floor of the senate during his scrutiny session. By engaging seven-point agenda, Sanusi has shown that CBN should be development conscious with respect to macro economics. For one he shows that a development agenda is on the ground and we can only make the agenda better but not deny it. Indeed contrary to the impression given by the banal media headlines, Sanusi has done more good to Yar'Adua's seven-point agenda than score of his ministers who parrot the figure as an appointment route rather than as deliverables for Nigerians. His suggestion that the agenda be downsized is in order given that in reality Yar'Adua administration has indeed focused more on energy and infrastructure in recent times. The return of another economist (the man with biggest picture) as distinct from the limited horizon of an accountant is expected to make some difference.

The point cannot be overemphasized; 'Central bankers read election results and not balance sheets'. It is early enough that Sanusi Lamido unlike his predecessor Soludo know that elections results (assuming Iwu's INEC makes the votes count!) are about macroeconomics, namely stable price, stable exchange rates, full employment, improved capacity utilization, debt management and not necessarily about bank consolidation which his predecessor rightly pre occupied self with. Indeed, only in Nigeria can the existing riotous macro economic variables, the most notorious being unemployment rate of 55 per cent, deliver 'landslide election results'! South Africa's Federal Reserve and its remarkable performance with respect to macroeconomics are central to the recent globally acknowledged victory of ANC government during the recently concluded election results. Thus, the issue in Sanusi's appointment is not the return of another economist (that is great!) to CBN but the economics of the new economist Governor.

The challenge before Sanusi is not to reinvent the wheel nor look for central banking model that has nothing to do with our miserable reality. The advice this writer gave his predecessor was to look inward. He should find out how late Dr. Clement Isong, Harvard trained economist, together with the then finance minister, late Chief Obafemi Awolowo managed the war economy without external borrowing and without inflation and naira devaluation. With existing level of unemployment, factory closures, low capacity utilization and social deprivations occasioned by poverty and Niger Deltalization of the whole land, the present day economy can indeed be likened to a war economy. We need a CBN that will be part of recovery and this call for activist bank regulator and *not* a passive CBN that bemoans economic decline through periodic reports of despair.

The Bank just marked its 50th anniversary. The question is how has it advanced the development or underdevelopment of the economy? The new governor must be wary of received wisdom. British colonialists (Fisher's Report in 1952) actually objected to setting up a Central Bank with full functions of managing the economy. Indeed, the World Bank favoured "Central Bank with limited functions." Nigerian nationalists however insisted on full-fledged Central Bank for Nigeria as a tool for economic liberation from exploitative dependency on London money and capital market, which explains the establishment of an Act of Parliament in 1958.

CBN must return to basics and take up the great challenges it was engaging in the 1970s and 1980s. The CBN must return to its core objectives of maintaining sound financial structure, promotion of monetary stability, safeguarding the value of naira and stable exchange rate and prove a financial adviser to the federal government in the areas of price and exchange rate management and employment creation. It is gratifying to read Sanusi acknowledging the achievements of Soludo. Lesson for the political elite from CBN corporate governance style: the cup is half full not half empty! The challenge lies in filling the cup. One critical area is bank consolidation. As great as that reform is, the issue is not just capital base but capital control. Beyond base build up, it is not over until real economy is grown with single-digit interest rate and certainly well valued naira.

Banks: Beyond the Bail Out[*]

With so much useful information on offer by the Central Bank of Nigeria (CNB) on the state of the country's banking system, the interest of yours truly remains purely academic. Many thanks to Lamido Sanusi, the new CEO of the CBN who in a welcome departure from his predecessor opted for full disclosures in place of playing legendary ostrich with seeming financial disaster waiting to happen. The former CBN governor, Professor Soludo, would ever remain an acknowledged enthusiast of bank consolidation via capital base expansion which radically transformed foot loose 89 banks with miserable deposits to some manageable 25 banks with expanded deposits. We must commend Sanusi Lamido for giving credit to his predecessor, Soludo, (an economist) for living a legacy of strong liquidity and bank capitalization. Very few successors have been so objective and fair with their predecessors as Sanusi has done. However at the height of recapitalization frenzy, some of us warned Soludo about the pitfall of making a fetish of capital base at the expense of capital management (read: corporate governance) and indeed capital control (read: economic development). Time is certainly longer than capital base illusion. Two years after consolidation was made an article of faith, Soludo's celebration of mega-bank as ends itself has proved a cup half empty. We undoubtedly witnessed remarkable capital base improvement from $3 billion of pre-consolidation era of 89 banks to some $7 billion dollars (with significant foreign investment inflows). Benefits of scale associated with size following consolidation were also recorded. Even Nigeria's capital reportedly goes global (assuming unexplainable ads and jingles on global network like CNN

---

[*] *Daily Trust* (Monday, August 24, 2009)

are anything to go bye). But judging by the new revelation by Sanusi, naughty "soft" corporate governance issues hunting the banks, namely asset-liability mismatch, capital inadequacy, weak internal controls, fraud and poor management, which in the first contributed to the past lingering distress syndrome in the banking sector persist.

The icon of Modern India, Mahatma Ghandi, once noted that: *"The world has enough for everyone's need, but not everyone's greed"*. Going by the countable few "defaulting customers" who owe as much as 747 billion naira ($4.71 billion) to countable five commercial lenders whose countable chief executive officers were fired last week, Ghandi's wisdom certainly sounds distant in Nigeria. Here in Nigeria, it seems with the erstwhile banking arrangement; there was enough for the greed of the few and almost nil for the needs of the multitude. Paradoxically, it is out of the commonwealth, (which in the first instance was not commonly shared or loaned) that a bail out of as much as ₦420 billion has been feverishly provided for the lenders to ensure they meet minimum capital requirements. Are we not again socializing the losses while the private gains associated with non-performing loans remain private? The point cannot be overstated: Sanusi Lamido has commendably and courageously acted the role of a sensitive and patriotic regulator who is on duty with pro active measures to avert a financial big bang with all the attendant mess. Hitherto his predecessor had pushed under the carpet critical issues of risk management and corporate governance of the banks. The devil is in the details. The disputed figures of the CBN with respect of how much are actually owned or lent or repaid might be devilish enough for some debtors to shout foul play. But what cannot be faulted are the arguments and facts of the CBN about a systemic corporate mess of the affected banks whose executives had reckless exposures to a capital market that has lost 70 per cent of its value. If the respective banks had corporate governance structures in place, the Boards of these banks should have made them to resign in the first instance. The NITEL privatization gamble of Mr Longe, one-time MD of First Bank was not as suicidal as that of the five executives before he was fired by the bank's board. With full disclosures that these banks account for 90 per cent of the discount widow, under provision of as much as ₦540 billion and average of nonperforming loan of over 40 per cent, CBN needs our support against bank damagers. Indeed the challenge lies in how to recommend same current leadership approach of the CBN and NDIC for other sectors of the economy.

Kenneth Galbraith, American economist once observed that the *'process by which bank create money is so simple that the mind is repelled'*. Delinquent banking which rests on captive government deposits (at a time the economy begs for stimulus spending!), foreign exchange "round-tripping", and speculation in capital market with bail out cheques tasks our imagination. One of the notable debtors revealed that the bank came on its own to hawk loan for him to buy "the shares on our behalf". Witness this:

> "...the Bank bought me 100 million units of shares that were worth N3.3 billion and I had shares with them before. They always hold the certificate as collateral because they know we have never defaulted. But this year, the share business went down, some of the shares we bought at N45 per unit have come down to N13. The share we bought for above N5 billion at that time are now worth N1.3 billion. Whose fault is it? It is not my fault. That is business. We have been in this business for so long."

With "business" like this we can see while poverty is mounting amidst misapplied capital. Pray what value has the debtor and his creditor added to the economy, wealth generation and poverty eradication? For too long we have paid lip service to corporate governance in which executives who preside over mess obtain cheap self awards in place of sanctions. Ordinary security men get fired for looking the other way while thieves call at night. Why then should corporate managers keep their jobs longer when at day time they watch as capital deposits under their care are being impaired? This then raises the issue of the nature of relationship between the regulator and the operators in the banking system. The difference was not as clear between the CNB as a regulator and the bankers in the recent past with the former seemingly playing the second fiddle. It is time the head wagged the tail as Sanusi is currently doing. Africa needs strongmen and strong institutions. It is not one or the other as Obama recently advised the continent. But above all, what Africa needs most is a new relationship between all actors in its market based on defined rules such that a regulator can and must call a spade a spade instead of calling it agricultural instrument, an expression of some compromise. As an adviser to government on the economy, a strong focused and an independent CBN is just in time.

Banks crisis: devil in the details[*]

The issues are familiar by now: ₦747 billion non-performing loans, corporate bad governance, insiders' dealings and sheer corporate impunity. Many thanks again to the CBN for living up to its brief as a lender of last resort. Without the timely bailout road (some ₦420 billion, $2.6 billion dollars) taken by both the CBN and NIDC, the alternative of a mass run on the affected banks is better imagined for the ordinary depositors and the economy as a whole. Even as sobering the running stories are, they are still preferred to total imminent collapse news and the attendant addition to national misery. This is the bigger issue often ignored by some hired (or are they non-performing?) writers who read conspiracy theories to simple timely regulatory function of the Central Bank. The details were predictably mouthful and mindboggling, tasking discernable imagination. When modern e-banking with its promised fool proof mechanism delivered so much contradistinction and mess, it's time we sought solace in some medieval wisdom and not in a *London's Standard and Poor* rating which dubiously chose to down grade Nigeria's credit ratings in the wake of CBN's commendable full disclosures. A Nigerian proverb has it that: "Money can make people laugh, but when they laugh, the foolish ones sometimes forget to close their mouths." Just witness Monsieur Jimoh Ibrahim, the owner of Global fleet and a star in the debt debacle. He reportedly laughed off CBN's list insisting that his indebtedness was ₦8 billion not ₦14.78 billions. Jimoh is notorious for his boisterous demagoguery as a business magnate even at the best of times. Thus if the worst of times brings out the best of what he's known for, he is only being

---

[*] *Daily Trust* (Monday, August 31, 2009)

himself. Of course the CBN had since replied Jimoh to address the substance of indebtedness instead on some unhelpful details. Jimoh Ibrahim certainly suffers no foolery. It takes some little wisdom to at least borrow so much out of others' people money and channel it to your own personal pursuit! After so many sermons about the virtue of borrowing, Jimoh has realised that CBN's message is not to criminalize borrowing as such but to make non-repayment expensive for borrowers. CBN's chieftains (without acknowledging it) must have again reigned down some Yoruba proverb on the debtors according to which: "He who borrows sixty kobo and fails to repay it loses the opportunity of borrowing seventy kobo." The good news is that he has since reportedly rushed to pay even as his mouth is still not yet closed, this time around to good cause and good measure too: after he served as an example to repay, he reportedly charitably counselled other debtors to pay up and complain later.

Talking about repayment, EFCC by the weekend disclosed that as much as ₦25.5 billion non-performing loans (NPLs) has been recovered from debtors. If there were no NPLs, certainly EFCC could do better to have invented some bad debtors anyway. The instant re-rating of EFCC from an organization which just three weeks ago was hitherto globally acknowledged to be "falling off" (apology to Hilary Clinton) to an organization "riding on" hitting the headlines is one detail worthy of studying after this bank saga. Mrs Waziri explained that the huge non-performing loans had enormous effect on the national economy. Nothing could be truer! Again devil is in the petty details: Waziri gave an example of an undisclosed businessman who secured a loan of ₦14 billion from one of the banks to export crude and as soon as the crude was sold, instead of paying back the loan went to Dubai to buy choice properties. How on earth did banks have so much exposure? As much as near ₦800 billion (4.7 billion dollars!), to just few debtors of questionable wealth generation impact? ₦14 billion to one singular borrower for a house in Dubai, not in Nigeria? In a country with paltry moribund sum of ₦1 billion for a so-called micro finance for the nation's poor multitude? Lagos state (with population of some 10 million) budgets (arguably one of the highest) ₦405 billion this year, (just half of non-performing loans to handful of corporate citizens). The non-performing loans of N747billion are almost thrice the internally generated projection (N288.9 billion) of Lagos state in 2009. The combined budgets of Delta (N233billion) and Akwa Ibom states (N195.3 billion) are just half of the banks' exposures to few debtors. Indeed the EFCC's recovered N25.5 billion from few re-paying debtors so far is half of the celebrated Enugu State's 2009 N60 billion "budget of pragmatic consolidation" proudly announced by Sullivan Chime, the state governor. The debt crisis must compel us to revisit our outworn poverty discourse. Poverty statistics at best say the obvious; *that the poor are poor* but at worse conceal the *obvious*; that *the rich are having more than they need*. Why should 80 per cent live on less than a dollar per day when the remaining 20 per cent (or better still), 5 per cent live on triple digits? Millions live on miserable minimum wages and pitiable micro-loan while few thrive on non-performing huge loans. We unfairly hold the poor responsible for their poverty while the real challenge lies on how to reverse the greed of the few through unbundling of scarce resources for reindustrialization, mass employment, job-*full* growth, progressive taxation, compulsory charity as enjoined by our religions and *above all capital control through appropriate monetary and fiscal policies that channel credit to many at fair interest rates.*

Paradoxically we are deepening and consolidating the widening class divide even by the EFCC's class conscious *Bail Terms*. Witness this: arrested debtors are expected to deposit the sum of ₦1 billion, in favour of the EFCC to secure the attendance of the accused person; A surety to the accused must be serving/current Minister of the Federal Republic of Nigeria who *will provide a landed property in Victoria Island, Lagos or Ikoyi or Maitama in Abuja or Asokoro in Abuja, whose title and value will be verified and found acceptable to the Commission."* The Commission's intent is certainly clear and difficult to fault: it is hard for the rich debtors to pass through the eye of the needle than they can return to kingdom of freedom. But the morality of the bail terns is questionable: if the seemingly performing rich bail out the non-performing rich with their rich assets located at rich corners of rich cities, are we not making reckless acquisition inadvertently addictive and even legitimate?

SAPs in Europe[*]

Africa was hit by balance of payment deficits in the 1980s. The continent witnessed huge external and domestic debts. Internal and external terms of trades also deteriorated while capacity utilization sharply declined. Flowing from the external orientation of most African economies, IMF and the World Bank (on the beacon of London and Paris clubs of creditors) imposed the infamous Structural Adjustment Programmes (SAPs). In Nigeria, the thrust of SAP (the policy trade mark of IBB military regime), included naira devaluation through the Second Tier Foreign Exchange Market (SFEM)-market determined exchange rate, privatization and commercialization, rationalization of tariff structures and subsidy (oil) removal. The impact assessment of SAPs in Africa runs into volumes of books. The writings on SAPS can fill a library dedicated to *underdevelopment* (note: *not* development) and poverty studies. The gathering of world leaders in history adopted the UN Millennium Declaration in 1999 committing their nations to a new global partnership to reduce extreme poverty and setting out a series of time-bound targets, with a deadline of 2015. That have become known as the Millennium Development Goals, MDGs. The MDGs which are the world's time-bound and quantified targets for addressing extreme poverty in its many dimensions-income poverty, hunger, disease, lack of adequate shelter, and exclusion-while promoting gender equality, education, and environmental sustainability came against the backdrop of the socio-economic havoc of two decades of SAPs in Africa.

---

[*] *Daily Trust*, 12th July 2010

The general consensus was that neoliberal/ shock therapy policy ideas contained in SAPs deepened more poverty, undermines domestic capacity for wealth generation and in fact set the process of de-industrialization in Nigeria and indeed in Africa from which recovery still proves illusory. In his classic book (2003) *Globalization and its Discontents,* Nobel Prize Winner in Economics, Joseph Stiglitz shows how IMF's inspired SAPs/reforms underdeveloped African continent while nationally inspired systematic and gradualist reforms transformed countries like China and Poland from poverty to prosperity. That book is a compulsory reading for those interested in genuine transformation of economy as distinct from privileging vested/class mafias in a society as promoted by IMF and World Bank SAP. *What is news today however is not the discredited SAPs in Africa. What is news is the paradoxical resurrection of the very notorious neo-liberal debt recovery policy dogma of SAP in Europe. Neo-liberal toolkit called SAP seems to have come (Europe and America) home to roost.* Various strands of SAPs are active implementation in Europe today. And that is official. UK's coalition government, (a mix bag of conservatives and liberal democrats) has just announced an "emergency" budget. The budget is premised on the twin austerity measures of massive cut in public spending, wage freeze, downsizing and higher consumption (VAT) taxes. The objective is to stem the rising tide of sovereign debt which has ballooned in the wake of last year's financial melt-down and feverish government bail-out for the global financial class. The debt-to-GDP ratios average 90 per cent in most countries of Europe and America. These ratios dwarfed the ratios of the countries of Africa in the 80s (where debt to GDP ratio averaged 50 per cent!) and made them less indebted compared to today's level of indebtedness of Europe and America. In fact in the case of America, debt to GDP ratio is as high as 100 per cent. *True to SAP's philosophy; the crisis in Europe is private and class driven but the solution is public bail out and public burden!; socialism for the rich (generous bail outs, capitalism for the mass (austerity measures!).* We are yet to witness mass protests and strikes in UK. The picture will be clear in October when more austerity measures are announced by the British coalition government. But we are all living witness to "SAP riots" and strikes that have crippled Greece and Spain respectively. Greece tops EU's Highly Indebted countries (HIC) as it were, with riots and even deaths. The country is almost on receivership and the brink of bankruptcy and even default on its sovereign debt if it does not cut on public spending. A critical look at the Austerity and loan agreement passed by Greek parliament make Greece looks like Uganda under SAP in 1980s:

> "An 8% cut on public sector allowances and a 3% pay cut for DEKO (public sector utilities) employees. Limit of €800 per month to 13th and 14th month pension instalments; abolished for pensioners receiving over €2,500 a month. Return of a special tax on high pensions. Changes were planned to the laws governing lay-offs and overtime pay. Extraordinary taxes imposed on company profits. Increases in VAT to 23%, 11% and 5.5%.10% rise in luxury taxes and taxes on alcohol, cigarettes, and fuel. Equalization of men's and women's pension age limits. General pension age has not changed, but a mechanism has been introduced to scale them to life expectancy changes. A financial stability fund has been created. Average retirement age for public sector workers has increased from 61 to 65. Public-owned companies to be reduced from 6,000 to 2,000."

Very soon, there may be poverty alleviation scheme for the Greek!

The critical questions today are: So the so-called developed countries are also as indebted? So the rich nations have also been living beyond their means? So the rich can also cry? The massive bail out by the governments of Europe and America might have increased the noise level of the budget deficits but it does not explain the fact that these countries have always been living above their means anyway. Whence then the IMF and World Bank which often wield the stick against African countries but look the other way while Europe and America over shoot their accounts? We are witnessing the tale of two clubs of debtors: one in Africa, another one in Europe. In fairness sovereign debts went into development and modernization in Europe and America. The trillions of dollar bail outs were meant to stabilize their economies. And the dividends are there to see as most of the economies including American economy are witnessing a recovery. However in Africa, most debts for which SAP was imposed were dubious in origin and even proved to be of dubious value. In Nigeria for instance, the 1978 $1 billion Euro-dollar was ostensibly meant for projects which included pipelines, cement factories, refineries, sugar projects and iron and steel. Studies have shown that disbursement and actual repayment of this loan had little to do with these listed projects. Also the debts of Europe were truly sovereign given that they ware owned to creditors at home. However in Africa, most long term loans were from abroad, mainly host of Western countries (Paris club) and private financial institutions (London club) which in turn informed the dictatorship of IMF/World bank conditionality. Lastly with all the burden of SAPs in Europe, the programmes are being driven democratic government compared to Africa where SAP was imposed by unaccountable dictatorships. In the former resistance against SAP continues as a matter of right while in the latter, especially Nigeria the struggle against SAP was criminalized, NLC was dissolved and regime of TINA (There Is No Alternative) suffocated the nation. Europeans may have nothing positive to learn from Africa in coping with the burden of SAPs.

Return of Development Economics[*]

Regrettably corruption economics has captured the imagination of Nigerians in the past three decades. Precisely, since mid-eighties! That was during the singular military regime that socialized and legitimized graft as an art of governance. For too long we are daily preoccupied with the task of catching public thieves, pretending to be recovering looted funds which paradoxically in turn get re-looted as was the celebrated reported cases of Abacha loot. The point cannot be overstated. Corruption and anti-corruption economics will not eradicate poverty, generate much needed national wealth nor make Nigeria one of the 20 leading economies by 2020 as favoured by Nigerian government. Assuming we have caught and even punished all the thieves and dealt with their mass counterparts: kidnappers, the question remains: have we really produced the necessary goods and services for the citizens? Have we delivered uninterrupted electricity? Have we provided water and housing among other mass of needs? The fundamental objective of the state principle as espoused in 1999 constitution is the welfare and security of the citizens not about catching thieves. *By all means please let's fight corruption. But let us also know that anti-corruption is just the means. The end is development.* What Nigeria and Nigerians need is urgently development economics. We must replace corruption economics that manifests in oil revenue sharing and eventual stealing with development economics. Development economics is defined here as economics of real production, value addition, reindustrialization (growing the real sector) job-creation and pulling the bottom millions out of the existing poverty.

---

[*] *Daily Trust*, 2nd August 2010

On Tuesday July 27, the Central Bank of Nigeria took a bold step with the announcement of the release of N130bn, out of the promised N200bn meant to refinance the manufacturing sector of the economy. Nigeria's economic crisis is crisis of production characterized by collapse of small and medium as well as large enterprises, idle and under-capacity utilization, unemployment, high production costs and un-competitive products prices. One of the critical success factors for development economics is financing. Before Sanusi Lamido's ascendancy as the Governor of the CBN, banks' consolidation did not translate to banks' credit allocation for the financing of the real sector of the economy. On the contrary, what the current bank reform shockingly revealed was gross distortions in banks' portfolio characterized by criminal insiders' abuse, short term lending for conspicuous consumption and scandalous on and off shore self-acquisitions. It is commendably that CBN has halted the drift in the banking sector, averted banks collapse, protected depositors, commendably named and punished banks rogue- executives and put risk management measures in place. But gratifying is the news that CBN now sets to pointedly lead by example to challenge the banks in refinancing the real sector of the economy. Banks are meant to finance long term development in a developing economy like ours.

It is refreshing last Tuesday in Abuja seeing the return of development economics. The development economics agencies are the CBN led by the Governor, Sanusi Lamido, the presidency represented by the Vice President, Arc Namadi Sambo, the Bank of Industry (BOI) led by Evelyn Oputu and Manufacturers' Association of Nigeria (MAN) led by Alhaji Burondo. The occasion was the signing ceremony of the initial N130 billion intervention funds for the real sector. Yours sincerely agreed with BOI's MD, Evelyn Oputu that the signing ceremony signified the CBN's policy response to the financing crisis facing the industry. The attraction of this intervention fund is its long term profile (15 years) and single digit interest rate (7 per cent).

From what we saw last week, Development economics is a win-win economics (everybody wins something) while corruption economics is a zero-sum game (looters take all, masses take nothing!). The CBN governor, Mr.

Lamido Sanusi, noted that the amount would be disbursed through designated banks. By doing so CBN fulfils its mandate to promote development while participating banks improve on their liquidity and above all beneficiary firms can recapitalize and retool and reenergize their production. In fullest of time jobs can be created and wage incomes are earned. CBN promises to disburse as much as N200bn out of the N500bn infrastructure fund meant to assist the real sector of the Nigerian economy before the end of the year.

With the release of the fund, therefore, the government, through the CBN, has demonstrated some measure of seriousness on its determination to re industrialize the country. However as significant as this fund is, the financial challenge is still much begging for trillions of naira intervention. According to the managing director/chief executive officer, BOI, Ms. Evelyn Oputu, a total of 377 applications had been received, with 84 per cent of the applications (totalling N130bn) already approved for disbursement. That says volume about the financial needs of manufacturers. In any case CBN disbursed trillions of Naira to intervene and commendably save few banks in the last one year. What is good for the money market is far more desirable for the industrial market!

If this financial intervention is complemented with electricity supply and protection of the domestic market through quality control, control of smuggling and dumping of fake and counterfeit products, then industrial recovery is under way. The beauty of development economics is the visibility of value adding development agencies, namely Central Bank of Nigeria, (CBN), Bank of Industry, (BOI), Manufacturers' Association of Nigeria, (MAN), Standard Organization of Nigeria, SON. The down side of corruption economics is the visibility of notorious agencies of dubious value, namely ICPC and EFCC. Let us promote the former agencies while we should give a time frame for the latter agencies to close shops. Development economics is sustainable while corruption economics is doomed and indeed terminal.

Between Bulls and the Bears*

The traditional image of typical capital market is that of a bustling, chaotic trading floor with aggressive traders at the top of their voices shouting "sell" and "buy". With the help of computerization, investors now trade directly from anywhere. This notwithstanding, stock market is still characterized by the *bulls*; those believe that the market is set to go up and the *bears* those who expect the prices to fall. The two are united by greed and fear which are regular trademarks of the capital market. It is however unthinkable that for whatever reasons, both the *bulls and the bears* of the Nigeria's stock market would be at each other's' throats as we have witnessed last week.

Before he was removed as the President of the Nigerian Stock Exchange (NSE) Alhaji Aliko Dangote, reportedly insisted that the Exchange was broke, saying it could no longer honour its obligations. According to him, NSE is currently dipping its hands in the Central Securities Clearing System (CSCS) accounts to borrow N900 million to support its cash deficit position. CSCS is a subsidiary of the NSE as well as the Clearing House of the Nigerian stock market. He said the 13th month salary for 2009 was not paid in December due to lack of funds and also that the prestigious Annual President Dinner did not hold due to financial crisis hitting the Exchange. He further challenged the management of NSE to submit itself for forensic audit by reputable auditing firms adding for good effect that most of the troubled banks also have audited accounts that were later found to be manipulated. He said: "I assure you that if it is done, the revelation in

---

* *Daily Trust*, 9th August, 2010

the banking industry will be a child's play when compared to the rot in the Exchange."

Promptly the NSE denied the news that it was insolvent. In his response, spokesman of the NSE, Mr. Sola Oni, rose in spirited defence of Exchange and said:

> "The Nigerian Stock Exchange is not insolvent. The organization is meeting all its obligations as at when due. The staff are not owed salaries and allowances. The retirees receive their cheques promptly. The Exchange does not owe any bank or individual. If there is any form of owing it could be that such a company is handling project that has not been completed. Even at that, the Exchange must have made some pre-payment. "No organization in Nigeria is fully insulated from the effects of global market downturn. The Exchange is certainly affected. But it has always been prudent in the management of its resources. As part of prudent management, the Council directed a downward review of staff salary and benefits in view of low revenue following global financial crisis. This does not imply insolvency. It is heart-warming to say that the market is recovering. This would enable the Exchange to upgrade its infrastructure the more."

Yours sincerely is not sure of what to make of the accusations and counter accusations of the bulls and bears of the stock market. *But one thing missing in this market drama is the plight of the ordinary investor caught in the war of attritions of NSE's gladiators.* The good news however is that both the embattled Chief Executive Officer (CEO) of the Nigerian Stock Exchange (NSE), Ndidi Okereke-Onyiuke and the accuser, the President Alhaji Aliko Dangote as well as other Council members have all been sacked by the Securities and Exchange Commission (SEC). A sole administrator has also been appointed to take charge of the Exchange to prevent a likely collapse of the market, following conflicts among the NSE elite and allegations of insider abuse. Many market watchers are of the opinion that the action of the regulatory authority, Security and Exchange Commission (SEC), headed by Ms Arunma Oteh, is coming too late too token. Two years ago, some of the Exchange's bad outcomes included collapsed prices of stocks (as a result of mass speculative greed). Many ordinary investors lost their fortunes. The dramatic 35% crash in stock prices was explained away as part of the global economic crisis for which nobody has so far offered official causation explanation. In fact no NSE/SEC chieftains were urged to resign either at the height of the market crash. Of course it was an open knowledge that their unofficial resignation, from their statutory regulatory functions, and insiders' greed nurtured the market crash. Taunted *"emerging"* Nigeria's capital market altogether turned to be nothing but a mere notorious "frontier", apparently for cheap feverish hot/hedge speculative funds as distinct from a market place for capital formation for an economy begging for development. At the centre of this capital deceit has been Ndidi Okereke, the hitherto sit tight DG of the NSE. She once boasted that Nigeria's capital market was an "investment destination" of "400 per cent-rate of return") which sounded like what the late American economist John K Galbraith once called "mass insanity". Before then the feverish/bullish activism of Ndi Okereke-Onyiuke- led Nigeria Stock Exchange (NSE) had led to scandalous infractions for which a good regulator must have raised a sledge hammer. She once desperately raised unsolicited funds for the campaign of Senator Obama for the Presidency of America. It would be recalled that in 2003 under the banner of *Corporate Nigeria,* the same crowd linked with capital market actually laundered money in billions of Naira for Obasanjo/Atiku Campaign fund in a less than transparent way (we are yet to know who gave what and why?). It is not clear what the rate of return on that singular controversial partisan investment was for its promoters. But chroniclers of that age of money impunity would certainly be unanimous to conclude that the corporate and financial recklessness of OBJ era which led to state promoted investment cronyism vehicle like *Transcorp* had its root in that undue monetization of electoral process boisterously openly backed up by corporate chieftains like Okereke and her crowd. The point cannot be overstated; what has proved useful recently in the money market (i.e., sanctions for sharp practices!) must even prove timely for the capital market. SEC must learn from the sweeping reforms of the banking sector and quickly move to sanitize the capital market. There cannot be an appropriate time than now that the chieftains of the market have moved from their sickening insiders' abuse to open market's wars of attritions.

Return of UNTL Kaduna[*]

Return of UNTL: In praise of governance. Some three odd years ago, (i.e. 2007) then Kaduna state deputy Governor, His Mr Patrick Yakowa disclosed while receiving the then visiting Minister of Petroleum resources Henry Ajimogobia to government house disclosed that: "The top management of the United Nigeria Textile Company (UNTL) last week informed me during a visit that the company will be closed down next week." Many textile mills in Kaduna, (the cradle of textiles) had closed down but that of UNTL assumed a special dimension, because of its size, production, employment and community impact. UNTL closure came at the time Kaduna state government had received the report on the Special Committee for the Revival of textile and cotton industries in the state. The Committee of which, yours truly was a member and chaired by the deputy governor was set up by Governor Arc Namadi Sambo to examine the problems of the industries and recommend measures for immediate revival. The summary pay-off of well over 5000 workers shocked the nation in general and the manufacturing sector in particular. Last Friday, Dec 3rd, UNTL was reopened by the Vice President Arc Namadi Sambo as an anti-climax of his active commitment of revival of industries in the state he once presided over and in Nigeria as a whole. The excitement and outpours of goodwill that greeted the roaring of the spinning and weaving UNTL mills contrasted with the attendant grief that trailed its deafening closure three years ago. Weekend event was a practical demonstration of the Vision 2020 which aims to make Nigeria one of the 20 leading industrialized economies. The Textile Workers' Union whose voice

---

[*] *Daily Trust*, 6th December 2010

198

has been consistently loud for the revival of the industry sees UNT return as a vindication of its constructive engagements and advocacy with the governments at all levels; presidency, Ministries, state governments, relevant agencies; Bank of Industry (BOI), Customs, Standard Organization of Nigeria (SON).

The return of UNTL signifies a return of governance just as its closure three years ago underscored the demise of governance.

UNIDO (United Nations Industrial Development Organization) (2003) study identified a number of critical success factors in industrial revival that included uninterrupted and cheap electricity supply, financing, policy consistency, standard enforcements, smuggling controls and patronage of locally produced goods among others. All these factors task our capacity to come to terms with good governance.

The singular effort of His Excellency, Vice President of the Federal Republic of Nigeria, Arc Namadi Sambo in the reopening of UNTL cannot overstated. Established in Kaduna in 1965, UNTL was a product of developmentalist post-colonial Nigeria championed by the late *Sardauna* of Sokoto, Sir Ahmadu Bello. Arc Sambo Namadi truly passes for a modern day Sardauna for helping tirelessly to reopen the UNTL and other factories which the late *Sardauna* helped to nurture. After the sudden closure due to a number of failure factors the Administration of Governor Namadi Sambo went into action in place of lamentations. Apart from personally leading a fact finding visit to the closed factories, in company of Federal Ministers, Arc. Namadi Sambo in 2008, he worked his talk with a construction of a 215 MW power plant dedicated to the industrial area of the State to boost the generation of power to help industrialization. He then brought the same zeal and commitment to the office of the Vice President. President Goodluck Jonathan's administration finally endorsed the intervention fund under the N100 billion for cotton/textile revival. This new deal was supervised by Vice President Namadi Sambo. The objective is to revolutionalize funding for the real sector and breadth life into the ailing industries. The fund is to be disbursed to beneficiaries at a concessionary interest rate of not more than 7 per cent with a tenor of 10 – 15 years. The deal worked out by the CBN and BOI covers lending and re-

refinancing of projects, restructuring of existing portfolios to manufacturers and support for investment in industrial clusters power supply. The return of UNT Plc. is premised on the realization of this cocktail of measures pushed by government. The sustainability of this reopening and further reopening of others depend on the continuous commitment of governments at all levels with supportive policies especially those aimed at the drastic reduction in the incidence of smuggling.

It was therefore reassuring when the Honourable Minister for Finance Olusegun Agaga made clarification on the reported lifting of the ban on the importation of textile materials on the eve of reopening of UNTL. According to him the ban on textiles that Nigeria produces locally remains in force. Domestic investors who operate under a very difficult condition like epileptic power supply cannot compete with smugglers. Import kills local industry and poses serious threat to the national economy. Nigeria must try to consume what it produces and produce what it consumes.

UNTL's history is about industry, productivity and quality prints, investment, positive economic climate, industrial policy consistency, mass employment, training and skills acquisition, research and development, market, consumption. Its reopening means not just new thousands of jobs but revival of hitherto depressed communities (Kakuri, Trikania and Nasarawa). With 10-000- workers when in full production, UNTL is a *"large, integrated, multinational conglomerate"*. I bear witness that development agenda (as manifested by reopening of UNTL) is a win-win agenda compared to corruption agenda. It was gratifying at the weekend seeing critical institutions such as BOI, Customs, SON, Ministry of finance united in cooperation to add value and reinvent the much talked about non-oil sector.

Naira valuation - in Praise of CBN[*]

Mr. Sanusi Lamido, the governor of CBN deserves national commendation for asserting the independence of the Central Bank in defence of the value and integrity of the Naira in the face of the policy attack (sorry, policy advice!) of the International Monetary Fund to the contrary. Yours truly has always been weary of neo-liberal policy that advocates unrestrained wholesome independence for the Central banking with spelling out the national responsibilities that go with independence. But Sanusi has shown with the assertion of CBN's independence from IMF's policy advice that there is nothing inherently good or bad with independent central banking as such. What matters is what the governor of the Bank makes of his or her independence; does he rise in defence of nationally agreed economic/development agenda or kowtows to vested interests either nationally driven or internationally inspired. Neo-liberalism aims to delimit the role of the state and government in determination of monetary and fiscal policies. The objective is to grant the central bank the "autonomy" to push through controversial policies of financial liberalization as it affects bank deregulation, interest rate liberalization and removal of exchange controls among. In recent past the autonomy under Soludo's CBN produced "Naira big-bang" redenomination policy under the high sounding *"Strategic agenda for the Naira"*, one policy disaster that is now part of part of history of non-strategic management. There was also the policy of Dollarization of state government accounts which ran into the brick wall of seven-point agenda of President Musa Yar'Adua. There was also the unnecessary increase in Monetary Policy Rate to 10.0 per cent

---

[*] 26 February 2011

ostensibly to tame inflation. Uncritical increase in MPR will further reverse the gains recorded in interest-rate management. The neo-liberal least resistance policy of managing inflation through hike in interest rate is at variance with current thinking in emerging economies that down ward push in interest rate is indispensable to economic recovery, economic competitiveness and employment generation.

It is to the eternal credit of CBN under Sanusi Lamido governorship that it independently refuses to be counted on the side of policy (unhelpful) policy dogma of the IMF. A developing country like ours, begging for reindustrialization, electrification, job creations and poverty eradication cannot crudely separate central banking from developmental and democratic aspirations of the people. Countries preoccupied with issues of development use their Central Banks to keep the economy on course through activist macroeconomics with respect to pricing, (inflation), exchange rates, interest rates, capacity utilisation, employment, debt management, intervention/support fund for targeted real sectors, etc.

The IMF had claimed that the naira was overvalued making a case for more exchange flexibility (read; devaluation). The International Monetary Fund (IMF) which with the global financial melt-down, has gone out of fashion has suddenly resurrected with familiar policy dogma in Nigeria. The basic monetary policy of neoliberalism is inflation targeting. The proponents of this monetary policy of inflation targeting hold that the objective of central bank is to anchor inflations expectations. IMF is indifferent to the fact that the need to constrain fiscal policy through cut in public spending further imperils economic growth and in our context undermines recovery all together. Neo-liberal monetary policy also advocates for positive real interest rates of investment. But the effect of real interest rate on savings and development is totally ignored. The truth is that where there is the need for urgent development like ours, negative interest rates are necessary stimulus. It is therefore refreshing that, CBN Governor, Mr. Lamido Sanusi, spoke for Nigeria by standing firm not to devalue the naira as recommended by the IMF, noting that the recommendation was "internally inconsistent."

IMF's recommendation, if accepted, would trigger higher inflation in the economy, he rightly noted. He said: "I have had this debate with the IMF, the recommendations they made are internally inconsistent. If we devalue the currency or we depreciate the currency, it adds to inflation." In his own apt words: "short-term shocks, which are a reflection of a global crisis especially, since it was driven by liquidity. And we know that, that liquidity was necessary." It is refreshing to read that CBN opposes the regime of inflation targeting." All talk of inflation targeting in the Central Bank of Nigeria is prohibited so long as I think that a developing country like Nigeria can pursue that. There are a lot of structural problems.

Of what benefit is a consistent devaluation to a mono-cultural economy that exports nothing beyond crude oil, the price of which is fixed by OPEC? What are the implications for inflation, capacity utilization and employment generation? By its singular display of independence, CBN has also shown that there is always an alternative to the notoriously unhelpful IMF/ World Bank policy prescriptions if we dare for once to look at the impoverished faces of our peoples rather than shining faces of the representatives of Bretton Woods institutions. Behind the legitimate protests and riots in Tunisia and Egypt are some illegitimate policy advices of IMF.

Depoliticising Anti-Graft War[*]

As an anti-corruption (sorry, a development) activist my commentaries in serial defence of EFCC and ICPC (in that order of importance) can pass for a lorry load. The defence of anti-graft agencies against corrupt forces is informed by the passion for *development, development and development.* We don't need a tutorial lecture from President Barrack Obama of United States of America about the link between corruption and development. Scarce public financial resources stolen by some few public officers would certainly not be available for education, hospitals and (certainly not in the least) for minimum wage for Nigeria's working poor. There is an inverse relationship between private accumulation of some few public officers and the worsening poverty of Nigerians. My last take in spirited defence of EFCC was when it's controversial "advisory" (note: not6 necessarily not prosecutor) list for political parties on the eve of the last elections was shot down by no other person by the then Minister of Justice and Anthony General of the Federation. Mr Mohammed Adoke, the Minister of Justice, had curiously openly come against an advisory list on accountability ostensibly complied by the EFCC. EFCC according to its Chairman Mrs Farida Waziri had posted on its web site a list of former public holders having varying accountability cases to answer. Yours sincerely had interrogated the then Minster as to; why a major attack against a non-controversial EFCC's list emanate from the office of Anthony General publicly paid to upgrade the list from advisory to accelerated prosecution? Paradoxically the EFCC was more on the defensive of the top-down shot down of its list than it was willing to stand to

---

[*] June 13, 2011

defend the list. Mrs Farida Waziri almost disowned her own agency's list when she inexplicably said she meant no offence (clearly defensive!) and she bore no responsibility for a posted list that has always been on the agency's web anyway. At the end of the day we never saw the so called list nor were the high profile names made available to the political parties as advisory list. What manner of war was it (against corruption) that the agency (EFCC) paid to prosecute the war was in itself on the defensive? What manner of war was it that the protagonist agency of this war felt shy from being on the offensive while the antagonists were as resolute and determined? That singular action created a crisis of perception about anti-corruption war. *Is this war an enduring commitment to halt the on-going graft in some high places or a partisan game of the political elite to settle some political scores in a partisan war of attrition?* This question begs for an urgent answer against the background of a new perception that the EFCC's acknowledged efforts at accountability were being politicised aimed at settling electoral scores that ought to be determined at the polls. The report that the new members of the National Assembly jeered the chairman of the Economic and Financial Crimes Commission (EFCC) Mrs. Farida Waziri and accused her of witch-hunting perceived political opponents of President Goodluck Jonathan has further created a crisis of perception for the EFCC. Some of the lawmakers challenged the EFCC Chairman to mention names of politicians prosecuted by the commission who were not perceived enemies of the federal government. Read Rep Abdulmumin Jibrin (PDP, Kwara): "Mention a single Politically Exposed Person (PEP) that was prosecuted without the person having problem with the federal government since the establishment of the commission in 2003." The reaction of Mrs. Waziri at the interactive session did not help matters either; as usual defensive: "I am my own person. I have never been asked by anyone to pick or drop anybody. My image is intact and I have never trumped up charges against anyone." She reportedly pleaded with the lawmakers that though they have made up their minds against the commission "because of the on-going case (that of Bankole), it is only the guilty that need to fear." We dare not pretend to be fighting corruption when in reality we inadvertently fuel the menace. Nigeria has just recorded a big slide in the race to the bottom of global corruption. According to Transparency International (IT) Nigeria emerged 134th of the 178 countries in 2010. In the latest position, the country slid four places from last year's position. Nigeria was ranked 28th among the 47 African countries surveyed. The CPI is a composite index, drawing on 13 different expert and business surveys. Surveys for the CPI were conducted between January 2009 and September 2010. Yet with all its ascribed respectability, the global hype about the celebrated Corruption Index is nothing but a perception. It is all about impression and perception. TI hardly offers any concrete evidence to show that America is less corrupt than Nigeria. However the perception is that corruption avoidance is higher in America than Nigeria, because the enforcement agencies are perceived to be consistent and principled in fighting graft. Mrs Farida has singular responsibility to change the perception that what we have at hand is not politicisation of anti-corruption war. *The current twin cases of the former Minister of Works, Hassan Laval and former Speaker Dimeji Bankole task the EFCC's sense of political/partisan neutrality and commitment to probity, not political witch-hunting.*

"Born Again" Ngozi Iweala?*

Before the global financial melt-down in 2007 and its local fallout of capital bubble burst in Nigeria, yours truly had taken strong exceptions to the doctrinaire market dogma of OBJ's economic reform agenda. That singular reform (note; not *development*) agenda privileged the capital and money markets at the expense of industry, social sector, labour market and national development in general. Then Minister of Finance, Ngozi Iweala was the pointed hard-nose, competent, neo-liberal economist of that singular economic team. She was indeed twice a Minister of the Federal Republic: Finance and Foreign ministries in quick succession between 2003 and 2007. She undoubtedly qualified as Nigeria's unofficial "Prime" Minister in a presidential system. Remarkably Mrs Ngozi Iweala brought guts to governance. She instituted transparency in national budgeting. Her singular insistence in publishing states and local government budgets was an act of subversion of state/local government corruption which promoted accountability and critical citizenry. Minister Ngozi commendably encouraged unfettered freedom to economic information well before the FOI Act. The huge human capital (intelligence, experience, skills, passion, values and commitment) she brought to governance and the remarkable value additions of her tenure (transparent budget process, periodic publications of federally allocated revenues and external controversial $18 billion debt write-off among others) would always be a reference point for public service delivery for some time to come. There are many ministers without standard. It was to the eternal credit of Iweala that she had standard. She was once hunted by the very standard of transparency

---

* July 11, 2011

she instituted. Recall the excess crude withdrawals controversy; some $17million withdrawn allegedly without national assembly knowledge in respect of the 2005 census (head count). A pro-active and offensive activist Minister for once was clearly on the defensive. Talking about standard, Iweala brought credibility to governance by knowing when to quit via resignation. In this part of the world, public officers hardly resign until they get booted out after which some of them are handed over to the police. Minister Ngozi whose intimidating credentials paraded multiple degrees in economics and public finance, was overnight sent to foreign ministry. Yours sincerely put up a bet that if she did not resign then employment relations and letters of appointment were worthless in Nigeria. What business could an economic technocrat with innate talent and passion for market dogma and well-acknowledged intemperance had to do with international relations, politics and diplomacy? I could not have imagined an Iweala brokering a peace deal between Hezbollah and Israel in a conflict which involved hostage taking, not debt –swaps or debt repayments. She taunted the card some "economic diplomacy" card as her policy trust in foreign ministry. But discernable observers who watched her in the wake of Israeli dastardly bombing of Southern Lebanon talking about the plight of Nigerians in Lebanon were unanimous that she was more eloquent and intelligent on debt deals of Paris/London clubs of creditors than theatres of wars that global diplomacy has assumed. There are many ways appointees are told that services are no longer required. It was good the former Minister knew when to quit OBJ administration. But so much for personal achievements and strengths of Iweala! She has since reapplied and indeed been offered the same job she left some three years ago. Paradoxically Minister Ngozi would only be assessed effectively based on the policy thrust of administration she once served. With nostalgia it is good to see Iweala back. With her African print she is a spectacular brand to see every Wednesday cabinet meeting. The critical issue however is what she has on offer for a nation begging for new policy ideas? The bane of the reform agenda she once championed; National Economic Empowerment and Development Strategy (NEEDS) was its ideological commitment to market reform as distinct from a pragmatic commitment to development. NEEDS was tall in rhetoric; a "new deal" with Nigerian people to reduce poverty with emphasis on the people's welfare, health, employment, education, political power, promising to make Nigeria the strongest economy in Africa. Listening to nominee Iweala on the floor of the national assembly pointing to imbalances in budgeting with respect to capital/recurrent expenditures further underscores the national vote of no confidence in the strategy of development she once taunted. Nigeria actually lost a decade of development, no thanks to uncritical neo-liberal policy instruments of liberalization, privatization, right sizing the public sector. Former Vice President Atiku Abubakar got it wrong commending her for saying the obvious. What is sobering is that the economic policies of OBJ, Atiku and Iweala (in that order) few years ago had made Nigeria ever more dependent on oil budgeting with Federal Government's current expenditure as much as 74 per cent of the national budget! *Nigeria needs new economic sound bites please.* Is Mrs Iweala offering us a new *born again* macroeconomics? Are we back to the discredited same old dogma of inflation targeting, recurrent expenditure bashing or job-targeting and stimulus financing? It is refreshingly new to hear her talking about job creation. What happened to the promised 7 million jobs of NEEDS? Are we to expect employment centred macroeconomic policies or employment blind trillion Naira budgets? Up to the eve of her departure from OBJ cabinet, the economic team actually pitched economic efficiency against economic democracy; the rich got richer without value addition whatsoever while the poor got enmeshed in the race to deeper poverty and joblessness. So much for the cliché; "Changing the way government do business". What of the way businesses are doing business in Nigeria? Are we for a productive economy propelled by electrification and industrialization or glorification of container/cargo/service economy? Sound good to read that the Minister supports the new minimum wage. If we must avoid the road to Tunisia or Tahir Square in Egypt, beyond minimum wage, labour market needs urgent bail outs in terms of decent mass jobs, enhanced pension, social security and social protection in general. For an over/fully employed Minister of finance like Mrs Iweala with one time controversial dollar denominated pay, she does not need a sermon on the burden of idle capacity for restless youths and under employment of their parents.

Islamic Banking- Time for Policy Discourse please*

Tons of written and verbal commentaries on the new (old) CBN's policy initiative on Islamic Banking could very well fill a banking hall of a bank yet to be licensed. Paradoxically most commentators so far are not disinterested commentators. Sorry, the commentators are not *interest-free* as the principle of Islamic banking envisages. On the contrary, the self-appointed protagonists and antagonists alike are motivated by anything other than banking and economics of which Islamic banking is just a specialization. What we have at hand so far is purely an avoidable and unhelpful clash of some petty religious fundamentalisms as distinct from informed disagreements arising from some structured policy discourse. The most outlandish is my colleague in the naughty business of weekly commentary; Mallam Bala Muhammed. His back page of *Weekly Trust* entitled 'Leave Our Bank Alone'[32] was vested interest-driven rather banking informed. His concluding remark sums up his religious preferences as distinct from CBN's announced policy guidelines. Witness him: "Let them leave our Bank, Jesus' Bank, God's Bank, alone! *Lakum dinukum wa liya din!*" *Haba* Bala! I have listened umpteenth time to the Governor of CBN, Sanusi Lamido Sanusi. According to him Islamic banking is all about financial inclusion and financial deepening for a nation begging for much needed financial resources for development. Exclusivist mind-set which informed such literary dictation such as *Leave Our Bank alone* does not in any way advance a policy discourse on the proposed Islamic banking as promoted by CBN. Islamic banking is all about financial inclusion, not financial exclusion. First

---

* July 18, 2011
[32] See 2nd of July

211

at the upstream! Only 20 per cent of Nigerians currently patronize banks. Islamic banking undoubtedly opens up a window of opportunities to capture more depositors who may be Muslims and non-Muslims alike. There is a shared value regardless of faith that we must in Nigeria work towards a cashless society. Islamic banking is one strategy to achieve this singular goal. Kenya is not an Islamic country. But Islamic banking has helped to improve financial inclusion and financial deepening there. At the down-stream end, Islamic banking is open to all just as any other forms of banking are opened to Muslims as long as you play by the rules of engagement and inclusion. Therefore Bala does not inadvertently need to pitch "Nigeria Christian clergy" against the Vatican which according to him already appreciates the "ethical principles" on which Islamic finance is based any way. The singular fact that the Vatican chooses to promote policy discourse rather than religious bigotry means that the challenge at hand is policy and policy discourse not clerical shouting matches and point scoring. Bala ought to therefore be more measured to explain the principles of Islamic financing to those yet to be converted, sorry to know, regardless of faith rather than throwing dart at the "lives of luxury; on fleecing their congregations; on buying private jets; on paedophilia; on gay bishops; and, closer home, on the daily 'Pastor-puts-in-family-way' scandals." Economics, calls for explanations, logical reasoning and persuasion not a smear campaign at others, a smear campaign that indeed mirrors the true lifestyles of all of us regardless of faith! Collapse of industries and poverty are not faith blind. The critical question is how Islamic banking makes a difference from the existing commercial/industrial banking in moving Nigeria forward open the path of development. It is time we engaged each other from the perspective of fundamental inclusive problems we all shared namely; unemployment, income, food, social and job insecurity rather than exclusive labels we carry; Muslims or Christians. India and China, for instance float zero interest banking that finances and propels textile industry from import substitution to export promotion. Yet neither China nor India carries the labels of Christian or Islamic countries. Similarly, my sister, Aisha Kabir Yusuf, muddled up the case for Islamic banking with her unhelpful legitimate religious prejudices. Witness her:

"In the final analysis, if Nigerian Christians want to establish banks that go with their 'no usury' Christian principle, then by all means they should apply to the CBN to register their 'Christian bank'. For now they are only raising hell over the 'Jewish bank', and amazingly the Jews aren't complaining."

Haba! From simple policy discourse about a form of banking which Islamic banking represents, Aisha has deviated into some unhelpful fundamentalism and even racism. What is "Jewish" about a bank? Is it because it is interest driven or manned by Jews? Is it all about our race, tribe or our faiths, economic preferences or piety? Many existing commercial banks are manned by Muslims managers. Does that qualify them as "Muslim" banks? Terms like; "Christian" bank, "Jewish" banking have nothing to do with CBN's new policy initiative. On the contrary, such terms only arm the chieftains of religious-industrial complex, such as the President of Christian Association of Nigeria (CAN), Pastor Ayo Oritsejafor, who irreligiously and certainly unfairly accused CBN governor of wanting to "Islamize" the country through Islamic banking. In terms of exclusive terms and categories the difference might not be clear between both the protagonists and antagonists of Islamic banking after all. But the challenge is for CBN to increase the tempo of its all-inclusive awareness campaign on its core inclusive albeit contentious policy initiatives, namely recapitalization of some banks, intervention development fund, non-interest banking, its autonomy and accountability and cash limit policy among others.

Privatization blues[*]

Last Saturday yours truly witnessed the formal closure of the Senate Ad hoc Committee on privatization in Abuja by the erudite and intensely engaging committee chairman, Senator Ahmad Lawan. My interest in this reflection therefore is largely academic. Some two weeks ago President Goodluck Jonathan inaugurated the reconstituted board of the National Council on Privatization (NCP). His singular regret that privatisation in Nigeria had not lived up to its billing as the answer to ailing state enterprises captured national imagination. It was a refreshing official developmentalist disclosure which for once happily departed from the boring stale constitutional amendments with bias for single term tenure elongation. The President said as much that the privatized firms had not been as "successful as Nigerians expected". However not few Nigerians including the President could have imagined wholesale *personalization* of the privatization process by some few local and foreign oligarchs through contrived assets undervaluation, bidding swaps, (witness winner and preferred winners), alleged bribes (what Nobel prize winner economist called Joseph Stiglitz rightly dubbed *"briberization"*), insiders" dealings, plain assets stripping, political dictatorship (in place of corporate governance), mass job destruction (as distinct from promised mass job creation), preferred foreign ownership and re-colonization (with Nigeria at 50!) in place of sovereign wealth. The newly reconstituted Council in consonance with the Bureau of Public Enterprise (BPE) Act of 1999 as amended, chaired by the Vice President Namadi Sambo, with statutory members like the Minister of Finance (vice chairman); Attorney Generation of the Federation

---

[*] August 15, 2011

and Minister of Justice; Ministers of Trade and National Planning; Secretary to the Government of the Federation; Governor of the Central Bank of Nigeria (CBN); Special Adviser to the President on Economic Matters; President of the Nigeria Labour Congress; Chairman of NACCIMA and Mrs. Bola Onagoruwa, Director General of BPE certainly have some urgent national tasks to do beyond the ordinary. I whole heartedly agree with President Jonathan that the NCP must revisit "the whole concept of privatisation" (President's words). *The bane of Nigeria's privatization process is that it was largely driven by discredited neoliberal ideology/market dogma as distinct from patriotic national development agenda.* Privatization entered the national lexicon through the notorious Structural Adjustment Programme (SAP) of the mid- eighties feverishly imposed by the IMF and World Bank in the wake of the economic crisis of the eighties. Nigerians patriotically rejected the IMF loan in 1986, (at a time indebtedness was promoted by the IMF and World Bank). But the international financial predators re-emerged through an adjustment (note; not developmental) program that contains cancerous discredited macro-economic policies such as naira devaluation, privatization and removal of subsidies. In 1999, former President Olusegun Obasanjo, a hitherto pragmatic and development oriented leader, got converted to the notorious same market dogma and arrogantly elevated a silly dogma to a state art. He declared that the state *had no business in business.* The likes of loose-cannon and unthinking public (note not private!) officers like El Rufai declared from the roof tops of the Bureau of Public Enterprise (BPE) (again note not from Bureau of their Private Enterprises!) that every state enterprise should be sold including some parts of the Villa buildings and even NTA and public buildings like 1004 to one monopoly called UAC! It is this singular ideological self-serving mentality that informed the wholesale impunity, disrespect for even Privatization law, we have witnessed in the last decade in the name of privatization. To therefore frontally clear the rots that have largely bedevilled the privatization process, we must de-ideologise the process and critically assess the process in the light of the nation's developmentalist challenges that include production of mass cheaper wage goods and service, national ownership of national resources, efficiency and competitiveness, mass employment of the youths and adults alike. *Nigeria's privatization is being hunted by its lowly origin. We must critically examine it in the light of the current development agenda.* It is completely wrong, illegal and irresponsible for government to have "delegated some of its responsibilities to the private sector over the period" as President Jonathan observed. Doing this we have unwittingly replaced allegedly subsidized and abused public monopolies with much more abused private monopolies which in turn thrive on the state subsidies and collapse of governance and regulation. Mallam El Rufai was particularly smart by half and not surprisingly crudely ideological when at this hour he still smears old public enterprises with exaggerated gulped N265 billion. This blue herring about public enterprises does not answer the critical questions of the moments! How much has the nation lost in terms of national income due to current privatization (sorry personalization) through the same serial waivers of payment of duties, tax holidays and pure assets stripping called public sales? Why the preference for foreign owners at less than market value? Rip offs done by state enterprises or private companies are rip offs! It is therefore not one or the other. I agree that some privately run cement factories are in production but what of privatized others that are under lock and keys? Few privatized companies that are working, what is their level efficiency? What is the level of their labour absorption? How many workers are they employing compared to pre-privatization era? How many jobs are destroyed, how many created? What is the level of competitiveness? Have we not replaced old public monopolies with private monopolies profiting from generalized chaos called competition as we are witnessing with airlines industry in which fare increases are in proportions with service arrogance and many at times service non-delivery? *Please what we need is policy balance and not policy dogma.* Let us follow agreeable national development agenda not "the books" of privatization according to the unaccountable sundry DGs of BPEs who at the recently concluded Senate Committee hearings make case shamelessly more for private owners and grabbers of public patrimony alike rather than rising to address legitimate public concerns from which they earn their pay. Judging by the self-denials and lack of acceptance of basic responsibilities by the former and current DGs of BPE it will be right to conclude that BPE itself has been privatized, (sorry personalized) regrettably and sadly too without public bidding! By the way how much does BPE worth in the market?

Reading the News ("oil subsidy" removal)*

Last Thursday (6th of October) in Abuja governors of Nigeria's 36 states at the National Economic Council, NEC, meeting reportedly backed the recent move by President Goodluck Jonathan to remove the controversial subsidy on petroleum products. Three days earlier, President Goodluck Jonathan reportedly forwarded to the Senate "a 2012-2015 medium-term Fiscal framework, MTFF and 2012 Fiscal Strategy Paper, FSP, with plans to begin the withdrawal of fuel subsidy from next year." President Jonathan reportedly stated:

> "A major component of the policy of fiscal consolidation is Government's intent to phase out the fuel subsidy beginning from the 2012 fiscal year. This will free up about N1.2 trillion in savings, part of which can be deployed into providing safety nets for poor segments of the society to ameliorate the effects of the subsidy removal."

First is the timing. A proposed over 100 per cent fuel price increase from January 1st 2012 can certainly not be a Presidential idea of a New Year gift for Nigerians. Certainly, not from the President who just barely last year promised all Nigerians a radical departure (a transformation agenda) from the existing mass misery. At 51st independence speech the President opened up with exhortation of Nigerians. Witness him:

> "I value all Nigerians. I see our youth who are looking for jobs and yet remain hopeful. I see the farmer, and fisherman, toiling everyday to earn a living. I see the teacher, working hard, to train our future

---

* *Daily Trust*, October 10, 2011

generations, with much sacrifice. I see the market women whose entrepreneurial spirit helps to generate income for their children and families."

Are these presidential alluring words from the heart of the President or disinterested business-as-usual pens of speech writers? Has the President reflected on the impact assessment of the proposed "subsidy removal" on millions of famers, fishermen, market women, he "values" so much? Secondly some observers drew my attention to the fact that the whole council of States which reportedly backed the President's proposal is indeed an unofficial definition of subsidy. All governors that attended that meeting travelled subsided either by air or by roads. Governance is actually a euphemism for subsidy, *ad-infinitum*, subsidized wives, subsidized children, subsidized aides, subsidized holidays, subsidized housing. Indeed the President and governors are tax free subjects in a country ostensibly looking for more revenue. So subsidy, however defined might not be bad after all, since all governors live on subsidy anyway? Must those demanding for equity not come with cleaner hands for once? Talking about equity and clean hands, the governors have rightly ganged up to oppose the so-called Sovereign Wealth Fund being proposed by the Federal government on the ground that it is unconstitutional. Pray what is constitutional with serial petroleum price increases which fuel inflation and costs of living and production? The fundamental objectives of state policy in 1999 constitution actually call for policies that must promote public welfare; "subsidy removal" violates that singular welfare spirit of the constitution. The Minister of Finance and Co-ordinator of the Economic Management Team, Dr. Ngozi Okonjo-Iweala, reportedly could not prevail on the governors to drop their decision to scrap the National Sovereign Wealth Fund, SWF, on the legitimate ground that the Federal government could not manage public funds for them in trust. How on earth can Nigerians have trust in the capacity of both the federal government and states to further manage additional so called (certainly unverifiable!) N1.2 trillion oil subsidy? Nine months into the fiscal year, the Minister of Finance, Dr Ngozi Okonjo-Iweala, last month stated that there was no record of implementation as far as the N4.6 trillion 2011 budget was concerned. Why additional ₦1.3 trillion to those who cannot account for whopping ₦4.6 trillions? Economic and Financial Crimes Commission (EFCC) just arrested three former governors over alleged fraud totalling almost ₦100 billion; Daniel (N58billion), Alao-Akala, (₦25 billion); and Doma, (₦18 billion). What trust can we have in some governors with additional freed funds when they have allegedly mismanaged previous public funds or when they can simply bolt away like Goje of Gombe to face up to simple challenge of accountability? Chairman of the Governors' Forum and Rivers State Governor, Rotimi Amaechi, had been hard put arguing that the said removal of the subsidy was long over-due, as the subsidy had only enriched very few Nigerians. Who on earth will the removal of subsidy enrich, 70 per cent living below poverty line? It's time we had a new development paradigm with new policy initiative. It is actually Nigerians that are subsidizing the government who indeed for now need a refund in terms of social security and rebates on public goods. Nigerians subsidize the government by providing boreholes and wells in the absence of public water supply. Nigerians buy generators and diesel in the absence of electricity supply. Nigerians provide for private security in the absence public security. Please let nobody mistake Nigerians' blood for oil subsidy that certainly is not yet proven to be there.

Not yet the End of History[*]

Last week of September Francis Fukuyama, a Stanford University professor and celebrated author of *The End of History* and *The Last Man* (a 1992 book, an expanded 1989 essay *"The End of History?"*) came to town. Precisely Abuja. Many thanks to Muregi Associates, an Abuja-based management, banking and financial consultancy services firm headed by my good friend and brother (in this *not-as-profitable* business of contest of ideas) Dr. Hussaini I. Mohammed. The forum was an international conference with the theme Development from Global Perspectives: Oil and Gas. It was a day like a decade at the prestigious Yar'Adua Centre, judging by the quantity and quality of historic development ideas canvassed covering critical success areas like Agriculture, oil and gas, corporate and national governance. Contract and exhibition of policy ideas in Abuja? That was quite novel and refreshing in the capital city notorious for weekly roads contracts approvals (executed more in the breach) by Federal Executive Council. A day's thoughts-for-food for once gave the capital city some face lift. It was interesting seeing eminent scholars in a city daily suffocated by combined forces of contractors, politicians, bankers, influence peddlers, assembly members and of course ghosts of Boko Haram as well as their partners in elusive search; police and the soldiers. Apart from Francis Fukuyama eminent scholars on parade included Professor Bob E. Osaze, the chairman of the occasion Professor Ibrahim Gambari, a former University Don, Ex-Foreign Affairs Minister and a Diplomat par excellence from the United Nations headquarters credited for the historic shuttle diplomacy that among others successfully led to the

---

[*] October 17, 2011

221

release of Pro-Democracy leader Ms. Aung San Suu Kyi (ASSK) from the military junta in Burma. The star guests were the former Head of State, Federal Republic of Nigeria General Muhammadu Buhari (Rtd) GCON and Chief Audu Ogbeh. General Buhari, just more like Audu Ogbeh, sounded professorial with his off cuff remarks from the heart, critical review of Fakuyama's 35 power points slides on *Corruption, Governance and Development.* The Guest lecturer, the renowned Japanese-American political economist, Professor Francis Fukuyama, is indeed an author of many books. However, *End of History and the Last Man* captured global imagination. By the way many thanks to Muregi Associates, for giving yours sincerely an opportunity to autograph my copy bought in late 1990s. The book's provocative thesis holds that after the deafening collapse of the former Soviet Union, what we in "the end point of mankind's ideological evolution and the universalization of Western liberal democracy as the final form of human government." For a day intellectual interactive session, time was a scarce commodity. It would have been excited to ask Fakuyama; what happened to his thesis is the light of the current universalization of global terrorism (its notable stars paradoxically invented in the West from Bin Laden to-you-know-them-all)? Can we talk of *an end of history* after even recent deafening *fall and fall* of global market capitalism and the attendant feverish resurgence of the state (note: state!) through intervention bail outs and unplanned budgets (a kind of bare-face "financial socialism" (socialism nonetheless for the money and capital market)? Whence the end of history when raw corporative class power, state connections and social relationships (and not necessarily the market) govern our new world as much as the old world under communism? Worldwide both the Wall streets and Main streets of global financial capitals are collapsing into one street of legitimate mass anger and protest against insiders' dealings, greed and plain money robbery thanks to Occupy protests of mass of peoples. Contrary to Fakuyama's prophesy, we might very well be witnessing the beginning of history rather than the end of history.

Talking of history, Francis Fakuyama was hunted by the spectre of history even down to Abuja. His 35 power-point slides about Nigeria amount to a rather simplistic narrative of developmental woes. Professor Ibrahim Gambari rightly problematized the Nigeria's poverty statistics better. It might very well be true that as many as 70.2 per cent of Nigeria's 150 million population lived below the poverty line compared to 17.2% in Indonesia in 2003. Professor Gambari rightly observed that within Nigeria poverty discourse was not as simplistic as Fakuyama repeated the old mantra of 70 per cent misery. He noted that there is poverty and there is poverty with some states out of 36 states of the federation necked deep than others. Yours truly holds that poverty statistics of the majority bellow the line does not even explain the wealth a nation. *We must consider the prosperity of the few above the poverty line before you can understand the poverty of many bellow the line.* Nigeria with well over 100 million poor, for instance produces, reportedly, the sixth richest man on earth. Nigeria is also fast growing country of few owning private jets and scandalously inclusive of religious clerics while their faithful climb Okada (commercial bikes!) after the alluring sermons. Poverty statistics at best say the obvious; *that the poor are poor* but at worse conceal the *obvious*; that *the rich are having more than they need*. Why should 70 per cent live on less than a dollar per day when the remaining 20 per cent (or better still), 5 per cent live on triple digits? Millions live on miserable minimum wages that are not paid and pitiable micro-loan while few thrive on non-performing huge loans. *We unfairly hold the poor responsible for their poverty while the real challenge lies on how to reverse the greed of the few.* Fakuyama's preference for binary discourse in terms of state versus-the market/ institutions versus the /persons, resources/policies is not helpful at all. Many thanks to General (sorry professor) Buhari for pointing out; strong institutions also need strong persons. Professor Gambari also made the point all the day that oil like any other resource is inherently not a curse, (as the new fad has it). The real curse is poor governance.

Between bankrupt states and Sovereign Wealth[*]

'States are not bankrupt, but...have no money!' And that is official! So, declared the chairman of the Nigeria Governors Forum (NGF) Chairman Chibuike Rotimi Amaechi, during the week. It is left for your imagination to discern between non-bankruptcy and running out of cash. Bankruptcy is a concept often associated with money, capital and industrial markets, not necessarily governance. Governor Amaechi may therefore be excused for making bankruptcy and lack of money as issues that are mutually exclusive. But that does not deny what bankruptcy is or what is not. For record purpose bankruptcy is an exit device for debtors who fail to meet debts obligations because of lack of money. One visible feature of bankruptcy is obviously lack of money. *Many states may not be under receiverships or bankrupt but they are actually indebted in trillions of Naira; both domestic and external debts.* And until there was a rule of deductions at source of federal allocations, scores of states were literarily bankrupt awaiting receiverships if they were corporate enterprises. According to the Debt Management Office (DMO), the 36 states of the Federation and the Federal Capital Territory (FCT) owed about $2.22billion (N333.05billion) in external debts as at June, 2011, almost half of national debt building up so soon after the much celebrated debt exit of 2003. The debt stock is party-blind. Indeed it is a kind of bi-partisan indebtedness. Lagos leads with external debt of $460.742 million, representing 8.54% of the nation's external debt; Kaduna State owes $175.433 million, representing 3.25%, Cross River, owes $124.022 million, representing 2.30% of the nation's external debt, and third leading

---

[*] October 31, 2011

debtor state. The debt profile of some other states are as follows: Abia State, $34.048 million, Adamawa State; $29.45 million, Akwa Ibom ($70.56 million); Anambra ($23.722 million); Bauchi ($58.8 million); Bayelsa ($28.77 million); Benue ($25.016 million); Borno ($14.036 million); Delta ($17.63 million); Ebonyi ($42.149 million); Edo ($46.92 million); Ekiti ($36.201 million); Enugu ($41.66 million); Gombe ($27.96 million); Imo ($52.32 million). In the period under review, Jigawa State's external debt was $29.120 million; Kano ($63.94 million); Katsina ($78.75 million); Kebbi ($51.644 million); Kogi ($36.203 million); Kwara ($48.557 million); Nasarawa ($41.35 million); Niger ($27.438 million); Ogun ($91.902 million); Ondo ($60.794 million); Osun ($65.332 million); Oyo ($93.990 million); Plateau ($26.974 million); Rivers ($36.501 million); Sokoto ($41.206 million); Taraba ($21.111 million); Yobe ($31.690 million); Zamfara ($27.186 million) and FCT ($37.664 million). DMO added that "these figures exclude arrears that only become obvious by the end of the year." Again if we weigh the debt burden of the states with their monthly Federal allocations, your guess is as good as mine as to if the states are bankrupt or not. Whatever the case might be, the truth may very well be in what Governor Amaechi did not say. He certainly did not say the states are viable or prosperous. Many thanks to the Governor of the Central Bank of Nigeria (CBN), Sanusi Lamido Sanusi who during the weekend improved on the narrative on the states. According to Sanusi, "the present political structures of Nigeria are too cumbersome and economically wasteful to guarantee rapid development of the country". On the occasion of the presentation of Professor Adamu Baike's book, *Against All Odds,* in Kaduna he reportedly and pointedly too asked the critical question; "do we need 36 States? That must be one singular question *against all odds.* Answer to Sanusi's critical question must come from all the communities that are still clamouring for creation of more states. Or, better still, we must ask the scores of candidates lining up for gubernatorial elections due next year in Bayelsa, Kogi and Adamawa states. Desperate candidates, for debtor-states that "have no money"! It is time we thought aloud outside the box of the narrative on the state as promoted by the state chieftains themselves. Governor Amaechi has eloquently made a case for a review of revenue formula in favour of the states. And that is the real problem. The impression is that the problem of the states is more money and that this money must come from revenue allocation (read; oil money). Of course the states need more monies and legitimately too from oil sovereign money. But there must also be full disclosures about the existing pattern of state resource allocations before we know what is bankrupting the states or why the governors have "no money". The CBN governor said states spend as much as 70 per cent paying salaries. What then about that? Workers pay taxes as they earn and the remaining sums are spent in the states on rents and food and diesel debts (since the pay does not meet basic needs anyway?) It is wrong to add the pay of thousands of non- value adding political appointees as over heads costs. What other projects do governors spend on that fuel the current indebtedness and possibly bankrupt them?

Rivers State Government was just reported to have concluded plans to "buy a helicopter at the cost of thirty million US dollars which is equivalent to about four billion, eight hundred million naira". If Rivers state is one of the states that "have no money" but could buy a "helicopter"" that "has a camera" at four billion naira, ostensibly to catch armed robbers, pray what would Rivers with money buy; launch satellites for aerial security surveillance across the state? Also in similar vein, Plateau State Government had reportedly "signed a N4.4billion contract for the construction of a new government house"". With billions of Naira casually thrown at non-critical mass of needs of impoverished peoples of the sates who on earth can disagree with Governor Amaechi that the states are not bankrupt but they "have no money"? Yours truly supports the governors in their protestation against what they dubbed 'illegal deductions' from the Federation Account by the Federal government. But have some of the governors for once pondered over the legality and above all, the morality and class character of some of their resource allocations?

BOI at 10 - Re-industrializing the country[*]

Last week, Bank of Industry (BOI) carried out a number of activities to mark ten years of its restructured existence. The high point of the anniversary activities included the official opening of its office buildings in Abuja and Lagos. The Abuja Corporate Headquarters of the Bank was on Thursday 22nd of December commissioned by President Goodluck E. Jonathan. Abuja commissioning coincided with a similar launch of the re-modelled head office in the commercial capital of Lagos.

Certainly the Bank is much older than its repositioned status date. BOI was reconstructed in 2001 out of the moribund Nigerian Industrial Development Bank (NIDB) Limited. NIDB was incorporated in 1964. It was part of the developmentalist Nigeria's financial architecture of post independent Nigeria. When the history of Nigeria's remarkable success story of the first two decades after independence is written, the role of old NIDB (with all its corporate governance fallings), through long term cheaper funding for industrial development must occupy a special chapter. It is right to say that BOI "is Nigeria's oldest, largest and most successful development financing institution". Its authorized share capital was initially set at N50 billion, but in the wake of NIDB's restructuring into the current BOI in 2001, it has been increased to N250 billion to reposition the bank "to address the nation's rising economic profile in line with its mandate." Following a successful institutional, operational and financial restructuring programme embarked upon in 2002, the bank "has transformed into an efficient, focused and profitable institution well placed to effectively carry out its primary mandate of providing long term financing to the industrial sector of the Nigerian economy". The strength of BOI is its activist corporate governance under the dynamic leadership of Ms Evelyn N. Oputu, the managing director and Alhaji Abdulsamad Rabiu, Chairman, as well as upbeat Executive Directors like Mr. Mohammed G. Alkali and Mr. Chris. C. Umeh. With its formidable corporate team, BOI is truly re-industrializing the country just as the old NIDB industrialized hitherto agrarian Nigeria economy emerging from British colonial underdevelopment. In 2007 the then Kaduna state deputy Governor, His Mr Patrick Yakowa broke the industrial obituary news of the sudden demise of *the largest textile mill in West Africa; United Nigeria Textile Company (UNTL)* in Kaduna, a company with billions of naira investment and thousands of employees. Many thanks to the resolve of the Vice President, Arc Namadi Sambo, President Goodluck Jonathan's administration finally endorsed the intervention fund under the cotton/textile revival plan. The new deal supervised by Vice President Namadi Sambo is to revolutionize funding for the real sector and breadth life into the ailing industries. The deal worked out by the CBN and BOI covers lending and re-refinancing of projects, restructuring of existing portfolios to manufacturers and support for investment in industrial clusters power supply. The sudden "resurrection" (as it were), of UNT Plc. last year, after three years of closure (with close to 1,500 direct jobs currently) is premised on the realization of this cocktail of measures pushed by BOI, CBN and government. *It can therefore be said that BOI in line with its motto; is "transforming Nigeria's industrial sector."*

At the anniversary commissioning, Evenly Oputu, the Bank's MD disclosed that in the last 10 years of its operations the Bank has approved 1,435 loans and investment totalling N165.74billion with considerable development impact on the Nigeria economy. According to her:

> "It is gratifying to note that in the last ten year BoI despite challenging environment, recorded appreciable stride in pursuit of its mandate and its evolution into a strong, dynamic and flexible development finance institution, DFI that proactively responds to the needs of entrepreneurs in Nigeria."

These achievements are indeed significant in a decade. But they all add up to a drop in the sea of industrial needs of Nigeria. With industry and manufacturing contributing miserably less than 4 per cent to the country's GDP and with paucity of long term funding as one of the critical success factors, there is need to further elevate the BOI beyond ordinary. *Jonathan's transformation agenda comes to grief without re-industrialization and after power supply (electricity) the most critical issue in re-indurtialization is long term cheaper financing.* The advantages of re- industrialization for Nigeria include lessening of dependency on imports, thus saving scarce foreign exchange. Where the economy is diversified, industrialization serves as a source of foreign exchange. It also serves as a source of mass sustainable decent employment for greater number of the population and invariably reduces income poverty. It is therefore refreshing that at the commissioning of BOI's corporate headquarters, apparently determined to promote and fund Nigeria's industrial sector, President Goodluck Jonathan rightly ordered the recapitalization of the Bank of Industry and directed that its equity be opened up to attract investors. The President reportedly directed the Minister of Finance, Ngozi Okonjo-Iweala and the Central Bank of Nigeria, CBN Governor Sanusi Lamido Sanusi to meet with the Minister of Trade and Investment, Olusegun Aganga with a view to coming up with modalities which would enable federal government increase the capital base of Bank of Industry. The sustainability of the reopened UNTL Kaduna for instance, and further reopening of others depends on the continuous commitment of governments through adequate funding of development banking institutions like BOI which of course must be complemented with other supportive and progressive policies such as drastic reduction in the incidence of smuggling. The challenge is to make sure that Bank of Industry (BOI) is sufficiently financed to make cheaper funds available to industries that are willing to modernize with clear cut performance criteria that include labour absorption and job retention. National Assembly must therefore appropriate more funds for the Bank. The existing commercial banks' short term funds with high interest rates make industry non-competitive. UNIDO has shown that high cost of borrowing in Nigeria increases working capital costs compared to other countries and that this is a major international cost disadvantage for producers in Nigeria.

What a New Year's gift?*

Yesterday being the New-Year day, my phone's in-box was filled with profound best wishes from Nigerians of all persuasions. None of these best wishes, included continuous power outages wish and new fuel price increase reportedly announced yesterday in the new-year. President Jonathan's 2012 message ends with the "best wish" to all Nigerians in the New Year celebrations. The reported news that the *"federal government has finally removed fuel subsidy"* reportedly making a litre of petrol, Premium Motor Spirit, PMS, to sell for N141 is therefore clearly anything but "best" wish for Nigeria and Nigerians in the new year. Any price increase is bad enough. But over 100 per cent increase of the price of petrol (an inelastic product for which there is no substitute for now in Nigeria) is one price increase clearly not meant to promote prosperity of the mass of Nigerians in the new year. *On the contrary, year 2012 with prohibitive increase in petrol price promises to further entrench despair and hopelessness the President sermonizes against in his new year address.* It is even worse and unacceptable Petroleum that the new product price dictation reportedly comes from Products Pricing Regulatory Agency (PPPRA) yesterday. A statement credited to PPPRA reads:

> " Following extensive consultation with stakeholders across the nation, the Petroleum Products Pricing Regulatory Agency (PPPRA) wishes to inform all stakeholders of the commencement of formal removal of subsidy on Premium Motor Spirit (PMS), in accordance with the powers conferred on the agency by the law establishing it, in compliance with Section 7 of PPPRA Act, 2004. "By this announcement, the downstream sub-sector of the petroleum industry

---

* January 2, 2012

is hereby deregulated for PMS. Service providers in the sector are now to procure products and sell same in accordance with the indicative benchmark price to be published fortnightly and posted on the PPPRA website. Petroleum products marketers are to note that no one will be paid subsidy on PMS discharges after 1st January 2012.

"Consumers are assured of adequate supply of quality products at prices that are competitive and non-exploitative and so there is no need for anyone to engage in panic buying or product hoarding.

The PPPRA in conjunction with the Department of Petroleum Resources (DPR) will ensure that consumers are not taken advantage of in any form or in any way.

"The DPR will ensure that the interest of the consumer in terms of quality of products is guaranteed at all times and in line with international best practice. In the coming weeks, the PPPRA will engage stakeholders in further consultation to ensure the continuation of this exercise in a hitch-free manner."

If this statement is true, then President Jonathan has further engendered the crisis of confidence and trust in governance. For one, a far reaching policy measure such as removal of petroleum subsidy cannot be so casually delegated to a discredited agency like PPPRA which is part of the chain of distortions of the price of imported product over the years. The President and notable members of his economic team have of late been visible discussing inconclusively with notable stake holders the issue of subsidy removal. It is therefore wrong to hijack the process of policy dialogue through a crude price dictatorship by PPPRA. Secondly there is a subsisting agreement, between the Nigeria Labour Congress (NLC) and the Federal government that legitimizes the product price at N65 per litre. Any arbitrary price increase that will fuel price riot and inflation remains arbitrary that must be resisted by Nigerians. President has just announced a bold emergency measures to curb the spate of violence in some parts of the country. Better late than never; what is clear is that these measures have raised the hope that the President is posed to guarantee physical security of lives and property. But these efforts come to naught if they are further undermined with economic insecurity measures such as prohibitive petro price increase.

UN, MDGs and Fuel Subsidy Removal*

Reportedly United Nations, UN has commended President Jonathan for withdrawing the subsidy on petroleum products, describing it as "a bold and correct policy". Speaking during a visit to President Jonathan at the State House, Abuja, the Special Adviser to the United Nations' Secretary General, Professor Jeffrey Sachs, was reported to have said the funds from the removal of subsidy would go a long way to rapid infrastructural development and the health sector. Also Sachs reportedly commended Nigeria's president for his conditional grants to local governments for the implementation of the Millennium Development Goals, describing it as "one of the most innovative schemes of using national resources for local government development." Really? Fuel price hike is a "bold and correct policy" according to the UN! Ordinarily the comment of Under Secretary Sachs should have been ignored as an unnecessary comic relief for a troubled UN looking for an escape from numerous challenges facing it with respect to its primary mandate of global peace keeping. With nuclear proliferation, senseless wars of attritions all over the world under its miserable watch, decimation of its member-states (witness Sudan) foreign imposed regime changes, observers rightly reason that the UN has enough preoccupation beyond petty meddlesomeness in petroleum product pricing in Nigeria. Of what relevance then is UN's reported support for fuel subsidy removal? For one the message is as significant as the messenger. First the message; that prohibitive fuel price increases occasioned by sudden withdrawal of subsidy on petroleum product would help the country meet the MDGs is the most unacceptable global official lip service to meeting the

---

*January 9, 2012

233

Millennium Development Goals (MDGS) in recent times. It would be recalled that the turn of the new Millennium offered another opportunity for Heads of Government and States to revisit the issue of development and underdevelopment. It was rightly observed that the dramatic growth and development of the twentieth century had not translated into prosperity for many but in many instance had entrenched poverty among many. In recognition of this fact, an unprecedented gathering of 189 Heads of States and Governments (including Nigeria's government) in 2000, signed on to a Millennium Declaration. The historic declaration was aimed at eradicating poverty, promoting human dignity, achieving peace, democracy and environmental sustainability in the twenty-first century. The Declaration enunciated critical eight Millennium Development Goals, 18 targets and 48 indicators that establish time bound targets for advancing human development. They are as follows:

Goal 1- eradicate extreme poverty and hunger by half in 15 years to the new century. Extreme poverty affects the proportion of the population that lives below a US$ per day;

Goal 2- achieve universal primary education- every child regardless of gender must complete full course of primary schooling;

Goal 3- promote gender equality and empower women- eliminate gender inequality in primary and secondary education by 2005 and to all levels of education by 2015;

Goal 4- reduce child mortality by two third between 1990 and 2015.

Goal 5- improve maternity health by reducing maternity mortality rate by two third between 1990 and 2015;

Goal 6 - combat HIV/AIDS, malarial and other diseases;

Goal 7- ensure environmental sustainability;

Goal 8- develop a global partnership for development.

The agenda set in 2000 was reviewed in 2005 and it was self-evident that many African countries, including Nigeria were far from attaining the goals. The incessant increases in the prices of petroleum products, as favoured by deregulation of downstream petroleum sector, impact negatively on poverty eradication which is the first of the MDGs no thanks to price inflation that erodes wage incomes in particular. Similarly high prices of kerosene make rural dwellers to cut down trees for energy, thus leading to de-forestation which undermines Goal 7 of the Millennium Declaration dealing with sustainable development. So what then is Sachs up to? Working towards the realisation of the goals or uncritically supporting policies that undermine national efforts to meet the goal?

Secondly is the messenger. Jeffery Sachs is not just an under-secretary of UN but also a famous development scholar who came to limelight with his passion for poverty eradication. He is the celebrated author of the best seller, *The End of Poverty*, how we can make it happen in our lifetime. He once argued that unequal global economic development occasioned particularly by the abysmal failure of Structural adjustment programme as recommended by IMF and World Bank in Africa called for re-theorizing of development with a view of solving the problems of the places where economic development is not working, where people are still off the ladder of development or are stuck on its lowest rungs. Happily President Jonathan has come to realise that contrary to UN claim this policy is far from being bold and correct. Thanks to the citizens who are protesting against unprecedented increase in prices of a product for which there is no meaningful substitute for. Indeed this policy is imposing more pain on the citizens and may take us away from meeting the MDGs. The bold measures Nigerians want must be the drastic cut in costs of governance (without value addition). Ironically the 25 per cent cut in executive pay (what of the legislative pay?) is nothing compared to 160 per cent in increase in price of petroleum products, a singular critical failure factor in worsening poverty since mid-eighties in Nigeria.

Nigerian Dangote changes the narrative[*]

Thursday, wholly Nigerian manufacturing Dangote group opened a one-billion-dollar cement plant at Ibese a hitherto wasteland of a century long reserve of lime stones and red soil in the bush of Ogun state. The commissioned plant is the largest of such in sub-Sahara Africa. There are two line plants of 3 million metric tons of cement per annum making Ibese to be 6 million metric tons per annum. With additional two lines in the works, its capacity increases to 12 million tonnes per year. *Last week's singular historic commission of the biggest cement plant in Africa, by Dangote group radically changed for better the recent orchestrated local and global Nigeria's magnified dubious story of despair and failure into a remarkable and commendable narrative of investment, hope and limitless opportunities.* It was indeed a week of contrasts. The very week Ibese plant opened, a so-called National Summit Group opened at the Sheraton 5-star hotel in Ikeja, Lagos. It was attended by notables (former Ministers, governors, Secretary to Federations, Senior Advocates, advisers, failed politicians, etc.) who without the Federal Republic of Nigeria, would not have been known anyway. Interestingly, the main agenda was not to add value to the Federal Republic that tossed them up from nowhere. On the contrary the preoccupation of the conveners was to increase the noise level of what the late Dr Bala Usman rightly dubbed a *"Campaign Against Nigeria"* by *"calling into the very basis of its corporate existence"*. The boring mantra of the need for Nigeria as a multi ethnic and religious society, to "sit and negotiate its status of existence as a nation," through a Sovereign National Conference, is too familiar as it is too silly to comprehend. But the old familiar tune nearly died down when Alhaji

---

[*] *Daily Trust*, February 13, 2012

Aliko Dangote chose to consolidate and deepen the Federation through massive investment, employment generation, national integration and community development that the Ibese plant commissioning represented. While the summiteers saw Nigeria as a debating society with their usual *talking* the talk (always from a 5-star hotel) about "true federalism" (as if there is a false Federalism) Dangote group from a remote village of Ibese saw Nigeria as a productive economy that must be self-sufficient in cement production by 2014. The chieftain of the national Summit and a former Presidential aspirant under the Social Democratic Mega Party (SDMP); Professor Pat Utomi from the rooftop proclaimed (like one American Professor John Campbell) that "the nation was on the precipice as it was in the 1960s-when the military took over the government.", Dangote group president, Aliko Dangote in contrast enthusiastically declared that: "With the commissioning of the Ibese plant, Nigeria has been transformed from major importer of cement to self-sufficient in production and export." Aliko added that: "We are working towards making the company one of the eight biggest producers of cement in the world."

At the inauguration President Jonathan commended the chairman of the Group, Alhaji Aliko Dangote, for his commitment to the industrialization of the country and for providing employment opportunities for people.

As guest at this historic commissioning, I bear witness to Nigerian renewed enterprise and reindustrialization of Nigeria with the potential of making the country a major exporter of cement and creation of direct 7,000 jobs for Nigerians. I also bear witness to import substitution in place of imports and dumping of cement. With the commissioning, the total capacity of Dangote Cement's is 20.25 million metric tonnes of cement per year. The Obajana cement (also driven by Dangote) has an installed capacity of 10.25 million metric tonnes per year, while Gboko plant currently produces four million metric tonnes. At a time there is abysmal dearth of national ambition, at Ibese I bear witness to amazing unprecedented corporate ambition. Aliko Dangote, president of Dangote Group, disclosed that with the plant commissioning; "We are marking the closing ceremony of cement import in Nigeria with the coming on stream of our he said, just before the final commissioning. Our long term ambition is to develop 46 million metric tonnes of production and terminal capacity in Africa by 2015. We want to become a truly pan-African champion in the sector, capable of competing globally with the largest cement companies in the world." At a time Nigeria and Nigerians are unacceptably getting insular running to their villages without asking what is chasing them, it is a refreshing story from Dangote about pan Nigeria and pan African investment that gives economic content to Nkrumah's political vision of United States of Africa well before Europeans conceived European Union. The cement business of Dangote Group not only generated revenues of $3billion in 2010 but has spread beyond the confines of Nigeria, to other African countries, including Benin, Cameroon, Cote d'Ivoire, the DRC, Ethiopia, Gabon, Ghana, Liberia, Senegal, Sierra Leone, South Africa, Tanzania and Zambia. The point cannot be overstated; industrialization delineates between growth and development of nations. The advantages of industrialization include lessening of dependency on imports, thus saving scarce foreign exchange. Where the economy is diversified, industrialization serves as a source of foreign exchange. It also serves as a source of employment for greater number of the population and invariably reduces income poverty. It gratifying to know that Nigeria is not only oil and gas rich but cement rich, thanks to government policy of backward integration and Aliko Dangote's bold and patriotic enterprise to take an advantage of a worthy policy. What is the role of manufacturing in the much talked about Vision 2020? Dangote group (a hitherto trading outpost) has shown that Nigeria, a country of 160 million can transform from a non-value adding, container-economy, exporting scarce jobs, importing everything plus unemployment to self-sufficiency in cements production and even export the surplus.

World Bank Presidency; Another Job or a Strategic Development Agenda?*

With the groundswell of national support for Dr. Ngozi Okonjo-Iweala for the presidency of the World Bank, an additional support of yours sincerely could turn out to be one support too predictably patriotic or nationally politically correct. And that is the real danger! Our preoccupation with undefined national concerns might very well make us lose focus of the real issues involved in the presidency or general operations of the World Bank. The most uninformed (and certainly unhelpful) so far is the support-message according to Abia State Governor, Chief Theodore Orji. In a statement issued by the governor's Press Secretary, Ugochukwu Emezue, Abia state governor devalued Iweala's bid to some kind of campaign for some affirmative action when he summed up the bid of the coordinating Minister of the Economy and the Finance Minister as her quest to become the "first female President of the World Bank". What has gender got to do with the presidency of International Bank for Reconstruction and Development (the original name of the World Bank) established in 1944, almost two decades before Nigeria got independence and some 40 years before the Beijing conference on women? For God's sake let us parade the globally acknowledged huge human capital (intelligence, experience, skills, passion, values and commitment) of Dr. Ngozi Okonjo-Iweala and not necessarily her gender. Even more unacceptable was the attempt to reduce the coordinating Minister, a globally renowned economist to a village-girl applicant seeking desperately for a job in Diaspora. Again witness Abia State governor; "all Abians at home and in the diaspora are solidly behind her, being

---

* *Daily Trust*, April 9, 2012

a worthy ambassador of Abia State...as a daughter of the state, this is the time to give her all the support she needs to succeed especially through prayers and other diplomatic means." This kind of local ownership (or is it privatization?) of Ngozi's candidature plays into bigger but equally intolerable American entitlement claim of the presidency of the World Bank. When parochialism squares to parochialism, old tested parochialism in this case US dated undemocratic version might prevail. Three notable former World Bank executives, namely Francois Bourguignon, Nicholas Stern and Joseph Stiglitz (Nobel prize winner) recently demanded that competition for World Bank presidency (long held by Americans since 1944) be made open and competitive. Narrative from Nigeria (assuming it matters at all since America still remains the leading controlling share nation) must also be seen and heard to be open and competitive, not as insular and parochial as that of the governor of Abia state. In any case once President Goodluck Jonathan had backed Iweala's bid, any state support is one support-overload that can weigh down the bid-lorry. But in all this global World Bank bid drama; what is the strategic interest of Nigeria and Nigerians? *Is it just another job for the already over employed Minister of Finance and coordinating Minister of the economy (and only herself alone!) or a move to advance the much trumpeted Transformation agenda of President Goodluck Jonathan?_* Not long ago we were inundated with some hysteria about the return of the very Okonjo-Iweala from the same World Bank to take up an expanded position as Coordinating Minister for the Economy and Minister of Finance in Nigerian President Goodluck Jonathan's new cabinet. The then World Bank President, Robert Zoellick, had said in a statement that; "Her desire to serve her country is truly a big loss for the World Bank but a major gain for Nigeria as it works to craft its economic way forward." What then suddenly happened to Ngozi's celebrated "desire to serve" her country when she so soon bids to return to Washington? Will her return not be a "big loss" to Nigeria and a "major gain" for World Bank? Whence then the patriotism in this global endeavour? President Jonathan was so up-beat while belatedly swearing in Minister Ngozi. The elated President made known what ordinarily should be meant for his memoirs; foreign Heads of state according to him patted him at the back for getting the former World Bank chieftain to his cabinet describing her acceptance of offer as a personal sacrifice not necessarily a national honour. Are we back again to personal ministerial carrier pursuit or national development agenda? Of what relevance is World Bank to Africa's development with or without an African as the Head? Both IMF and World Bank have been more notorious of late for Executive personal scandals than grand economic plans for global economic recovery. The Asian financial melt-down of the 90s and deafening financial global melt down of 2007 took place in spite of the two Brettons Wood institutions. The two institutions are themselves begging for reforms. We should therefore not make a cheap fetish of the presidency of the World Bank. As a student of labour market, serial appointments of Okonjo-Iweala in quick self-succession to the very same official position (some dynastic appointments without a royal entitlement) tasks imagination. First is her ease of labour market entry and labour market exit. For a country in which many jolly-citizens parade all the degrees, namely BA, BSC, PH.D but without the real thing; *jobs*, an over-employed Mrs Iweala (with job in waiting, jobs in deferment, job in bid) calls for a critical rethink of unemployment theories. What kind of labour market it is in which one person is so over employed while many are idle and even under employed? It is a scandal that with a country that showcases close to 50 per cent open unemployment, we are concentrating so much authoritative allocation of resources (power) in one woman, sorry, one unofficial prime applicant albeit with mouthful portfolio; coordinating Ministry of the economy. Mrs Iweala's priority promise of jobs, jobs, and jobs hits the nail on the head for a country of mass unemployment. However nobody will take her serious until she in the first instance sheds her current job-full portfolio overweight.

In defence of CBN's autonomy[*]

The Senate holds today a public hearing on a controversial bill to amend the Central Bank of Nigeria (CBN) Act of 2007. The bill has reportedly passed the second reading at the Senate and House of assembly. It aims at altering the current corporate governance structure of CBN from relative independence and autonomy in budgeting to some incoherently defined dependency and subservience on the national assembly. Twin issues of concern for the legislators are the composition of the Board membership as well as its budgeting process. The National Assembly reasons that the subsisting CBN Act allows the Board Chairman, who is the CBN Governor, "unfettered" powers to approve its budget without referring to the National Assembly. Hence the need to get him removed as chairman of the board, and (in his/her place bring) an outsider and possibly a politician as chairman. Legislators are also bent on removing Deputy Governors who are also executive directors of CBN as members of the board. The bill also seeks to divest the Board of the power to consider and approve the annual budget of the bank. The legislators are insisting that the Fiscal Responsibility Act of 2010 supersedes the CBN Act of 2007 in mandating the bank to submit its annual budget for national assembly approval. Sen. Enyinnaya Abaribe (PDP- Abia) who seconded the bill said "We have powers to make laws for the CBN. The CBN cannot on its own choose which law to obey."

The bill, according to its sponsors, would enhance transparency and entrench the principle of check and balances in the administration and operations of the Bank. CBN has since cried foul

---

[*] May 28, 2012

about the on-going legislative process aimed at undoing some of the clauses of the CBN Act. The apex bank holds that contrary to the impression that membership of the CBN board of directors is dominated by appointees from within the institution; members of its board are indeed appointees of the president and are confirmed by the very national assembly. It also insists on its right to independent budgeting as contained in the subsisting CBN Act; its accounts are duly audited by the Accountant General of the Federation (AGF). It also said it employs the services of two international reputable accounting firms in the preparation of the accounts.

The Director, Corporate Communications Department, Mr. Ugochukwu Okoroafor, said: "The financial year of the CBN ends on the 31st of December of each year and the audited annual accounts is usually ready in February in line with the provisions of Section 50 (1) of the CBN Act. No 7 of 2007." On the board composition, Okoroafor declared that: "Sections 6 (1) and (2) of the CBN Act 2007, provide for 12 members of the Board; five internal and seven external. The Governor and the four Deputy Governors comprise the internal membership. There are seven external non-executive members, among who are two institutional members. Consistent with the provisions of the CBN Act 2007, the non-executive members constitute a clear majority of the Board of the CBN. All members of the CBN Board are appointees of the President of the Federal Republic of Nigeria and are confirmed by the Senate," Devil is in the details of the arguments for or against the proposed bill to amend the CBN Act. But observers cannot make a dispassionate analysis until we weigh the detail arguments either for or against the proposed bill against certain basic principles of analysis. The bane of the current proposed legislative meltdown (note: not oversight function) of the CBN Act is the inability of the legislators to appreciate the principle of independence and autonomy of all institutions of state and indeed civil society in a democracy. It is a common knowledge that "central bank is an institution that manages a country's currency, money supply, and interest rates. It also regulates the operations of commercial banks and some other financial institutions.

Monetary policy goals of central banks include price stability, attainment of high employment rate, macroeconomic economic growth, exchange rate stability and maintenance of balance of payment equilibrium. The CBN's core mandate of ensuring a non-inflationary growth calls for high degree of independence.

We can certainly interrogate the quality of the autonomous power of the CBN under any of its governors but nobody including the legislators dare questions the principle of independence of CBN for the economy. The current legislative ambush of the CBN Act, through some feverish selective amendment of board membership and budgeting process clauses, amounts to a leap back to the discredited era of military dictatorship during which decree-overload became a substitute for robust policy debate. Many Nigerians including yours sincerely share different views about the ways and manners CBN had exercised its renewed autonomy since 2007. Some including the then Executive took exception to the instant Naira Re-Denomination policy of CBN in 2007. But the government never made a move for a vindictive legal assault on the Act legitimizing apex bank's autonomy. Many Nigerians hail the CBN's consolidation of banks as well as independent bail-out funds for some distressed banks that have protected depositors from the misery of banks' collapse. CBN's activist intervention funds for textile, agriculture and automobile subsectors have also added considerable value for an economy begging for recovery. All this positive development could not have been possible if the CBN waits for the ever acrimonious budgetary process of the national assembly or some politically correct Board of party card carrying members. Independence of CBN is consistent with global practices. Autonomy which is good for national assembly is even more desirable for a critical institution like CBN. We can disagree with specific policies of the Bank and even the styles of its Governors, but we dare not undermine the autonomy of the institution itself.

Crude oil theft or industry collapse?*

The latest buzzword in the dictionary of Nigeria's oil industry abysmal/deafening failure is crude oil theft. It is now an "oily" fashion (as it were) for visible government and corporate oil chieftains to impress on us all that crude oil theft is getting out of hand. The Shell Petroleum Development Company (SPDC) has particularly increased the noise level of the "worsening state of crude oil theft in Nigeria." According to Shell, Nigeria had been losing about $5 billion annually to the activities of illegal oil bunkerers operating in the oil fields located in the coastal parts of the country. An estimated 150,000 barrels of crude oil valued at $13.5 million is said to be stolen daily by the oil thieves believed to have links with some individuals in the country and an international oil cartel backed by some foreign countries. The managing director of SPDC and Chairman of the Shell Group in Nigeria, Mr. Mutiu Sumonu, reportedly told the opening of a three-day public hearing on the frightening rise of illegal oil bunkering activities in the Niger Delta region at the public hearing organised by the Joint Committees on Petroleum Resources (Upstream) and Navy in the House of Representatives. The incident of crude oil theft had degenerated from the occasional and haphazard operations of some local thieves to a well-coordinated syndicate of criminals who are prepared to do anything to obtain the ill-gotten crude oil he said. Witness him: "The scale of crude oil theft now is more than what the oil companies can handle. It is extremely pervasive now. If you over-fly the whole of our operational areas in the Niger Delta, you will see canoes, barges and illegal refineries all over the place." Also recently in Lagos the

---

* *Daily Trust*, July 2, 2012

Minister of Petroleum Resources, Mrs. Diezani Alison-Madueke, said the rising incidence of bunkering bordered on the security of the nation and the economy. In terms of losses, she said, "the country is losing approximately 180,000 barrels of oil equivalent daily at this time. Of course, to the nation, if you look at the international cost for a barrel, it will be estimated at $7billion yearly." The Minister of Finance, Dr Ngozi Okonjo-Iweala, further disclosed that Nigeria lost $14 billion in 2011 to both oil theft and fraud in the allocation of a controversial fuel subsidy.

In an interview with *Financial Times* of London, the Finance Minister said the trade in stolen oil led to a 17 per cent fall in official oil sales in April, or about 400,000 barrels per day. "We have to get very serious about the bunkering issue. If we can stop the amount that is stolen, we can beef up the excess crude account faster," she said. At the much discussed presidential media chat, President Goodluck Jonathan described Nigeria as the only country in the world where crude oil is stolen at an alarming rate. Pray with these serial identifications of the problem of the "cancer" of crude oil theft, whence the solutions to halt the criminality? The bane of Nigerian governance discourse in recent times is its paralysis by analyses. Our leaders are tall in academic identification of problems but miserably short in proffering doable solutions. Beyond saying the obvious that crude oil theft is mainly a Nigerian brand, perpetrated by "common criminals", the President has not proffered a "common" solution talk less of an uncommon radical presidential solution. True to her management style by Task Force, the oil Minister has just inaugurated a new industry joint task force, JTF, (comprising of the Police and the Armed Forces, in collaboration with the Ministry of Petroleum Resources, the Nigerian National Petroleum Corporation, NNPC, as well as multinationals and indigenous operators) ostensibly to stem the menace that is deepening by the day. Meanwhile the security agencies, namely (the Navy, Civil Defence Corps) are trading blames at the House public hearing while the oil thieves are united in closing the entire oil industry from the upstream. The danger of oil theft cannot be over emphasised. Nigeria became an oil producing nation in the 60s just with production of 5,000 barrels per day. A daily theft of 150,000 barrels not captured in our ever dubious national oil receipts means we have degenerated from being a promising oil producing nation to increasingly hopeless crude oil stealing nation! But the crude oil theft by those the President called "common criminals" is only a tip of the rot of the collapsing oil industry.

The entire petroleum industry has performed below expectations and not few hold that the sector is a failure. The industry is characterized by wastage, corruption, (recent $6 billion subsidy scam!) low productivity and unchecked dominance of foreign multinationals. Shell cries about crude oil theft but like all other oil companies, it is debatable if they all account properly for their own production also. Nigeria remains the weakest link within OPEC as her incessant pressures for oil export made her to exceed quota thus undermining world crude price. In terms of Nigerianization, know-how and upstream technology the initiative still remains with foreign multinationals while local content is abysmally low and in many areas the scandalous gas waste underscores the referred failure of upstream operation. Very little progress had been made in terms of technology for exploration and production activities remains valid today. Nigeria government is yet to move from 'income generating' to 'industry control', as government still remains passive tax collector while the oil companies predominate. In 2000 there was a scandalous discovery of twenty hidden oil wells by Engineer Hamman Tukur-led National Revenue Mobilisation Commission in which Nigeria reportedly lost as much as N280 billion to illegal operation by multinationals, underscoring a complete erosion of marginal government control of the upstream operation. May be we should be more worried about an uncommon total industry collapse (see Algeria, Saudi Arabia, Iran, Venezuela) than "common" oil theft by "common criminals".

Budgets for Beginners*

George W. Bush, Former American President humorously once said; "It's clearly a budget. It's got a lot of numbers in it." If we define national budgets as mere packs of some figures, Nigeria can certainly go for an Olympic medal for lot of figures that pass for national budgets. 2012 budget contains scores of figures. For one, it is a trillion naira budget 4.9 trillion naira, an increase of 6 per cent over that of 2011. Budget 2010 was 4.6 trillion naira. Indeed in the last decade Nigeria has been posting multiple digit budgets! Some figures in 2012 budgets include some N398 billions for statutory transfers, N2.47 trillion for recurrent expenditure, 1.32 trillion for capital expenditures and 1.560 billion for debt servicing! With this huge financial sum, Nigerians legitimately expect accelerated recovery of the Nigerian economy as a matter of necessity if we were to be consistent doctrine of necessity that enthroned President Goodluck Jonathan. Nigeria has been voting trillions Naira budgets in the past 10 years without any positive impact on the economy and public welfare.

Nigeria's budgets are always predicated on the same old parameters - oil production capacity (of 2.35 million barrels per day in 2010 compared to 2.48 million barrels per day in 2012) oil price benchmark (of $57 per barrel in 2010 compared to 70 dollars benchmark price for 2012) and an average exchange rate of N150 to the US dollar in 2010 compared to N155 to the US dollar in 2012. Inflation Rate was put at 9.5 % in 2012 compared to 11.2% in 2010 and Real GDP Growth at 6.1% in 2010 budget compared to 7.2 % growth rate in 2012.

---

* *Daily Trust,* August 6, 2012

Almost Nigeria' budgets are industry shy or better still industry blind! You hardly know the expected industrial capacity utilization that would drive the growth targets.

Unfortunately Nigerian budgets are silent on clear cut concrete economic parameters to measure the performance of the budgets such as the expected level of capacity utilisation, number of jobs to be created. After a decade of so much official rhetoric about economic diversification, Nigeria is still wholesale oil dependent. Whence then the promised escape from oil dependency and diversification of the economy? It is time we reversed the worsening unemployment situation due to mass factory closures.

Nigeria's budgets are the most "politicised" estimates of annual national expenditures and incomes with an eye on sharing, corruption as distinct from development in recent times. For once in 2010 since the commencement of the Fourth Republic, an ailing President did not perform the formality of personally laying the government's financial plan before the National Assembly. Also for the first time, the two chambers separately received the budgetary proposals from the Federal executive. Some equality in disunity for the two chambers! Ironically the two chambers expectedly were united in legislating a bloated padded increase of N600 billion (almost a trillion). In other words the two chambers received the estimates separately but they were united in bloating it up almost with unanimous Yes vote.

The recent controversy over the level of the per cent implementation of the 2012 budget is true to the politicisation of budget process in Nigeria with so much heat rather than real search light on how the budget impacts on development. Whether the budget is 15 per cent implemented, 20 per cent or even 100 per cent, the critical question is how many jobs have been created? What is the level of electricity supply? How many people have been taken out of poverty line? How many industries have been revived? The National Assembly should start asking correct questions while the executive should start giving the correct answers.

Still in defence of CBN's autonomy[*]

The House's Committee on Banking and Finance sets to go the road the relevant Senate Committee seemed to have discovered to be unhelpful and unpopular early in the year.

Today, there will be another public hearing on the controversial bill to amend the Central Bank of Nigeria (CBN) Act of 2007. The bill aims at altering the current corporate governance structure of CBN from relative independence and autonomy in budgeting to some incoherently defined dependency and subservience to the national assembly. Twin issues of concern for the legislators are the composition of the Board membership as well as its budgeting process. The National Assembly reasons that the subsisting CBN Act allows the Board Chairman, who is the CBN Governor, "unfettered" powers to approve its budget without referring to the National Assembly. Hence the need to get him removed as the chairman of the board, and (in his/her place bring) an outsider and possibly a politician as chairman. Legislators are also bent on removing Deputy Governors who are also executive directors of CBN as members of the board.

The bill also seeks to divest the Board of the power to consider and approve the annual budget of the bank. The legislators are insisting that the Fiscal Responsibility Act of 2010 supersedes the CBN Act of 2007 in mandating the bank to submit its annual budget for national assembly approval.

The bill, according to its sponsors, would enhance transparency and entrench the principle of check and balances in the administration and operations of the Bank. CBN has since cried foul

---

[*] *Daily Trust*, October 22nd, 2012

about the on-going legislative process aimed at undoing some of the clauses of the CBN Act. The apex bank holds that contrary to the impression that membership of the CBN board of directors is dominated by appointees from within the institution; members of its board are indeed appointees of the president and are confirmed by the very national assembly. It also insists on its right to independent budgeting as contained in the subsisting CBN Act; its accounts are duly audited by the Accountant General of the Federation (AGF). It also said it employs the services of two international reputable accounting firms in the preparation of the accounts.

CBN said:

> "The financial year of the CBN ends on the 31st of December of each year and the audited annual accounts is usually ready in February in line with the provisions of Section 50 (1) of the CBN Act. No 7 of 2007." On the board composition, "Sections 6 (1) and (2) of the CBN Act 2007, provide for 12 members of the Board; five internal and seven external. The Governor and the four Deputy Governors comprise the internal membership. There are seven external non-executive members, among who are two institutional members. Consistent with the provisions of the CBN Act 2007, the non-executive members constitute a clear majority of the Board of the CBN. All members of the CBN Board are appointees of the President of the Federal Republic of Nigeria and are confirmed by the Senate."

Devil is in the details of the arguments for or against the proposed bill to amend the CBN Act. But observers cannot make a dispassionate analysis until we weigh the detail arguments either for or against the proposed bill against certain basic principles of analysis. The recurring proposed legislative meltdown (note: not oversight function) of the CBN Act is clearly unhelpful. We must encourage and indeed help our legislators to appreciate the principle of independence and autonomy of all institutions of state and indeed civil society in a democracy. It is a common knowledge that central bank is an institution that manages a country's currency, money supply, and interest rates. It also regulates the operations of commercial banks and some other financial institutions.

Monetary policy goals of central banks include price stability, attainment of high employment rate, macroeconomic economic growth, exchange rate stability and maintenance of balance of payment equilibrium. The CBN's core mandate of ensuring a non-inflationary growth calls for high degree of independence. We can certainly interrogate the quality of monetary policies emanating from the autonomous power of the CBN under any of its governors. But we must not question the principle of independence of CBN for the economy, just as we must all rise up to defend the autonomy and independence of the legislature in a democracy. The current legislative ambush of the CBN Act through some feverish selective amendment of board membership and budgeting process clauses, amounts to a leap-back to the discredited era of military dictatorship during which decree-overload became a substitute for robust policy debate. It is encouraging that out of the scores of memoranda to the senate during its last public hearing on the controversial bill, none supported the proposed amendment.

On the contrary, all stakeholders upheld the principle of Central Bank Independence (CBI). Many Nigerians including yours sincerely share different views about the ways and manners CBN had exercised its renewed autonomy since 2007. Some including the then Executive took exception to the instant Naira Re-Denomination policy of CBN in 2007. Recently most Nigerians including yours truly took exception to the proposed controversial Naira redenomination of 2012. These policy contestations are healthy. But they are certainly not excuse for a legislative move for a vindictive legal assault on the Act that had long commendably legitimized the apex bank's autonomy. Many Nigerians hail the CBN's consolidation of banks as well as independent bail-out funds for some distressed banks that have protected depositors from the misery of banks' collapse.

CBN's activist intervention funds for textile, agriculture and automobile subsectors have also added considerable value for an economy begging for recovery. The recent regained strength of the value of the Naira to the dollar is also commendable. All this positive development could not have been possible if the CBN waits for the ever acrimonious budgetary process of the national assembly or some politically correct Board of party card carrying members. Independence of CBN is consistent with global practices. We can disagree with specific policies of the Bank and even the styles of its

Governors, but we dare not undermine the autonomy of the CBN itself.

Re-industrializing Nigeria[*]

Tomorrow, Tuesday 20th of November is "Africa Industrialization Day", a day set aside annually "to stimulate the international community's commitment to the industrialization of Africa." With 160 million population (potential industrial consumers indeed) a quarter of Africa's population and abundant minerals (being the primary raw materials for industrialization for a wide range of industries) re-industrializing Nigeria means re-industrializing the great continent of Africa. Iron ore and a host of other locally available metallurgical raw materials are globally utilized for the local iron and steel industry. Nigeria is endowed with these mineral resources in abundance.

The immediate past World Bank's Vice-President for Africa, Mrs. Oby Ezekwesili, recently did a gross national disservice to Nigeria's development and industrialization discourse. She was reported to have said that: "I am one of those Nigerians who are praying for Nigeria oil to dry up so that our government can quickly take immediate actions towards diversifying the nation's source of revenue. Alternative to oil should emerge immediately to cure the oil politics in our nation." It was unhelpful to give in to cheap despair because of gross mismanagement of oil revenue. In any case Mrs Oby could be rightly accused of being part of ruling elite perpetrating the resource curse tragedy. After all she had been given more than one chance to diversify the economy and clear the mono-economy mess as a former Minister, (the last portfolio being Mineral resources) and a member of high sounding economic team of Obasanjo's administration. The truth is that crude oil and natural gas are the

[*] *Daily Trust*, November 19th, 2012

basic for the petrochemical and fertilizer industries. There is inherently nothing bad with crude oil and gas or any other raw materials such as cotton. See how the Chinese are in raw material global hunt to propel their industrialization. On the contrary, with Nigeria's proven oil reserves estimated at 35.5 billion barrels, as at March 2011, and proven gas reserves estimated at 187 trillion Nigeria like Indonesia and Malaysia (oil producing nations too!) should be an industrialized country. The UK is an oil-producing nation, but oil revenue constitutes less than 2 per cent of its national income. UK does not pray that its oil dries up, rather it is delighted that it oils its economy with oil through value adding activities; i.e. *industrialisation.*

We should not lazily pray that oil and gas dry up (more so after few of us must have fortunately "oiled" ourselves up stairs up to the World Bank). What we must do is to ensure a developmentalist state led industrialisation process that must urgently fix the existing four refineries (Port Harcourt I and II, Warri, and Kaduna), build more refineries, raise the existing intolerable zero-combined capacity utilization, produce refined products and create jobs for the army of Nigeria's unemployed. Our prayer should be to halt the on-going criminal wholesale products importation with all the attendant criminal corruption and job exports. What is good for oil and gas (I.e. Value addition) is also good for textile, automobile, agriculture, iron and steel sectors, chemical and construction, etc.

The point cannot be overstated that Africa Industrialization Day is celebrated on November 20 each year. On this day, governments and other real sector organizations in many African countries examine ways to stimulate Africa's industrialization process. It is also an occasion to draw worldwide media attention to the problems and challenges of industrialization in Africa.

As part of the activities in Nigeria a select group of private sector trade unions from the textile, construction, agricultural, chemical and non-allied, steel and engineering, petroleum and natural gas, is organizing a series of activities to mark the 2012 edition with activities that include a Roundtable and Press Conference and Rally on Monday 19th November and on Tuesday 20th November 2012 in Abuja respectively.

The Abuja roundtable brings together policy makers from strategic Government institutions, members of Federal Executive, National Assembly, experts on policy investment and trade issues and selected private sector unions affiliated to the Nigeria Labour Congress (NLC) and the TUC. Significantly too this round table provides the appropriate platform to present the draft report of a study carried out by the group with the support of Friedrich Ebert Foundation on the state of industries and employment in Nigeria.

In the last decades, some unions, including yours sincerely (Textile Workers Union) have been consistent in the campaign for the revival of the Nigeria textile industry. The timely response of CBN, under the activist leadership of CBN governor, Sanusi Lamido Sanusi, which through development financing (Bank of Industry BOI,) had helped to stimulate the hitherto closed United Nigeria Textile Plc in Kaduna to operation. Today UNTL which has re-engaged over 1500 workers on account of Bank of Industry intervention fund.

Nigeria must just reindustrialize if it must be part of the 20 leading economies in 2020. The drivers of Nigeria's growth should not necessarily be services (often of dubious value such telecoms) but real goods through value adding activities that must create jobs. If America under President Obama jealously protects America industries with an eye on jobs, jobs and jobs, Nigeria with open unemployment of 50 per cent must wake up and industrialize and get Nigeria and Nigerians back to sustainable employment, income earnings and poverty eradication.

Fuel Pricing - State or the Market?*

It is time for both anniversary and reflection on last year week long protest/national strike led by NLC/TUC/civil society coalition, following the arbitrary prohibitive hike in the price of petroleum product.

Legitimately the scale and the outcomes of the protests have so far dominated the anniversary discussions. Rightly too, people have demanded for justice for those who lost their lives in the struggle for appropriate people friendly petroleum products pricing. However there are also critical policy issues the strike raised which hunt the nation until the federal government faces up to the challenge of good governance and development in general. For the labour movement, last year's strike was a continuation of similar strikes of 1988 and 2000 over the notorious issue of fuel pricing.

Last year's strike/protests just as the previous ones have re-opened the debate about the role of the state and market in Nigeria's socio-economic development. The orthodoxy of adjustment programme promoted both by the IMF and World Bank had pitched the market and the state against each other as if they are mutually exclusive. It is, however, interesting to note that even as these international financial institutions favour a roll-back of the state, it is still the state that is often called upon to rescue the market in cases of failure. We were told that government had no business in business, yet it is government that is often called upon to increase price of petroleum product (note: not to reduce the price). The truth is that there is nothing inherently good in wholesale deregulation as being propagated in the past decades. The short-coming of wholesale

---

* *Daily Trust,* 14th January 2013

deregulation is seen in the unprecedented failure of banks in Nigeria in recent past and the role of the state through the CBN to save the financial market. This shows that the unregulated market could become an obstacle to development as banks' executives in the absence of adequate supervision, misappropriate customers' deposits. The state intervention in the aviation in recent times shows that unregulated aviation industry could encourage market abuse through cutting corners by operators with all the attendant implications for safety of lives. This underscores the need to fashion out appropriate policy mix that will allow for some liberalization in all sectors not just oil and gas but not beyond the permissible limits of control by the government. John Ralston Saul (1995) has said that "the most powerful force possessed by the individual citizen is her own government."

With specific reference to petroleum products, historically, major petroleum marketing companies used to be the main source of petroleum products' supply. Multinational companies transported and distributed the products relying on their distribution and retail outlets. Many thanks to the functioning railway of the 1970s early 1980s. It was an era of deregulation (as it were) in which Nigerians paid market-determined prices for products. Prior to 1973, seven marketing companies controlled marketing and distribution of the products. Macroeconomics was also favourable; exchange rates were then relatively stable thus allowing for planning on the part of major petroleum marketing companies to source products from imports.

However this arrangement was not sustainable given that it was dependent on the profit and market imperatives of the oil marketers that included Shell, BP, Mobil, AGIP, Esso and Total. The rate of consumption of petroleum products soon exceeded the capacity of Nigeria Petroleum Refinery Co. Ltd. (NPRC) owned by Shell and BP to deliver products to the economy. Above all, the arrangement was import-dependent. Global cost inflation in 1973 undermined the capacity of marketing companies to deliver imported products at affordable prices. The country's economic activities expanded in the seventies such that private companies could no longer cope with increased demand for products. This resulted in erratic supply of petrol and kerosene and ultimately acute scarcity of the product. The shortage was endemic and created social and economic dislocation in the country. This market-failure made government to venture into petroleum products marketing and distribution.

The concern by government to overcome the then total dependency on oil companies led to policy shift towards some regulation. Government therefore introduced uniform pricing, after constructing a 3000km pipeline distribution network linking all the refineries in Port Harcourt (expanded in 1971), Warri (commissioned in 1979), Kaduna (commissioned in 1980) and Port Harcourt II (commissioned in 1988) to satisfy domestic demand, strengthen self-reliance and avoid a situation in which the oil companies could hold the country to ransom. The question then is, will Nigerian government once again take a leap backward into the dark days of wholesale dependency on oil companies or strive to move from the old status of oil rent collector to that of industry control that will maximize national benefits?

Yours truly believes that Nigeria must strengthen the institutions of the market as well as that of the state, i.e. good governance. Petroleum products supply has always been an acid test for successive governments in Nigeria. The supply and distribution of petroleum products will considerably put to test the ability of government to deliver on promised democratic dividends. This is the enduring lesson of 1988 and 2000 strikes as well as that of last year. The real issue is fixing the refineries, building new ones and making Nigerians pay for Made-in-Nigeria products, with domestic labour absorption (employment) not the existing high prices for imported fuel that lead to export of jobs (unemployment).

Creating Mass Jobs through Local Industry Patronage Bill*

Today the Senate Committee on Investment, under the chair of Senator Nenadi E. Usman, conducts a public hearing on the Local Industry Patronage Bill 2013. The bill:

> "seeks to make it mandatory for the Government ministries, Departments and Agencies to give priority to local manufacturers and indigenous companies in the procurement of goods, works and services and to prohibit the exclusion of locally produced goods in the procurement process and for other related matters."

Sponsored by Senator Moh'd Shaaba Lafiagi, this is one developmentalist bill if enacted into law could make a positive impact on re-indutrialization efforts of the Federal Ministry of Trade and Investment, revive distressed industries, increase capacity utilization and above all create mass decent jobs for the millions of the unemployed youths. There are scores of reasons why industries are collapsing. They include poor infrastructure, notably poor electricity supply, high costs as well as short tenure of funding, policy summersaults, addictive waivers (read; corruption), raw material crisis and complete lack of local patronage of locally manufactured goods. It is commendable that the Local Industry Patronage Bill being sponsored by Senator Lafiagi creatively singles out the critical success factor of enhanced local patronage as a way of reviving industries.

With trillions of Naira annual budgets, Nigeria remains a great spender in Africa. The critical questions are, are we buying made-in-Nigeria goods and services or we are just promoting capital flight

---

* *Daily Trust*, 25th March, 2013

through uncritical spending bias for imported goods and services? I agree with the principle of this Bill that it is time we translated the policy pronouncements of successive governments aimed at industrializing our country through practical legislative intervention. In 2003, we hosted the 8th All African Games in – Abuja (COJA) with billons of Naira. The fiesta turned out to be another avenue for capital flight. BMW South Africa reportedly gave 900 cars "free" to COJA in an attempt to outbid Nigeria PAN in Kaduna. To what extent did SA BMW's method conform to ethics of competition and level playing field in international trade? How free were the free cars by a company in business for profit? What was the implication of that singular uncritical cheap opening of Nigerian market mean for industrial capacity utilization, job creation in Nigeria? Meanwhile while PAN was closed, COJA hosted by Nigeria refuelled South African economy. We were also eager to build a new stadium and throw billion dollars at peace keeping operations world -wide, but what values are these operations adding to Nigerian economy in terms of job creations and industrial expansions? For instance, which Nigerian companies would supply tarpaulins for our peace keeping military men and women in Mali? Who airlifts them? Nigerian airlines or outsourced airlines?

In the 1970s, at a time it was not fashionable to patronize Africa and even more fashionable to ape Europe and America, our legendary Anikulapo Kuti sang "Buy Africa". His contention was that prosperity would elude Africa without patronage of its products and ideas by Africans. Over 30 years after that rude lyrical awakening, Nigeria had uncritically enlisted in the World Trade Organization (WTO), a club of trading nations without products to trade but with multiple dumped products to buy. The result today is that Nigeria has become a huge market for dumped products from Europe and China leading to factory closures, unemployment and poverty true to Fela's foresight. I share the patriotic as well as smart economic insights of the proponents of this timely Bill that:

"Americans use American cars, same with Koreans and Japanese. The question then is why is it that Nigerian government officials cannot use cars either produced or assembled in Nigeria? Most household items as well as cars used by various foreign embassies here in Nigeria are brought in from their home countries as a matter of deliberate policy to patronize their home made products, but the reverse is the case in Nigeria. The Indonesian public officers are made to wear locally produced fabrics to work twice a week. India refused to use colour television until they started producing in India. Occasionally, some of our leaders attempted to adopt locally made dresses as their official attires in order to encourage Nigerians to patronize locally made fabrics. As commendable as this is, it falls far short of what is required to keep our local industries alive."

We need to push local patronage by force of law not because it is just patriotic but because it is economically sensible and desirable.

For instance, let *all* uniforms, for primary/secondary schools, the Armed Forces, Police, Immigration, Customs, be procured from local manufacturers and sewn locally. This will increase capacity utilisation and reduce unemployment in the country and ultimately help in reducing crime in the country. Government officials (top-down) should be made to wear locally produced fabrics at all public functions to encourage the populace to buy made in Nigeria

In conclusion, if this bill is passed into a law and effectively monitored and implemented, then Nigeria will be on her way back to re industrialisation, employment to the teeming unemployed youths, increased Gross Domestic Product (GDP) and source of revenue earner to government in form of taxes, levies, rates. All nations proudly patronise their goods and services to create jobs and wage incomes, why not Nigeria?

Reindustrializing Africa - in Praise of Aliko Dangote[*]

"We can't be any longer just participating in global value chains as producers and exporters of primary products and importers of finished products"- Rob Davis, Minister of trade and industry, South Africa (The Africa Report, Oct 2013).

> "We believe industrialization is the key to Nigeria's economic prosperity and we also believe Nigerians should drive the industrialization process. As a practical demonstration of our business philosophy, we have massive investments in the real sector both within and outside the country. Currently, we have over 13 subsidiaries in Nigeria and operations in 14 other African countries." Aliko Dangote: 'Nigeria Beyond Oil' at the 2013 9th All Nigerian Editors' Conference held in Asaba, Delta

Wednesday, November 20th marks 2013 Africa Industrialization Day (AID). Africa Industrialization Day is celebrated on November 20 each year. It is a day dedicated by governments and other organizations in many African countries to examine ways to stimulate Africa's industrialization process. It is also an occasion to draw worldwide media attention to the problems and challenges of industrialization in Africa. In the age of systemic corruption and absence of development agenda, social scientists in Africa might very well know the meaning of graft by route than they would be able to define Industrialization. Many thanks to the United Nations Industrial Development Organization (UNIDO) which plays an important role in coordinating events on or around Africa on

[*] *Daily Trust*, Monday November 18, 2013

Industrialization Day with special effort to unite leaders or representatives of as many African countries as possible to stimulate discussion on the industrialization of Africa and assess the progress made in the past year. *Aid* happily returns us back to *Development Economics 101* in Africa. The point can therefore not be overstated; Industrialization is the "...the process of transforming raw materials, with the aid of labour and capital goods, into (1) consumer goods and services (2) new capital goods which permit more goods (including food) to be produced with the same human resources..." Industrialization is at the heart of development discourse. Industrialization delineates between growth and development of nations. The advantages of industrialization include, creation of sustainable mass decent jobs, lessening of dependency on imports, thus saving scarce foreign exchange and enhanced government revenue through company taxes. The campaign for Industrialization by the nationalist leaders at independence in the 1960s was part of the decolonisation process. Under colonialism African colonies were producers of raw materials and consumers of goods and services from the metropolitan Europe. We are all familiar with how according to Walter Rodney, "Europe underdeveloped Africa" through deliberate denial of value additions, exportation of raw materials and dumping of finished products. It was to the credit of Africa's founding fathers that a decade after independence, they commendably reversed dependence, built factories, trained the hands, mass-employed millions, produced goods and services through value additions which a century long colonialism denied. In Nigeria, we recall today with nostalgia, the great industrial estates of Ikeja/Ilupeju, Sharada/Bompai Kano, Trans Amadi of Port Harcourt, Aba and Enugu industrial estates as well as Kakuri, Nassarawa industrial estates of Kaduna among others. In the case of Ghana, late Kwame Nkrumah as far back as 1961 in addition to scores of factories such as the Black Star Line, beef factory, Kumasi jute and shoe factories, Aboso glass factory, Kade match factory audaciously established Tema Oil Refinery even without discovery of oil and gas then! African founding fathers certainly had a vision of beneficiation and worked their vision through aggressive industrialisation and internal articulation of their economies which in the 1960s and 1970s which made them ahead of countries like China, India, Indonesia in terms of manufacturing value added. Alas today, we are inadvertently back to deindustrialization of the colonial era. Africa is a resource rich continent yet it has low levels of industrialisation, with materials being exported in its raw forms. Some African leaders gullibly agonize about 'resource curse' when the founding fathers long foresaw resource blessings, promoted strong industrial policies that recognized manufacturing as a key engine of growth for national economies.

UNIDO (2004) shows that manufacturing industry in sub-Saharan Africa (SSA) lags behind other developing regions in almost all measures of economic development, namely income per head, industrialization and agricultural productivity. The distribution of manufacturing activity in SSA, measured by the dollar value of manufacturing value added (MVA), is highly skewed. Indeed with the exceptions of South Africa and Mauritius, MVA per head in the 15 most industrialized countries is very low. South Africa is the only country in which manufacturing plays a major role in both domestic output and exports, while Mauritius, an island with a population of only1.2 million inhabitants, is best described as an export platform. Nigeria that once in 1970s and early 1980s boasted of robust manufacturing sector contributing as much as 25 per cent of GDP has fallen down on manufacturing ladder to less than 5% of GDP relying on extractive sector of oil and gas with very little value addition. Against this background, we must single out Alhaji Aliko Dangote as the new African re-industrialiser. Undoubtedly the richest man in the continent, but what increasingly marks Aliko out is his commitment to value addition and beneficiation to the abundant raw materials in the continent. African development observers were recently excited about the bold corporate decision of the Dangote Group, the West African conglomerate to blaze the trail in Re-industrialising Africa through an unprecedented investment of $9billion in oil refinery and petrochemical complex in Nigeria. The refinery located at the Olokola Liquefied Natural Gas (OKLNG) Free Trade Zone in Nigeria would be Nigeria's first private and Africa's largest petroleum refinery, with a projected daily production output of 400,000 barrels a day, the same capacity of the combined 4

Nigerian government-owned refineries in Port Harcourt, Warri and Kaduna. It is refreshing that Dangote Group of industries is changing the narrative of the continent from that of 'resource curse' to resource beneficiation, value addition and mass employment through industrialisation. If we add the Dangote cement new plants in Cameroon, South Africa, Zambia and similar factories in Congo, Ethiopia and Tanzania, we might be witnessing investment patriotism/ investment pan Africanism which the founding fathers of Africa envisioned but was wrongly abandoned for the discredited IMF/ World Bank's inspired adjustment programme (read; deindustrialization) of the mid-eighties.

Privatization or Petroleum Industry Bill (PIB)?*

The Bureau of Public Enterprise (BPE) recently gave credence to the earlier statement credited to the Minister of Petroleum Resources, Diezani Alison-Madueke in London according to which the federal government had concluded plans to sell off its four state-owned oil refineries before the end of the first quarter of next year. My dear friend, the Head of Public Communications of BPE, Mr Chigbo Anichebe, announced two weeks ago that President Goodluck Jonathan had approved the privatisation of the nation's four refineries in keeping with the economic reform programme of his administration. Very few observers of the petroleum sector would disagree with the Minister Diezani Alison-Madueke that government in recent times in particular "had not done a very good job over the years" in the business of running major infrastructure refineries inclusive. What with wholesome products importation? What with gross under capacity utilization of the refineries? What with poor or controversial book keeping, endless start-stop Turn-Around-Maintenance (TAM), start-stop products scarcity and corruption of varying dimensions? But even at that many observers of the petroleum sector also wonder aloud if the immediate priority of the industry now is another emergency privatisation or the passing of the decade long much awaited Petroleum Industry Bill (PIB). The point cannot be overstated; whether privatised or state own, the industry cannot operate within the context of an obsolete and deficient legal framework. It is a sad commentary that the principal legislation for

---

* *Daily Trust*, Monday December 30, 2013

the industry, (which remains the primary source of financing the economy) is the moribund Petroleum Act, enacted in 1969, over 40 years ago when the industry was at its infancy. Petroleum Industry Bill (PIB) has been in the works for over a decade. It has passed through 6th and 7th assembly of the senate and the House without the bill not being passed to law. The star word Nigerians want to hear from Minister Diezani is the immediate passing of the PIB, not the emergency privatisation without an appropriate legal framework.

With its acknowledged shortcomings and some clauses begging for improvement, I bear witness that the PIB is still adjudged today to be one of the most important legislative bills in the history of the country due to the critical role of the petroleum sector in the Nigeria economy. Yet the arguments for or against the bill have not in any way featured in the current government/opposition parties' wars of attritions. Indeed I search in vain for a mention of an important historic piece of governance legislation called PIB in the two notorious letters of both former President Olusegun Obasanjo and President Goodluck Jonathan. The absence of the PIB in both OBJ's and GEJ's shows that the quarrels are certainly not about the Nigerian people or better still not about transforming the petroleum sector. Yet it is an open knowledge that Crude oil receipt accounts for "about 80 per cent of total government revenue, 95 per cent of foreign exchange earnings, about 16 per cent of Gross Domestic Product (GDP), and four per cent of total employment – thus making Nigeria one of the most oil-dependent economies in the world." Why then will a proposed law that is meant to institutionalize transparency, accountability and attract new investment and even unbundle the NNPC does not invoke a sense of urgency? Can we truly have a genuine privatization of the refineries without an appropriate modern legal framework like PIB? Is the proposed privatization meant to enhance production, create more jobs or is it another opportunity for public assets' stripping and insiders' dealings that will be of benefits to a few and a loss to the nation? If we are yet to reap the benefits of the power sector privatisation, how can the Nigerians be convinced that emergency privatization of refineries will not worsen the products supply crisis, lead to massive job losses and foreign dependency. Given that privatisation of the refineries was done under President Obasanjo without clear cut transparency and subsequently reversed by President Yar'Adua, in the absence of PIB, how transparent and sustainable can the new feverish privatization be?

The highlights of the Petroleum Industry Bill (PIB) include creating a conducive business environment for petroleum operations; enhancing exploration and exploitation of petroleum resources in Nigeria for the benefit of the Nigerian people, optimising domestic gas supplies, particularly for power generation and industrial development; establishing a progressive fiscal framework that encourages further investment in the petroleum industry while optimising revenues accruing to the government; establishing commercially oriented and profit driven oil and gas entities; deregulating and liberalising the downstream petroleum sector; Promoting transparency and openness in the administration of the petroleum resources of Nigeria; Promoting the development of the Nigerian content in the petroleum industry; Protecting health, safety and the environment in the course of petroleum operations; and attaining such other objectives to promote a viable and sustainable petroleum industry in Nigeria which certainly must include putting an end to the criminal oil theft. Significantly too, "the PIB is meant to create a legal and regulatory framework that is 21st century compliant and engender sweeping reforms of our oil and gas sector - create new institutions to govern the operations of the industry; break the NNPC into three main companies with a fully-capitalised and profit-oriented National Oil Company; and institute a new fiscal regime amongst others". All these objectives are laudable enough to preoccupy the Minister compared to the unstated objectives of an emergency privatisation. The proposed privatization of the refineries also raises issue about our approach to reform. Must we promote an immediate effect approach (18 months!) reminiscent of the military era or gradualist Approach associated with most democracies? If we cannot pass PIB in ten years, why selling off refineries in 18 months?

How duty waivers under-develop Nigeria*

Nigeria has lost a staggering sum of N1.4 trillion (almost have of the annual national budget!) on import waivers in the last three years. And that is official! According to the Nigeria Customs service under the officially supervised waiver regime "more than 65 per cent of incentives on export were for questionable goods". PREMIUM TIMES quoted a new document by the Customs Service according to which hundreds of billions of naira are being lost to the Federation Accounts "as authorities recklessly grant import/export incentives on unapproved goods from rice to fish to kolanuts, with no significant bearing on the economy". With manufacturing and value adding activities contributing less than 4 per cent to the Gross Domestic Products (GDP), Nigeria has long assumed notoriety as a "container economy". Nigeria increasingly is emerging more as an "imports destination" than an investment destination; everything is imported from petroleum product to toothpicks, from presidential jet to policy ideas!

Taxes levied by the government in relation to imported items are referred to as import duties. In the same vein, duties levied on export consignments are called export duties. In the 70s and 80s Nigeria was truly a productive industrialising economy. Excise duties collectable from factory gates of functioning industrial estates in industrial cities of Lagos, Kano, Kaduna, Enugu and Port Harcourt dominated the major sources of Customs revenue. Indeed Customs services maintained visible presence in the factories to collect taxes of local value chains. However with the so called liberalization of the economy and abandonment of Industrialization agenda, import

---

* Monday January 27th, 2014

duties assumed special importance. It is bad enough that we have replaced a productive economy with an importing economy. We run the economy based on wholesale import of finished goods and export of raw materials in the classical version of Lugardian economy 100 years after amalgamation of the colonial economy. It is however clearly unacceptable that we cannot and indeed refuse to tax these imports (some of them luxury goods such as armoured cars) under the regime of unacceptable waivers. Addictive waivers give undue advantage to importers and impoverishes local producers who operate under high cost environment which cannot be passed on to consumers.

During the public presentation of the 2014 budget in Abuja last Monday, Minister of Finance, Ngozi Okonjo-Iweala, has said that the 2014 budget envisaged a net collectible revenue of N7.50 trillion. Mrs. Okonjo-Iweala, who is the Coordinating Minister for the Economy also accepted as much that the expected collectible revenue represented a 9 per cent reduction from the N4.1 trillion in 2013. The revelation from the Nigeria Customs Services (NSC) however shows that the revenue loss to the Federation last year arising as a result of waivers is more than what has been officially acknowledged. By the time we add duty waivers to oil theft and depletion of Excess crude account, we may be having at hand a disintegrating economy caused by a policy suicide called political waivers the beneficiaries of which are the government cronies who just make money at the expense of local jobs and public revenue.

The present dispensation of wholesale waivers regime has inadvertently legitimized the status of Nigeria as a non-productive corrupt economy that is avoidably loosing scarce revenue, jobs and local goods and services to waivers. The NCS has rightly compared the government's present management of export grant to the well-abused fuel subsidy pointing out 65 per cent of beneficiaries that received the grant for goods not approved by the government, which ordinarily should be limited to raw materials, machinery and spare parts. It is legitimate for Nigeria as a developing economy to have policies that favour the growth of its local companies, through such selective policies like tax breaks for local companies, even official ban of goods in which we have comparative advantages and waivers for machineries that are needed to produce goods at home. Thus economic waivers are good for the economy, once they are targeted towards local production and not to benefit rentier importers. Waivers granting policy had been in existence in Nigeria as means of fostering businesses with potential for value chain development. Indeed the economic waiver that encourages local production should be retained. There are also statute waivers as spelt out in protocols within ECOWAS for instance.

It is refreshing to note that question 15 of the 50 questions posed by the House of Representatives on the economy deals with the management of waivers policy. The Co-ordinating Minister for the Economy and Minister of Finance, Mrs. Ngozi Okonjo-Iweala was asked to produce a detailed report on the exact amount of money Nigeria lost to import duty waivers between 2011 and 2013. She was also directed to provide the full names of the beneficiaries; what the waivers were used to import; and the justification for granting such duty exemptions. Nigeria awaits public hearing on this singular question dealing with waivers. What is also clear is that the management of waivers policy is too important to be left with the executive alone. One of the policies that undermine most local textile mills apart from wholesale smuggling and lack of electricity is waivers for imports of finished textile products at a time local manufacturers cannot break even.

The Economy: Rebased or Transformed?*

We have been promised the transformation of the economy but we seem to have a Rebased economy instead.

Of course there are those who would argue that rebasing and transformation are not mutually exclusive. Some would even say rebasing (which accurately and commendably reflected changes in the Nigerian economy in the last two decades) is a function of a transformation. Maybe. But certainly rebasing and transforming an economy are not the same. The former is in quantitative terms while the latter is in quantitative terms. The United Nations defines rebasing as the "process of replacing present price structure (base year) to compile volume measures of GDP with a new or more recent base year." Quantitative Nominal GDP at current prices does have its usefulness though. In quantitative terms, we are now the biggest centre of goods and services in the continent. The Godliness is in the details for Nigerian economy. According to Yemi Kale, the DG of the National Bureau of Statistics, on paper (i.e. in nominal terms,) the size of the economy expanded by more than three-quarters to some estimated 80 trillion naira ($488 billion) for 2013 compared to some $262.6 billion. Conversely the devil is in the details for South Africa which has been beaten to a second position in economic activities at some World Bank's 2012 estimated GDP of $384.3 billion. To this extent, the new Rebased figure for Nigeria legitimizes Nigeria's Super Eagles serial defeat of Bafana Bafana in the round ball tournament. But the real economy is certainly not football tournament. Nigeria undoubtedly leads in nominal GDP no less as it is the current champion of the African Cup of Nations for

---

* Monday April 14th, 2014

football. But in real quantitative terms, South Africa's economy is stronger. Its GDP is driven more by value adding manufacturing activities compared to Nigeria's economy. According to United Nations industrial Development Organization, UNIDO manufacturing industry in Sub-Saharan Africa (SSA) lags behind other developing regions in almost all measures of economic development, namely income per head, industrialization and agricultural productivity. The distribution of manufacturing activity in SSA, measured by the dollar value of manufacturing value added (MVA), is highly skewed. Only ten out of 45 countries have an MVA of one billion dollars or more, while just one country, South Africa, accounts for 27.3% of the subcontinent's total MVA. In Nigeria, manufacturing accounts for less than 4%t of the GDP. Nigeria's new numbers came interestingly from marginal services such as movie; the music industry and the telecommunication sector, which all combined to push Nigeria's economy over that of South Africa. Even at that, the local content of these services is debatable. In fact South Africa's economy drives Nigeria's newly captured activities such as telecoms and music and movie industry (given that we must still watch better Nollywood films if only we pass through SA's DSTV. All these mean that under these new nominal figures, South Africa is still ahead of Nigeria in qualitative terms. Indeed Nigeria still parades lower per capita GDP of just 1000 dollars far less than South Africa at $6,800. Rebasing therefore does not mean Nigerians are better off than South Africans. Indeed we are worse than South Africa in prosperity. Two-thirds of Nigerians still live below poverty line. Electricity is still a luxury while lives are daily unavoidably wasted to poor health and transport facilities. The list of activities captured under the rebasing must have increased to 46 from 33 previously to include "telecommunications and information services, publishing, motion picture, sound recording and music production and broadcasting, arts, entertainment and recreation, financial institutions and insurance as well as real estate". However the rebasing must also indicate many manufacturing activities that have disappeared in the last two decades. Which then now raises the issue of transformation that President Jonathan promises. This administration will be better assessed in terms of promised transformation agenda dealing with power supply, agriculture and beneficiation in the extractive industries such as oil and gas. With wholesale importation of tooth picks to petroleum products, textiles to furniture, it's certainly not yet a transformed Nigerian economy.

Godwin Emefiele - enter another Player-Turned-Referee

'Central Bankers Read Election Returns, Not Balance Sheets' - Robert Z. Aliber

Today another chapter is added to the history of Nigeria's central banking with the ascendancy of the former group managing director/chief executive Zenith Bank Plc, Mr. Godwin Emefiele, as the new governor of the Central Bank of Nigeria (CBN). It is a sad commentary that terror news hits the headlines in today's Nigeria not necessarily the foreign reserves, exchange rates, inflation, capacity utilization and unemployment figures (and all those naughty macro-economic issues, CBN is called to fix!). Mr. Godwin Emefiele's historic assumption of office today is certainly hunted by the spectre of security challenge. Apart from the predominance of news associated with insecurity, in a double jeopardy, the controversial exist of his predecessor Mallam Sanusi Lamido Sanusi, casts dark shadow on the emergence of Mr. Godwin Emefiele as the 11th governor of the Central Bank of Nigeria. Regrettably the attendant litigations in regular and industrial courts on the summary termination of Sanusi Lamido Sanusi may be more news worthy than a new tenure at the apex bank. And that is perhaps the first riddle for Mr. Godwin Emefiele; how to make sure that his process driven and relatively easy entry (appointment and Senate confirmation) will not be inversely related to his smooth exit. Interestingly analysts are quick to point to the difference between Sanusi and the new entrant, Emefiele. The latter we are told is level headed while the former was intemperate. May be. While we are unhelpfully inundated with their respective profiling, the point cannot be overstated that both Sanusi Lamido Sanusi and successor actually have a lot in common. Sanusi and Emefiele are both one time players in the banking sector before they are called upon to become regulators at the CBN. Sanusi came from First Bank while Emefiele until recently was the group managing director/chief executive Zenith Bank Plc. Very few players have passed the acid test of being regulators. Will Emefiele conclusively pass this singular acid test? Mallam Mai Bornu was the first indigenous Governor of the Bank in 1963 who retired from its service in 1967. He came from the CBN where he had worked before. The most celebrated CBN Governor was Clement Isong appointed by Yakubu Gowon as Governor of the CBN in August 1967, an office he held until September 1975. He was also a regulator by work experience. He was credited with successful prosecution of the war economy during the Nigerian Civil War (July 1967 – January 1970) and even managing the subsequent oil boom without incurring unnecessary debts and even daring to debts to accumulate enough foreign reserves. The new historic assignment puts to test Emefiele's professional experience and commitment to the alluring mission of the CBN which reads that by 2015 (next year) CBN is expected to *"be the model central bank delivering price and financial system stability and promoting sustainable economic development."* Mr Emefiele is encouraged to read and re-read the provisions of the CBN Act of 2007 of the Federal Republic of Nigeria which charge the Bank with the overall control and administration of the monetary and financial sector policies of the Federal Government, namely ensuring monetary and price stability; issuing legal tender currency in Nigeria; maintain external reserves to safeguard the international value of the legal tender currency; promote a sound financial system in Nigeria; and provide economic and financial advice to the Federal Government. Central banking worldwide has been likened to a good (economic) driver, which must keep an eye on the road and maintain steady hands on the wheel for a good (economic) ride. Countries preoccupied with issues in development use their Central Banks to keep the economy on course through activist macroeconomics with respect to pricing, (inflation), exchange rates, interest rates, capacity utilization, employment, debt management, etc. This is the point the new CBN governor must bring to the fore. It is reassuring that Emefiele is committed to development financing. He was reported to have said that his immediate priority is beyond financial system stability to cover macroeconomic stability using the development banking model. He was reported to have said that:

> "We will be focusing on achieving macroeconomic stability by holding exchange rate strong using various monetary policy tools as well as keep interest rate low/affordable for businesses that require finance. We will also be focusing on development banking to support the growth of the real sectors of the economy particularly agriculture and the manufacturing sectors."

Nigerians are however more interested in the numbers than policy rhetorics. The existing interest rates are certainly not industry friendly. Rebased GDP without enhanced job opportunities to be driven by industry means growth without development. CBN must move from inflation targeting to Employment-targeting. A greater weight must be placed on employment and job creation to ensure economic security as well as physical security. Mr. Godwin Emefiele is encouraged to consolidate on the gains of his predecessors and overcome their shortcomings. We wish Mr Emefiele a rewarding tenure that will certainly be judged by lower interest rate, increased foreign reserves, more jobs, full capacity utilization and stable Naira value. The credit for today's smooth transition at the CBN despite the court cases over the controversial exit of Sanusi goes to the acting governor of the bank, Mrs. Sarah Alade, who has been holding the fort since February. Mrs. Sarah Alade has given practical effect to the meaning of institution-building.

It's Africa Industrialization, stupid![*]

Last Thursday, 20th November marks 2014 Africa Industrialisation Day. The United Nations General Assembly declared November 20th of every year since 1990 as a day "to stimulate the international community's commitment to the industrialization of Africa". The 2014 commemoration of the Africa Industrialisation Day takes place under the theme: 'Inclusive and Sustainable industrial development; Africa Agro Industry for Food Security'. In almost all the capital cities of the Continent that signed on to this important day, it was business as usual (with mass importation of finished goods, export of raw materials, not local production) with little renewed commitment to local value addition and beneficiation. It seems only the "stupid" Africans could be preoccupied with industrialization! The "wise" Africans are more concerned with the ever vicious scramble for nomination forms for 2015 (with respect to Nigeria)! But many thanks to the Nigeria's trade unions notably a select group of private sector trade unions and unionists from the textile, construction, agricultural, chemical and non-allied, steel and engineering, petroleum and natural gas under the banner of NLC and IndustriALL global union, who took to the streets of Abuja raising the banners of industrial development, job creation and local value addition. Ironically as the mass manifestation of the trade unionists was going on, many members of the Federal House of Representatives including all members of the House Committee on Industry, Trade and Investment were jumping the fences of the National Assembly for an emergency sitting, not on the collapse of existing industries and the attendant mass unemployment, not on increasing power

---

* Monday November 24th, 2014

outages after privatization of electricity, but on the controversial extension of emergency rule in the Northeast. On the same day, President Goodluck Jonathan was reportedly in London to preside over a meeting of Nigeria's Honorary International Investment Council (HIIC) which opens there on Friday! We must certainly think global to attract foreign investment, but the point cannot be overstated that local value adding activities must take place on the African continent not in the heartland of Europe which once "underdeveloped" Africa. On the President's entourage were key ministers including the Minister of Industry, Trade and Investment, Dr. Olusegun Aganga expected to lead industrialization discourse at home. There was a round table discussion in collaboration with Friedrich Ebert Stiftung (FES) on Wednesday with focus on the recent privatization of PHCN and the recently launched Nigeria Industrial Revolution Plan (NIRP) by the federal government. The round table frowned at the conspicuous absence of key Government Ministries and Agencies that were invited to the Roundtable particularly the Ministry of Industry, Trade and Investment. Our Development emphasis of Africa must be on beneficiation. Africa is endowed with raw materials but not adding value to them. We export raw diamonds and gold and import wrist watches, ear rings and neck laces. We export crude oil and import petroleum products. We export cottons and import finished fabrics including second hand clothes. My Mobile phone in boxes are daily full of non-value- adding news that as many as 30 ships carrying containers filled with goods are expected to arrive at Lagos ports!. Africa should stop being exporter of raw materials and jobs but producer of manufacturing goods and retainer of mass decent jobs. Let us produce what we consume and consume what we produce. Nigeria commendably recently launched National Industrial Revolution Plan (NIRP) focusing on 10 critical sectors that include textiles, food and beverages, chemical, automobile, petroleum sector among others. President Goodluck Jonathan should ensure the full implementation of the NIRP in partnership with all critical stakeholders including Labour. The new automotive policy shift in the automobile industry which puts restriction on importation of different cars to the country is welcome if it adds value locally. There cannot be industrialization without electrification. The power sector reforms must urgently translate to affordable uninterrupted electricity for the industry. Africa share of world's GDP is scandalously still less than 1 per cent 50 years after independence. Even with rebased GDP, Nigerian manufacturing sector has failed to undergo the critical structural transformation necessary for it to play a leading role in economic growth and development. Manufacturing share of GDP has remained less than 4 per cent, contributions to foreign exchange earnings have been minimal, and the share of employment and government revenue generated have been low.. Nigeria is still having jobless growth. Growth is not driven by manufacturing. Dumping, Counterfeiting and unfair trade practices are the norms. With all the acknowledged efforts in the Agric sector, our import bill though has reduced to some ₦906 billion from the ₦2.3 trillion, is still dangerously high.

The recent announcement of austerity measure by the Finance Minister Dr. Okonjo-Iweala shows Nigeria must urgently diversify. We suffer the problem of resource curse such that a drop in the crude oil price has totally altered the parameters of the annual budget. Nigeria does not need austerity measures but accelerated implementation of the Nigeria Industrial Revolution Plan to grow the non- oil sector. We should build on the strengths of Nigeria's raw materials, large market and abundant human resources and minimize the weaknesses of policy inconsistency and weak Infrastructure to grow the non- oil sector. In this respect we must commend the investment patriotism and pan African orientation of the President/Chief Executive of Dangote Group of industries, Alhaji Aliko Dangote. Dangote Group of industries is changing the narrative of the continent from that of 'resource curse' to resource beneficiation.

Aliko Dangote is said to be the richest man in Africa. But what is even more significant is that his wealth is based on value adding manufacturing activities ranging from production of cement, sugar and flour among others. We also recognize and commend the efforts at the State levels particularly of States like Osun with the establishment of Omoluabi Garment factory and Kano State where Governor Rabiu Musa Kwakwanso is setting up garment factories in the 44 local government areas of the state.

NAIRA - Dictatorship of the CBN

"Central Bankers Read Election Returns, Not Balance Sheets' - Robert Z. Aliber

Last week, the Central Bank of Nigeria (CBN) announced the devaluation of Naira by N13 as part of its dictated measures ostensibly to strengthen the nation's economy. The CBN Governor, Godwin Emefiele, disclosed the devaluation after a meeting of the Monetary Policy Committee. (MPC). The MPC consists of the Governor of the Bank as the Chairman, the four Deputy Governors of the Bank, two members of the Board of Directors of the Bank, three members appointed by the President; and two members appointed by the Governor. MPC in number compares with the Central Working Committee of the Communist Party of the collapsed Soviet Union and true to type its method is far from being democratic.

Under the new monetary dispensation, Naira now exchanges for N168 instead of the old official rate of N155 to one U.S. dollar. According to the CBN governor, MPC also decided to increase the Monetary Policy Rate (MPR) by 100 basis point from 12 per cent to 13 per cent. The MPR is the rate at which banks borrow from the Central Bank to cover their immediate cash shortfalls. It is an open knowledge that the higher the cost of such borrowing, the higher the rate at which banks advance credit to customers. The conventional wisdom has it that central bankers as monetary advisers to government should pursue policies with an eye on public welfare not necessarily on balancing the book as the MPC members did recently. CBN wrongly targets inflation rather than targeting real production and employment creation.

In fact CBN Governor, Godwin Emefiele seems moves in the opposite direction of the global trends of lowering interest rates to boast productivity and create jobs. Yours sincerely searches in vain for any known modern democracy where votes truly count and few months to a general national election, the Central Bank for whatever reasons, would arbitrary devalue the national currency and at the same time hike the interest rates (already in injurious double digit!). When we add already less than 50 per cent capacity utilization in the real sector, 50 per cent open unemployment a drop in foreign reserve, from these miserable macroeconomics could lead to an electoral retrenchment of any democratically elected government. As a consistent supporter of the autonomy of the CBN, the latest dictatorship of injurious macro-economic variables of 8% naira devaluation and increase in interest rate challenges all Nigerians to watch how the CBN exercises it's autonomy and to whose interest. The CBN governor said the decision to lower the value of naira against the dollar was to strengthen the currency. How devaluation strengthens the naira beats imagination. For an import dependent economy for inputs and finished goods of varying brands, devaluation puts further pressures on naira value.

The often-repeated declared objectives of monetary policies are stable external value of the naira, domestic price stability and a viable external balance of payment for the country. The recent announced measures would certainly fuel inflation and undermine price stability. Certainly you cannot talk about price stability when at a stroke you record such per cent devaluation that further puts pressure on inflation rate officially put at 12 per cent by the government. Certainly the objective cannot be improved capacity utilization given that manufacturers now need more money to oil their ever-rising production cost for imported inputs, no thanks to devaluation. For a new CBN that has promoted in recent times development financing as one of the requirements for sustainable economic growth through various intervention funds at single digit interest rate, a return to hike in interest rate only privileges the money market operators and punishes the real sector of the economy. The challenge lies in how the CBN must urgently resume its regulatory role especially with respect to the foreign exchange market. CBN must return to basics.

It must return to its core objectives of maintaining sound financial structure, promotion of monetary stability, safeguarding the value of Naira and stable exchange rate and prove a financial adviser to the federal government, in the areas of price and exchange rate management. As a banker of last resort and financial adviser to the federal government, the new governor of the CBN must impress on the government to drastically cut the costs of governance which truly puts pressure on the value of the naira in the face of dwindling oil revenue. CBN must promote policies that will grow the real sector of the economy and lessen the scandalous dependence on oil revenue. It must re look the twin mutually destructive measures of devaluation and increase in interest rate. The new upward review of interest rate will definitely discourage borrowing by small and medium business enterprises and will not help in reviving the collapsed businesses. Sustainable mass industrial jobs cannot be assured under the monetary regime of naira devaluation and high interest rate.

Delayed Salary payment as Wage Theft*

"A just wage for the worker is the ultimate test of whether any
economic system is functioning justly"
- *Pope John Paul II*

How do leaders serve their people? They may pay good wages and
treat employees with respect.
- *John C. Maxwell*

With open unemployment rate of almost 50 per cent, few workers
who have jobs are privileged in Nigeria in recent times. Mass workers
of the old good working Nigeria have long been endangered, no
thanks to downsizing in the public sector and collapse of hundreds of
industries in the private sector. Mass unemployment is bad enough.
But even worse too is the fact that few available jobs are getting
precarious. Many workers are outsourced. Many are casuals who get
hired and fired at the will by profit-driven employers. Few workers
are permanent employees with pensionable jobs. The old slave
masters at least kept slaves permanently. Some modern employers
simply rent workers. Even more unacceptable is the fact that
increasingly some workers are denied adequate wages and paid
irregularly and even not paid at all.

It is the truism of working life that working people work in
order to earn money to pay for food, housing and school fees among
others. Yet, increasingly in Nigeria, access to adequate and regular
wages is no longer guaranteed contrary to the spirit and content of
the Constitution and the country's labour laws. In many states of the

---

* Monday December 29, 2014

Federation as well as many Federal ministries as well as MDAs, non-payment of wages has led to huge wage arrears. In some cases, such as Benue state, Governor Gabriel Suswan true to eighteenth century trans-Atlantic slave master's mentality said he could not pay salaries running up to three months. Large wage arrears have been rightly likened to debt bondage and slavery.

The point cannot be overstated that delayed payment of salaries of working men and women is wage theft. It is an economic crime. Some of the employers in the public sectors are Governors who are also politicians. They actually just recently duly paid all their delegates for their respective political parties' Conventions from which some serving governors emerged also as senators in waiting. Who paid their these indulgent bills while they are yet to pay the legitimate earnings of workers as at when due. There is no doubt that the short fall in the oil revenue and serial oil theft had adversely undermined the revenue profiles of most states. But the unacceptable delayed payments preceded the recent scandalous non- payment and delayed remunerations. Above all, we have not heard of the non-payments of the executive over-bloated pays of some these defaulting governors. Indeed some of these governors still travel with their long convoys of Jeeps to private terminals to board chattered flights even in the face of dwindling revenues. ILO standards on wages most ratified by Nigeria address these problems by providing for regular payment of wages, the fixing of minimum wage levels, and the settlement of unpaid wages in case of employer insolvency. Some of them include Labour Clauses (Public Contracts) Convention, 1949 (No. 94), and Protection of Wages Convention of 1949 (No. 95). Delayed payment is double jeopardy for the affected workers because the problems of Naira devaluation and rising prices (inflation) mean arrears eventually paid, worth less than the delayed pay. For instance, the current N18,000.00 national minimum wage at the exchange rate of N150 to $1, writhed some $120 per month in 2010. However with the devaluation of the currency and current exchange rate of almost N200 to $1, minimum wage has dropped to as low as $90 dollars per month, a shortfall of $30. When we take into consideration the rising inflation it is clear the real income of the working people has declined by over 50% within the last four years. Nigeria now has working poor whose monthly pay can hardly take them home because of government unstable policies. Nigeria certainly cannot be developed with working poor or working beggars who live on delayed worthless pay. Austerity measure must first reflect through reduction in costs of governance and not delayed legitimate pay of working men and women.

Index

Printed in the United States
By Bookmasters